TSQ Transgender Studies Quarterly

Volume 6 ∗ Number 4 ∗ November 2019

Trans Futures

Edited by micha cárdenas and Jian Neo Chen

ARTS & CULTURE

BOOK REVIEWS

General Editor's Introduction

Figure 1. "Border Fence under Construction," Calexico, CA, July 6, 2018. Taken by author.

> We can't take you anymore. Our country is full. So turn around—that's the way
> it is.
> —President Donald Trump, April 5, 2019

On April 5, 2019, Air Force One flew over the lush green agricultural fields of the Imperial Valley located in the southeastern corner of California, on the US-Mexican border. As the plane began its descent into the Naval Air Facility in El Centro, California, President Donald Trump was greeted by a personal message carved into a nearby alfalfa field—"Trump 2020" (Morales 2019)—a field-sized billboard forecasting a desire for a future win for Trump in the 2020 presidential election, a future that portends the continued nativist, racist, homophobic, and transphobic attacks that have already become one legacy of the Trump administration.

This is not the first time that the agricultural bounty of the Imperial Valley has been used as a tool of propaganda. In 1915, D. W. Griffith used the cotton fields of Calexico, California, to stand in for the plantations of the Reconstruction-era South depicted in his historic and controversial film *The Birth of a Nation* (1915). The political landscape depicted in that film, characterized by a white supremacist ethno-nationalist insurgency and "rife with visions of intimidation, voter suppression, and racial division," resembled that of 1915, a year in which there were more lynching of African Americans than there had been in the previous ten years, as much as it did that of the 1870s or, for that matter, as it does our own (Blakemore 2015; Du Bois 2007: 120). Just as the ascendency of Trump fueled both a diffuse resistance movement and the naked racism that led to violence in Charlottesville and elsewhere, *The Birth of a Nation* (originally titled *The Clansman*) similarly incited two movements—the formal rebirth of the Ku Klux Klan, the post–Civil War Southern white supremacist and anti-Black racist paramilitary group described as "the most vicious terrorist organization in the history of the United States" (Franklin 1979: 431), and the National Association for the Advancement of Colored People's fight against the film, which "mobilized thousands of black and white men and women in large cities across the country" outside the South, many of whom were unaware of the existence of the new civil rights organization (Lewis 2009: 331). Motivating these movements was a pressing sense that the future itself was somehow at stake for differently racialized groups of people.

Calling attention to Calexico standing in for the cotton fields of the Deep South also highlights how the southern border of the United States has long functioned as a landscape for imagining the nation's futurity—and to whom that future belongs. When the US Border Patrol was first established in 1924, as part of a xenophobic retreat from foreign entanglements after World War I and a concomitant wave of hostility to immigrants and foreigners, a significant number of patrollers were members of the resurgent Ku Klux Klan, which was active in border towns from Texas to California (Grandin 2019: 164). The policing of the southern border over the past century thus offers a scene in which to see the interrelated histories of various forms of genocidal dispossession targeting Indigenous, Latinx, and Black lives deemed unfit to participate in the collective life of the nation.

It was during Trump's visit to Calexico that he relayed his message of "no future" for thousands of potential asylum seekers when he spoke the words: "We can't take you anymore. Our country is full. So turn around—that's the way it is." In doing so, he gave voice to what micha cárdenas and Jian Neo Chen, the guest editors of this special "Trans Futures" issue of *TSQ*, call the "linear and universal times of settler colonialism, white supremacy, and heteropatriarchy." They—and the authors and artists whose work they publish in this issue—challenge us to contest the inevitability of Trump's assertion that "that's the way it is." In asking us to ponder, "What will be in the times to come? What will *I* be in the times to come? What will *we* be in the times to come?," they challenge us to imagine the very possibility of trans futures and to imagine trans lives in relation to other forms of vulnerable and precarious life.

While carving "Trump 2020" into the agricultural terrain of the southwestern Imperial Valley expresses one vision of the future, another can be seen in the land itself and the life it supports—the alfalfa in which that message is expressed grows rapidly and is harvested frequently, and the message it was made to bear was quickly and easily erased. Desired futures can be unwritten. The enhanced segment of the border wall (fig. 1) that Trump came to Calexico to celebrate is but a physical manifestation of a far more extensive anti-immigrant policy that is far more difficult to efface. The presidential photo-op on the border was in fact prefatory to an order issued by Attorney General William Barr ten days later, on April 15, 2019, that forces tens of thousands of asylum seekers to remain detained indefinitely—their futures suspended—while waiting for removal proceedings to conclude unless granted parole. Given that this new policy does not apply to unaccompanied minors and families, it will disproportionately affect queer and trans asylum seekers and other unmarried, childless individuals.

The border wall that Trump fetishizes and the policies that seek to translate the fantasy it represents into a social reality can be understood as attempts to protect the nation from "gendered and racialized bodies that move through borders of all sorts, from the metaphorical gender boundaries so often invoked in transgender transition narratives to the national borders involved in immigration" (Beauchamp 2012: 72). The recent death of Roxsana Hernández, a Honduran transwoman who was detained after requesting asylum and who died after suffering abuses while in immigration enforcement custody in the Cibola County Correctional Center in New Mexico,[1] tragically exemplifies the violence that falls especially heavily on those whose bodies cross multiple kinds of borders. Their movements toward a desired future on the other side—a future of possibility and potentiality expressed through the metaphors of travel, home, and migration that are persistently invoked to describe transgender identities and bodies, as well as the embodied experience of crossing a geographical border—are all too often brutally terminated.

As cárdenas and Chen note in their introduction, futurity, transness, and crossings both literal and metaphorical supply—despite the death wishes often directed at them—a "felt horizon" that continues to solicit movement toward it, whose unfilled promises cry out to be redeemed. How utopian is it to think that Trump's border wall will ultimately prove to be no match for the brilliant interventions made by the authors in this issue, which draw attention to the kinds of "trans and queer relational and embodied practices of survival, reproduction, and transformation that move beyond what can be captured by [state] regimes" (Chen and cárdenas in their guest editors' introduction)? Speaking in Calexico in a roundtable about immigration with members of his administration and local and regional law enforcement officials, Trump boasted that his new wall was thirty feet high, heavily reinforced, hard to climb, sharp on top, and built of steel slats spaced close enough together to prevent a body from passing through but far enough apart to see what was happening through the gaps. "I think it looks fantastic," Trump said, "very see-through, so you're able see the other side, which is a very important element" (White House 2019). Trump was no doubt imagining the ability of the US surveillance apparatus to penetrate Mexican space, but a wall always has two sides. As you engage with the visions of trans futures that fill the pages of this special issue, think of the see-through border fence that cannot but help, despite itself, to offer a sight line to the far horizon, an elsewhere that remains imbued with potential.

Francisco J. Galarte is assistant professor of gender and women's studies at the University of Arizona, where he teaches Chicana/Latina studies and transgender studies.

Notes

1. In May 2018, Roxsana Hernández was detained after presenting herself for asylum at the San Ysidro, California, port of entry. She had traveled with other transgender migrants as part of a migrant caravan. Days after Hernández presented herself and was detained, she was rushed to an emergency department in Chula Vista, California. There she was diagnosed with cough, congestion, fever, and unmedicated HIV. Hernández was not admitted for medical care, nor was her condition monitored. She did not receive medical attention until she was gravely ill, and an independent autopsy revealed that she was also physically assaulted and abused while in custody (Rosenberg 2018).

References

Beauchamp, Toby. 2012. "The Substance of Borders: Transgender Politics, Mobility, and US State Regulation of Testosterone." *GLQ* 19, no. 1: 57–78.

Blakemore, Erin. 2015. "'Birth of a Nation': One Hundred Years Later." *JSTOR Daily*, February 4. daily.jstor.org/the-birth-of-a-nation/.

Du Bois, W. E. B. 2007. *Dusk of Dawn: An Essay toward an Autobiography of a Race Concept*. New York: Oxford University Press.

Franklin, John Hope. 1979. "'Birth of a Nation': Propaganda as History." *Massachusetts Review* 20, no. 3: 417–34.

Grandin, Greg. 2019. *The End of the Myth: From the Frontier to the Border Wall in the Mind of America*. New York: Metropolitan.

Lewis, David Levering. 2009. *W. E. B. Du Bois: A Biography*. New York: Henry Holt.

Morales, Julio. 2019. "Trump Comes to Calexico, Tells Illegal Migrants: 'Turn Around.'" *Imperial Valley Press*, April 5. www.ivpressonline.com/news/local/trump-comes-to-calexico-tells -illegal-migrants-turn-around/article_ba62d916-5823-11e9-903a-03843e294080.html.

Rosenberg, Eli. 2018. "Transgender Asylum Seeker Roxsana Hernandez Was Beaten before Her Death, According to New Autopsy." *Washington Post*, November 27. www.washingtonpost .com/nation/2018/11/27/transgender-asylum-seeker-was-beaten-before-her-death-according -new-autopsy/.

White House. 2019. "Remarks by President Trump in Roundtable on Immigration and Border Security: Calexico, California." April 5. www.whitehouse.gov/briefings-statements/remarks -president-trump-roundtable-immigration-border-security-calexico-california/.

Times to Come

Materializing Trans Times

JIAN NEO CHEN and MICHA CÁRDENAS

What will be in the times to come?
What will I be in the times to come?
What will we be in the times to come?

This special issue performs a claim to trans futures—a claim that imagines the reconstructed social realities and worlds made possible through the materializing of trans times. Critical trans studies and trans political struggles intervene in the spatial-temporal orders that determine and regulate the borders of knowledge, life/death, embodiment, movement, and social value established to secure the heteropatriarchal white settler state, liberal civil society, and the territories of the national body. Trans studies and politics activate the multiple temporalities of body-mind-sense, social vitality, and memory embodied and imagined through gender by trans practices that exceed the spaces and times of the state, society, and nation. We use the term *trans* to recognize multiple embodiments, expressions, and identities of gender nonconformity and variance that surpass—and potentially decolonize—racially constituted white, binary gender/sex, while maintaining links to *transgender*'s resistant repurposing of Western psycho-medical science and to *trans**'s broad inclusiveness based on the algorithmic command to "trans everything."

This issue began from a desire to question and imagine our collective trans futures, and to question the idea of futurity itself. Beginning with commitments to trans of color studies and to decolonization, the call for papers for this issue brought in articles that imagine futures of transfeminist solidarity, tropical aliens, and new understandings of Black and trans solidarities that challenge the trans/cis binary. The concept of the future that colonizers, such as the colonizers of Australia, brought with them demanded an absolute devotion, argue Anna Tsing,

Heather Swanson, Elaine Gan, and Nils Bubandt, editors of *Arts of Living on a Damaged Planet* (2017: G7). They write, "Moving toward this *future* requires ruthless ambition—and the willingness to participate in great projects of destruction while ignoring extinction as collateral damage. The settlers looked straight ahead as they destroyed native peoples and ecologies" (G7). We reject the inclusion of trans people in a Western colonial narrative of progress that serves only to make countries like the United States appear progressive, or generous, in the granting of rights. In reality, those rights are always conditional and are used to reinscribe colonial frameworks of land ownership and to identify who is worth protecting, and who is not.

If trans implies a movement from one gender toward a different location, then transness is always imbricated with forward time and cannot exist without linear, teleological time. Yet if we imagine transness to be not about a crossing from one location to another but about a multidirectional movement in an open field of possibility, then time and its direction become more fluid. The assemblage model was used by Brian Massumi (2002) as a way to escape the capture of the grid of identifications for a more mobile space of affect. Jasbir Puar (2007; 2017) takes up that model to analyze fluid dynamics, such as a bomb explosion in which human, machine, and energy become blurred together in an instant that challenges presumed divisions of matter, describing how the sheer speed of movement can break down categorical designations such as male, female, human, machine, cis, and trans at the molecular level.

The multiple times of trans elude the linear rationality of history and visible subjects of knowledge. Trans uses of cultural forms, including literary and popular memoir, live performance, documentary film/video, and digital media, highlight trans practices of embodiment, identity, and social relation that remain outside cisgender spatial-temporal orders of reality, even as they lay claim to realness, with different degrees of access (cárdenas 2011). In *Redefining Realness: My Path to Womanhood, Identity, Love, and So Much More* (2014), Janet Mock uses the unruliness of memoir to convey episodes in her coming-of-age as a Black Native Hawaiian trans girl displaced by the social assignment of gender across different institutions, geopolitical locations, and histories of racial gendering. Her storytelling proliferates senses of past, present, and future to embody the different temporalities of self-understanding, identification, and memory that constitute trans experience: "When I say *I always knew I was a girl* with such certainty, I erase all the nuances, the work, the process of self-discovery" (75). Trans memoirs and cultural genres intervene in dominant culture's reduction of transgender (and transsexual) experience to linear narratives with temporal continuity (Amin 2014; Salah 2017), organized around medical and state-determined gender/sex change through surgery, hormone replacement therapy, and identity documents. These narratives overwrite the expansive practices of gender transformation beyond and within surgery, hormone replacement, and identity marking, which give expression to trans identities outside/within visible social orders of reality (Halberstam 2005). The dominant culture's diminishing of trans temporalities to the visible and calculable attempts to regulate and assimilate trans experiences into the times and spaces of the state, society, and nation (Haritaworn 2015; Spade 2011; Puar 2017).

Trans temporalities also intervene in what can be captured in the other natural, universal order of time considered dialectically opposed to the rational modernity of the heteropatriarchal settler colonial state, liberal civil society, and territorial national body (Mbembe 2003; Bruyneel 2007; Derrida 1992). Trans practices of body-mind-sense and gender transformation stage and potentially rework binary cisgender—structured through whiteness—as a fundamental fault line defining the human and the territorial national body at the threshold between nature and culture. In *Asegi Stories: Cherokee Queer and Two-Spirit Memory* (2016), Qwo-li Driskill addresses the mapping of heteropatriarchal gender and sexual systems onto Cherokee and other southeastern Indigenous bodies, lands, and histories through European invasions and colonization, beginning with Hernando de Soto's sixteenth-century southeastern expedition. Driskill interweaves Indigenous temporalities and cosmologies of nonbinary gender, same-sex love, and political community into the contemporary landscape of the Southeast territories—a naturalized landscape that relied on enslaved Africans for its European settlement. Gloria Anzaldúa (1987) has extended the mixed aesthetics of the borderlands in the Anglo and Spanish colonized southwest territories to create a different set of images that mythologize queer and gender-nonconforming Chicana/Latina survivals in *Light in the Dark/Luz en lo oscuro: Rewriting Identity, Spirituality, Reality* (2015). The Aztec figure of Coyolxauhqui and the Nahuatl concept of nepantla communicate the necessity of decolonizing limited perceptions of reality to embody different worlds and to reconstruct identities fragmented by twenty-first-century manifestations of colonial histories (Anzaldúa 2015). The decolonial methods created by Driskill and Anzaldúa contend with the imposition of heteropatriarchal conceptions of gender and sexuality that allow for the genocidal dispossession of Indigenous, Latinx, and Black forms of embodiment and political collectivity and the colonial cultivation of "natural" settled territories, family, and nation in the United States and Americas (Pérez 1999; Barker 2017). Indigenous two-spirit and decolonial trans of color practices and imaginations draw from temporalities of gender, sexuality, and social relation that exceed—and remain submerged within—the colonial opposition between the modern and natural times of gender (Gómez-Barris 2017). In *Black on Both Sides: A Racial History of Trans Identity* (2017), C. Riley Snorton offers a dynamic racial archive of transness that remembers the conditioning of the modern world and its social orders of being, value, and time on the transubstantiation of blackness as nonbeing (Wynter 2003). His counterhistory traces Black gender transitivity as fugitive expressions of the fungibility and ungendering of blackness within captivity and freedom (Hartman 1997; Spillers 2003). Kale Bantigue Fajardo's queer ethnography of Filipino seafaring masculinities, including tomboy masculinities, in *Filipino Crosscurrents: Oceanographies of Seafaring, Masculinities, and Globalization* (2011) describes the multiple, shifting racial masculinities adapted by the migrant Filipinos who work on the ships that transport 90 percent of the world's current commodities. The oceanic times and spaces shaped by the neoliberal global economy; the Philippine state; and Spanish, US, and Japanese colonialisms—and navigated through the variant gender practices and intimacies of Filipino seafarers—complicate the transpacific frontier that has expanded the US empire beyond its continental territories beginning with Hawai'i, Guam, and the Philippines in 1898 (Trask 1999; Hau'ofa 2008; Bascara 2006; Go 2011).

What will be sensed in the times to come?
What will I sense in the times to come?
What will we sense in the times to come?

Inspired by queer of color critique, trans of color studies can offer other configurations of race, gender, sexuality, and decolonization. Looking to Jose Muñoz's statement, "Queerness is not yet here. . . . Put another way, we are not yet queer, but we can feel it as the warm illumination of a horizon imbued with potentiality. . . . The future is queerness's domain," invites a similar consideration of transness as felt horizon. We do not presume queerness and transness to be necessarily separate. A decolonial trans of color figuration understands that transness both is not yet here and has always been here. The multiple temporalities of trans of color critique can be seen in the decolonial acknowledgment of the injustice of the present, which sees that present as emerging from a past colonial encounter and works for futures that will exist after racial capitalism's totalizing logics. Similarly, transness and gender nonconformity often imply a disjunct time, in which an assignment at birth is retroactively rejected, and a present embodiment is understood as needing to become otherwise in the future.

Trans futures are surprising and unpredictable, if the contents of this issue are any indication. Perhaps trans futures, instead of looking like pink neon, blue-gray steel, and shining glass, look like bone and blood, like impure ecologies of mixing and contamination, like reimagining kinship to include beings with manufactured bodies, like clones and robots.

The contributors in this issue perform futures for trans studies and trans struggles by introducing times and spaces of trans critique, experience, and imagination that challenge conventions of discipline, genre, method, and perception. They also intervene in efforts to produce normalized transgender subjects. LaVelle Ridley's discussion of *Tangerine* (dir. Sean Baker, 2015) reads Mya Taylor's singing performance in the film as producing a moment of reprieve—a moment to breathe—away from the experiences of antiblackness, transmisogyny, anti–sex work respectability, and capitalism faced by Black trans women and visually captured in the film. She suggests that this moment of singing offers embodied practices and knowledge of Black trans existence beyond the binary of resistance and assimilation. Krizia Puig crosses times in their article, using an Anzaldúan method blending theory, poetry, fiction, and autobiography, and adding layers of media as well, in ways that continue to challenge the presumptions of academic discourse. Puig conjures futures of alien embodiment, which recall Anzaldúa's ritual of becoming alien, yet sees them as heading (back) into the stars. V Varun Chaudhry's essay considers the future possibilities of solidarity between trans studies and activism and Black feminism, based on the gendering of Black women in excess of white heteronormative categories, as theorized by Saidiya Hartman, Hortense Spillers, and C. Riley Snorton, in large part because of the fungibility forced on them by racial capitalism (Hartman 1997; Spillers 1987; Snorton 2017). Rox Samer proposes a practice of vidding, or remixing existing videos, sounds, and texts, as a form of research and argument through creative practice. They describe how this form has been used previously, as well as how they have created their own vids to articulate possibilities of transfeminist futures from the television show *Orphan Black*. Vick Quezada uses mixed media to create a visual encounter with the submerged histories of settler colonialism that have shaped hybrid Indigenous-Latinx consciousness in the Americas. Their artwork in this issue—which is also featured on the cover—brings Indigenous temporalities and worlds of materiality, interconnection, and gender to the surface of the visible image.

Contributors to the issue examine the neoliberal administrative technologies that have expanded the settler colonial state's capacity to control and diminish trans lives and to render trans futures less than possible. They identify the bodily, spatial, and temporal regimes that regulate which, and how, trans people will be included in the state's vision of society and nation. They also describe and envision trans and queer relational and embodied practices of survival, reproduction, and transformation that move beyond what can be captured by these regimes, which have been fundamentally shaped by histories of empire, racism, heteropatriarchy, colonialism, capitalism, and ableism. Ren-yo Hwang counters linear accounts of prison reform and the carceral state from sovereign capital punishment to their most recent liberal revision in carceral care, which claims to humanize the treatment of those incarcerated. Rather than sig-naling progress, carceral care, they argue, intensifies violence in ways that con-tinue the long history of pathologizing Black femme subjectivity. Using ethno-graphic vignettes to document their collaboration with Aliya Sanders and other trans women inside the California public prison system, Hwang offers a relational mode of endurance and care that defies the deadening effects of carceral care. Olivia Fiorilli discusses the 2017 ban on the state's mandatory sterilization of trans people as the prerequisite for legal gender recognition in France as an extension of—rather than departure from—the state's efforts to eliminate the possibility of trans reproduction, especially for trans women, and to preserve reproductive futurity for cisnormative women and men. By analyzing the regulation of trans reproduction, gender-affirming medical processes, and gender identity markers through interlocking legal, public, and medical systems since the 1950s, Fiorilli shows that liberalized state recognition for trans people in France continues to annihilate trans futures, including the denial of self-determined gender, enforce-ment of cisnormative bodily uniformity, and barred access to one's own repro-ductive capacities. Marie Draz explores the less visible temporal management of gender self-determination by the state through gender documentation practices in the United States and United Kingdom. While she acknowledges the important shift toward trans, nonbinary, and intersex self-identification enabled by the California Gender Recognition Act of 2017 and the earlier UK Gender Recognition Act of 2004, she calls attention to the legislations' attempts to exact the promise of gender fixity over time through gender classification and identity documentation that serves colonial racial state building. Bess Collins Van Asselt provides a critique of neoliberal education models, particularly the Advancement Via Individual Determination (AVID) program, aimed at training students from marginalized socioeconomic classes for college success beginning as early as kindergarten. Asselt describes the regimented temporal advancement, gender embodiment, and social interaction—modeled after white upward mobility—required by the AVID curriculum and their eviction of trans and queer Black youth and youth of color.

Authors in this issue explore the specific temporalities and practices of trans, nonbinary, and gender-nonconforming gender transformation, transition, and naming. J de Leon's essay understands the act of renaming oneself, and the adoption of new pronouns, as a collective gesture of futurity that wills a future self into being, in collaboration and community, when the name and pronoun(s) are spoken by others. Hil Malatino sees the time of waiting to transition to an imagined properly gendered state as the interregnum, a time akin to Lauren Berlant's cruel optimism, and contrasts that time with the critical utopian worlds of messy joyful survival seen in works of fiction by trans women authors Kai

Cheng Thom and Torrey Peters. In the place of agonizing waiting for futures of joy, joy promised by seeing the happiness of others on social media, Malatino gestures to futures in which trans people love and care for each other.

There are a number of aspects of this issue on trans futures that we wanted to be otherwise. We regret the lack of Indigenous and two-spirit authors in this issue and wish to see two-spirit futures addressed in an issue to come. Additionally, we acknowledge that the majority of the essays included are from authors based in the United States. While that may be an effect of both of the editors living in the United States, we acknowledge that we could certainly have done more to expand the field of trans studies internationally.

We thank *TSQ* general editors Susan Stryker and Francisco Galarte and managing editor Abe Weil for giving us the opportunity to bring together this special issue and for their guidance and support. We appreciate the contributors who gifted this issue with their work and the peer reviewers who provided generous and attentive feedback on submissions.

We feel the imperative to imagine trans futures in the face of so much violence, which only presents death as our collective future. Together, the authors and artists in this special issue not only imagine livable futures for trans people but also call into question the linear and universal times of settler colonialism, white supremacy, and heteropatriarchy. They imagine trans times as containing pockets of slowness, dead-end diversions, and the openness of multiplicity. They perform a claim to trans futures that opens up the possibility of materializing the reconstructed realities and worlds of trans times.

> *What will be done in the times to come?*
> *What will I do in the times to come?*
> *What will we do in the times to come?*

Jian Neo Chen (*they/he*) is associate professor of queer studies in the English Department at the Ohio State University. Their first book *Trans Exploits: Trans of Color Cultures and Technologies in Movement* (2019) explores the displaced emergences of trans of color cultural expression and activism through performance, film/video, literature, and digital media by the second decade of the twenty-first century. Chen serves on the editorial board of *TSQ*.

micha cárdenas, PhD, is assistant professor of Art & Design: Games & Playable Media at the University of California, Santa Cruz. Her book in progress, "Poetic Operations," proposes algorithmic analysis as a method for developing a trans of color poetics. cárdenas has coauthored *The Transreal: Political Aesthetics of Crossing Realities* (2011) and *Trans Desire/Affective Cyborgs* (2010).

References

Amin, Kadji. 2014. "Temporality." *TSQ* 1, nos. 1–2: 219–22.

Anzaldúa, Gloria. 1987. *Borderlands/La Frontera: The New Mestiza*. San Francisco: Aunt Lute.

Anzaldúa, Gloria. 2015. *Light in the Dark/Luz en lo oscuro: Rewriting Identity, Spirituality, Reality.* Edited by AnaLouise Keating. Durham, NC: Duke University Press.

Barker, Joanne, ed. 2017. *Critically Sovereign: Indigenous Gender, Sexuality, and Feminist Studies.* Durham, NC: Duke University Press.

Bascara, Victor. 2006. *Model-Minority Imperialism*. Minneapolis: University of Minnesota Press.

Bruyneel, Kevin. 2007. *The Third Space of Sovereignty: The Postcolonial Politics of U.S.-Indigenous Relations.* Minneapolis: University of Minnesota Press.

cárdenas, micha. 2011. *The Transreal: Political Aesthetics of Crossing Realities.* Edited by Zach Blas and Wolfgang Schirmacher. New York: Atropos.

Derrida, Jacques. 1992. "Given Time: The Time of the King," translated by Peggy Kamuf. *Critical Inquiry* 18, no. 2: 161–87.

Driskill, Qwo-Li. 2016. *Asegi Stories: Cherokee Queer and Two-Spirit Memory.* Tucson: University of Arizona Press.

Fajardo, Kale Bantigue. 2011. *Filipino Crosscurrents: Oceanographies of Seafaring, Masculinities, and Globalization.* Minneapolis: University of Minnesota Press.

Go, Julian. 2011. *Patterns of Empire: The British and American Empires, 1688 to the Present.* Cambridge, MA: Cambridge University Press.

Gómez-Barris, Macarena. 2017. *The Extractive Zone: Social Ecologies and Decolonial Perspectives.* Durham, NC: Duke University Press.

Halberstam, Jack. 2005. *In a Queer Time and Place: Transgender Bodies, Subcultural Lives.* New York: New York University Press.

Haritaworn, Jin. 2015. *Queer Lovers and Hateful Others: Regenerating Violent Times and Places.* London: Pluto.

Hartman, Saidiya V. 1997. *Scenes of Subjection: Terror, Slavery, and Self-Making in Nineteenth-Century America.* New York: Oxford University Press.

Hau'ofa, Epeli. 2008. *We Are the Ocean: Selected Works*. Honolulu: University of Hawai'i Press.

Massumi, Brian. 2002. *Parables for the Virtual: Movement, Affect, Sensation.* Durham, NC: Duke University Press.

Mbembe, Achille. 2003. *On the Postcolony*. Berkeley: University of California Press.

Mock, Janet. 2014. *Redefining Realness: My Path to Womanhood, Identity, Love, and So Much More.* New York: Atria.

Pérez, Emma. 1999. *The Decolonial Imaginary: Writing Chicanas into History.* Bloomington: Indiana University Press.

Puar, Jasbir K. 2007. *Terrorist Assemblages*. Durham, NC: Duke University Press.

Puar, Jasbir K. 2017. *The Right to Maim: Debility, Capacity, Disability.* Durham, NC: Duke University Press.

Salah, Trish. 2017. "'Time Isn't after Us': Some Tiresian Durations." *Somatechnics* 7, no. 1: 16–33.

Snorton, C. Riley. 2017. *Black on Both Sides: A Racial History of Trans Identity.* Durham, NC: Duke University Press.

Spade, Dean. 2011. *Normal Life: Administrative Violence, Critical Trans Politics, and the Limits of Law.* Cambridge, MA: South End.

Spillers, Hortense J. 1987. "Mama's Baby, Papa's Maybe: An American Grammar Book." *Diacritics* 17, no. 2: 65–81.

Spillers, Hortense J. 2003. *Black, White, and in Color: Essays on American Literature and Culture.* Chicago: University of Chicago Press.

Trask, Haunani-Kay. 1999. *From a Native Daughter: Colonialism and Sovereignty in Hawai'i.* Honolulu: University of Hawai'i Press.

Tsing, Anna Lowenhaupt, Heather Anne Swanson, Elaine Gan, and Nils Bubandt. 2017. *Arts of Living on a Damaged Planet: Ghosts and Monsters of the Anthropocene.* Minneapolis: University of Minnesota Press.

Wynter, Sylvia. 2003. "Unsettling the Coloniality of Being/Power/Truth/Freedom: Towards the Human, after Man, Its Overrepresentation—An Argument." *CR: The New Centennial Review* 3, no. 3: 257–337.

Imagining Otherly

Performing Possible Black Trans Futures in Tangerine

LAVELLE RIDLEY

Abstract In this article the author focuses on Mya Taylor's singing performance as Alexandra in the 2015 comedy-drama film *Tangerine* as a performative index of black trans women's futures. Contextualizing her performance within the larger, dangerous world for most black trans sex workers that the film portrays largely without critique, the author argues that this scene offers Alexandra, and black trans viewers of the film, a brief reprieve from the anxieties of social and state oppression and allows her (and us) to breathe, and within that breath to imagine toward radical futures that resist the binary of resistance and compliance, to imagine otherly. The author draws on black trans studies, black feminist theory, and black cultural and media studies to articulate how this film as a unique and crucial moment of black trans cultural production also offers us a key moment in theorizing black trans epistemology.

Keywords black trans women, trans futures, film, imagination, black trans epistemology

"The Audacity to Breathe": An Affective Approach to Black Trans Possibilities

Only a few months into my transition as a black trans woman, I saw a new movie on Netflix called *Tangerine*.[1] My partner, a white trans man, encouraged me to watch it, and I agreed only if we made a date of it. During the hour-and-a-half film, we laughed, cried, and argued about politics. Once the film was over, we were transformed by the beauty of the actors' performances. Not only did Mya Taylor (Alexandra) and Kitana Kiki Rodriguez (Sin-Dee) give stunning performances, but we were fortunate to watch black trans women portray black trans women on screen: self-representation that is revolutionary (though it should not be). Although visibility and representation are challenging concepts in trans studies and politics, exemplified by Che Gossett and Juliana Huxtable's (2017: 45) critique of visibility as "a scattering of people without any redistribution of power," I found extreme satisfaction, both personally and intellectually, in observing these women portraying experiences of existing within the matrix of antiblackness, misogyny, transphobia, and whorephobia they themselves have

TSQ: Transgender Studies Quarterly ★ Volume 6, Number 4 ★ November 2019
DOI 10.1215/23289252-7771653 © 2019 Duke University Press

endured because it signaled a moment of varied self-recognition. We are all black trans women—me, Taylor, Rodriguez, and their characters—and yet our narratives are not homogenous, though we fall similarly under routinized enactments of power. As Marquis Bey (2016: 34) writes in his essay on black transfeminist thought, "my corporeality is the vessel through which I understand the world"; therefore, witnessing these characterizations signals an important moment for meditating on the conditions of possibility for black trans women to move, gesture, and imagine toward the future. *Tangerine*, specifically Alexandra's singing performance scene, maintains the possibility for black trans people—viewer and character alike—to imagine and express forms of knowledge and ways of existing with systems of domination that do not rely on the binary of resistance and assimilation.

Tangerine centers its trans characters in a way that does not posit them as villains, tricksters, or sinners, but as complex women who live difficult, though sometimes humorous, lives. Nonetheless, the film portrays the daily violences experienced by Alexandra and Sin-Dee as natural and expected—they are black trans women and sex workers. The expectation of violence and oppression illustrates what C. Riley Snorton and Jin Haritaworn (2013: 66) term "trans necropolitics" or "the discursive and representational politics of trans death and trans vitality." This signaling of the precarity of black trans life is echoed by black trans activist Lourdes Ashley Hunter's (2015) bold assertion that "every breath a black trans woman takes is an act of revolution." Even further, Hunter's declaration is animated by its resonance with the 2014 murder of Eric Garner, during which he repeated, "I can't breathe." The inability to breathe, to aspirate, structures black and trans life, and I offer the concept of "imagining otherly," in part, as a way to think through how the reprieve, the ability to catch one's breath, that illustrates Alexandra's singing performance structures how we might think of black trans futures and knowledges. Imagining otherly seeks to suggest an epistemological escape from the precarious confines that trans necropolitics posit.

In this essay, I focus specifically on one scene: Alexandra's singing performance. The part of the scene I discuss begins with Alexandra pacing outside the club called Mary's to her covertly handing money to the doorman after performing. I suggest the performance in this scene offers the clearest articulation of imagining otherly, which functions as both a survival tactic and epistemological framework for addressing the possibilities that lie in moving beyond the polarizing ways of engaging with power: to resist or comply. Imagining otherly attempts to reveal the pathways to other radical forms of possibility for black trans women's futurity by thinking, as Kai M. Green (2015: 196) writes, "toward possibilities outside of those that have been deemed permissible by the state." Imagining otherly provides an alternative framework for thinking about the stakes of black trans representation in media by foregrounding the possibility of escape to some imagined elsewhere, a knowledge project that, I hope, uniquely positions black trans people's engagement with futurity instead of reveling in the supposed arrival of equality and change that ideas such as the "transgender tipping point" herald.

Instead of focusing merely on the ramifications of representation, this essay questions what black trans epistemology looks like and what value we might find in black trans knowledge. As the editors of the *TSQ* special issue "The Issue of Blackness" claim, they see "Black feminist theory as essential to black trans theory and to transgender studies. Black feminist thought, labor, and commitment have been essential to the de/construction of gender and sexuality" (Ellison et al. 2017: 166). Understanding that these fields are interlocking is paramount to developing black trans political and epistemological stances. Certainly this project already has academic and creative roots. Scholars, artists, and activists such as Miss Major Griffin-Gracy, Matt Richardson, C. Riley Snorton, Kai M. Green, Dora Silva Santana, Tourmaline, Che Gossett, Marquis Bey, and others have laid critical foundations for thinking about how the experiences of black trans people matter.[2] This essay seeks to engage with black feminist and trans studies by centering the forms and contours of knowledge produced by black trans sex workers in *Tangerine* and offering a way of reading their visual presentation that suggests a divorce from constricting forms of resistance and engagement with oppressive structures.

"Out Here It's All about Our Hustle, and That's It": Staging Black Trans Imaginations

Released in 2015 by Magnolia Pictures, *Tangerine* follows two black trans sex workers—Sin-Dee Rella and Alexandra—on Christmas Eve in Los Angeles. Sin-Dee has just been released from a twenty-eight-day stint in jail and, upon catching up with her friend Alexandra, discovers that her pimp/boyfriend Chester has been cheating on her with a white "fish," meaning a cisgender woman. Enraged, Sin-Dee storms across Los Angeles in search of this fish and Chester, the quest from which the film's hilarity stems. This other woman's whiteness and cisness heightens the viewing audience's awareness of Sin-Dee's blackness and transness. Sin-Dee's return from jail further notes the perilous connections black trans women—those who are sex workers, in particular—have with carceral power. That her boyfriend—whose relationship to Sin-Dee cannot be divorced from his position as her pimp—is cheating with a white cis woman plays into seemingly commonplace situations in which black trans women are found only on the periphery of permissible desirability, easily replaceable by those with more racial and sexual capital.

In her pursuit of this fish—whose name is Dinah, as Sin-Dee expertly uncovers—Sin-Dee drags an unhappy and disapproving Alexandra along. As we see throughout the film, Alexandra expresses disdain toward Sin-Dee's never-ending drama. Despite revealing Chester's infidelity, Alexandra wants nothing to do with Sin-Dee's revenge, thus complicating her relationship with her friend. The crusade to find Chester's lover takes the viewers around the block, encountering several of the "girls," as in other black trans women who engage in sex work. Despite her reluctance to accompany Sin-Dee on this quest, Alexandra goes along, using the opportunity to pass out flyers advertising a singing performance she will give at Mary's. While passing out the flyers around the block to the girls, Alexandra's request for an audience takes on a doubled tone, both pleading and commanding. In the same breath, Alexandra asks the girls, "Please be there tonight. Don't disappoint me," and then employs the forceful refrain "Mary's at 7:00! Mary's at 7:00! Mary's at 7:00!" This doubled tone, accompanied by assertive pointing and a stern facial expression hidden behind sunglasses, also signals an insecurity Alexandra has with trans women of color in the film, including Sin-Dee. The girls hesitantly agree to come, and Alexandra carries on with Sin-Dee in search of Chester and his lover. Later in the film, Alexandra encounters a different group of girls on the block and yells, "Don't forget my performance at 7:00!" followed with a hushed "Ugly ass bitches." Behind her back, the girls sneer at Alexandra, saying hurtful things about her body and undesirability. During Alexandra's request for an audience, the camera focuses on her body language—she walks quickly and rigidly on the sidewalk, keeping her interaction with the girls to a minimum—and the way she expresses both anxiety and impatience with members of her community, indexing Alexandra's visual and verbal relationship with the girls. Encountering the girls here matters because they do not appear later at the performance. The requested presence and received absence evidence the discordant relationship among trans women of color in *Tangerine*.

While Alexandra advertises her performance and interacts with a few clients, Sin-Dee has finally found Dinah and holds her hostage. We see the two women riding the bus to Donut Time, and the camera cross-cuts to Alexandra as she paces outside Mary's, hoping someone shows up for her performance. As if by telepathy, Sin-Dee realizes the time and quickly exits the bus with Dinah and heads to Mary's. Upon entering the nearly empty club, Alexandra, Sin-Dee, and Dinah head straight to the bathroom, where the lighting is dim but colorful. Alexandra struggles with her makeup, her anxiety on full display. Sin-Dee helps her "fix her mug," or apply makeup, reminding her, "That's what everybody's looking at." This gesture further complicates Sin-Dee and Alexandra's friendship, seemingly moving away from its discordant nature.

As the performance begins, the staging and close-up shot of Alexandra singing attempts to capture the performance as a respectable demonstration of talent. Sitting on a small stool on a small stage in front of a microphone stand with silvery tinsel, Alexandra, wearing a red dress and red lipstick, begins to sing. As she sings, with a red curtain draped behind her, she maintains a stiff pose and emotionless facial expression. She has both hands placed on her knee, legs crossed, facing the crowd, proving her ability to not only perform well but also exude proper femininity. Alexandra's posturing illustrates a performative adoption of "respectability politics, heteronormative standards, and class privilege," what Julian Kevon Glover (2016: 340) terms "transnormativity." Alexandra's attitude toward Sin-Dee and other trans women in the film and performance of apparent respectability index a desire for upward mobility, to gain reprieve from the hegemonic systems that oppress her. But I do not believe that is going on here. Rather, I argue that the visuality of Alexandra's performance registers how imagining otherly provides an escape route from those hegemonic systems. Here, I draw on Juana María Rodríguez's deployment of fantasy to underscore the complex maneuvers that imagining otherly offers. In her book *Sexual Futures, Queer Gestures, and Other Latina Longings*, Rodríguez (2014: 26) draws on the work of Judith Butler, Leo Bersani, and José Esteban Muñoz to establish fantasy's function as "an escape from the real-world materiality of living, *breathing* bodies, but as a way to conjure and inhabit an alternative world in which other forms of identification and social relations become *imaginable*" (italics added). For Rodríguez, "queer understandings of sexual futures" (27) depend critically on the ability to fantasize, to "inhabit the imagined elsewhere of a radical sexual sociality" (26). She principally draws from Butler's (2004: 29; italics added) "critical promise of fantasy," which, in *Undoing Gender*, she describes as that which "allows us to imagine ourselves and others *otherwise*." I italicize these key words of Rodríguez and Butler to textually lay bare the ways in which my conception of imagining otherly is indebted to the concept of fantasy, how systems of domination and polarized responses to that domination—resistance and compliance—are pivoted on otherwise, approached in differently imagined ways. Understanding the process of imagining otherly through the valence of fantasy clarifies that Alexandra is not simply striving for a transnormative self-presentation but actively demonstrating a possible and alternative pathway for a black trans sex worker. This articulation interrupts hegemonic discourses on representation, illustrating Che Gossett's (2017: 185) claim that "blackness ruptures trans representability, respectability, and visibility." Other paths, such as singing the song "Toyland,"[3] become clear and possible by imagining otherly.

The song "Toyland" is an apt choice for Alexandra's performance, not only because the events of *Tangerine* take place on Christmas Eve but also because the song lyrics evidence the necessity of imagination, given the impossibility of moving toward Butler's otherwise. The song illustrates how wonderful the land of Toyland is for little boys and girls, who will never want to leave once they enter.

The song creates an image of a place without struggle where one can flourish. Through the song's imagery as a fantastical escape mechanism, I contend, Alexandra desires Toyland and imagines herself there, producing an alternative reality and an alternative future for herself. Alexandra deploys Toyland as a "freedom dream," a truly utopic place where she could imagine a life other than the one the film's narrative plans for her and fulfill Robin D. G. Kelley's (2002: 2) belief that "the map to a new world is in the imagination." Considering Toyland as a utopia allows the viewer to understand that imagining herself within or as moving toward this place is made possible only by its artifice. Alexandra can dream toward Toyland because she will never truly reach it, though, as L. H. Stallings (2015: 211) reminds us in *Funk the Erotic*, "It is only in recognizing one's mythical status that the process of making inventive futures can begin." Alongside freedom dreams, Kai Green's deployment of *tranifestation* provides a generative way of understanding how Alexandra's performance imagines otherly and marks the impossible-possible of Toyland. He claims, "*Tranifesting*, or transformative manifesting, describes the theories, methods, and modes and forms of self-representation that attempt to call into being flexible collectivities or groupings whose articulation transforms normative understandings of race, gender, sex, and sexuality" (2013: 300).

Alexandra's performance allows her to move away from the transmisogyny, antiblackness, anti–sex work sentiment, and capitalist forces that impact her experiences throughout the film and produce an alternative future via imagination of other paths. This process of disidentifying with the interlocking systems of power that negatively impact her life reveals her performance to be both a personal freedom dream and also a veiled survival tactic. Alexandra widely advertised her performance to the girls on the block to form strong(er) bonds of community among black trans women and to also perform other futures for them. If witnessing one black trans woman give an excellent singing performance was enough to convince another girl to chart a new path, then Alexandra's mission would be accomplished, and such a manifestation might draw the community even closer together.

Once the performance is done, Alexandra pays the doorman for allowing her to sing, revealing the lengths that black trans women must go through to even demonstrate their chances for other kinds of existence as well as the impossibility of reaching any kind of Toyland. This monetary exchange signals the complex relations between the materiality of black trans women's lives and the limited, though productive, ways by which they aspire, fantasize, and imagine otherly. Indeed, Alexandra's performance scene stands out as a captivating cinematic moment that showcases not only the vocal talents of a black trans woman but also her capability to adapt to a different kind of environment, one in which she might flourish and find fulfillment. Understanding Alexandra as tranifesting a different path by imagining otherly also allows us to perceive how Alexandra is creating a new (form of) knowledge with her performance. This scene is critical because while the rest of the film upholds the hegemonic epistemological relationships between black trans women and state power—depicting scenes of poverty, abjection, and sexual violence, for instance—Alexandra's performance provides a tiny reprieve, a moment for viewer and character alike to imagine otherly. This scene takes a break from those strict, grounded sources of interlocking oppressions for black trans women who engage in sex work and allows Alexandra to perform "survival and breathing and [the] possibility of transfeminine desire amid and beyond our social and material conditions" (Raha 2017: 632). The estimations and analyses I have outlined allow us to understand how, in a way, this scene does not make sense with the rest of the film. It divorces itself from the hegemonic outline for black trans women's lives that *Tangerine* generally upholds and makes its own sense, producing its own knowledge about what potential such lives carry. Performance, it would seem, is also not a luxury.[4]

Toward a Black Trans Epistemology

Alexandra's performance not only illuminates how imagining otherly signals a critical engagement with systems of domination that limit the possible pathways for black trans women; it also signals its epistemic function, meaning that this engagement with imagining the future is a process of knowledge production. Thinking through imagining otherly, fantasy, freedom dreams, and tranifesting, we might ask what Alexandra's performance tells us about knowledge, its production, its articulation, and the stakes a black trans epistemology has for black trans women. How does her performance gesture toward different approaches of embodied black trans knowledge? Performance can be a method for political expression and a veiled survival tactic. Advertising her singing performance was a way for Alexandra to demonstrate that she had the capability of transforming her life and of doing things differently in service to her own desires and joy. This is why I claim tranifesting specifically as a framework for imagining otherly as well as an epistemological function that points us toward understanding how black trans peoples' labor and value might lead to alternative trans futures. The performance scene allows viewers to see that other paths are available to black trans women, even when they have to forge them themselves.

Love, specifically in its "forms of care and support," as articulated by Nat Raha (2017: 637), provides another ground on which to theorize black trans epistemology. In their article "'She Came to Liberate': Janet Mock and Revolutionary Love among Trans Women," Timothy S. Lyle (2017) explicates Mock's first memoir *Redefining Realness* and offers the term *revolutionary love*, a concept they note as first articulated during the black arts movement, to describe how trans women of color (most importantly, those who were sex workers) showed love to Mock as a young black trans girl and helped her create and understand community. Discordant understandings of community are another facet of black trans meaning making in *Tangerine*. It illustrates what Raha (2017: 637) defines as radical transfeminism, an analytic and praxis that helps trans women (of color) "through working together, over and across material precarity." This specific kind of love permits both a discordant relationship between the girls as well as a solid defense and protection of each other. While Alexandra prepares herself for her performance in the club bathroom, Sin-Dee uses the toilet and wipes her urine-stained hands on Dinah's hair, demeaning her as they take up space together. Mirroring this encounter, Sin-Dee, having learned that Alexandra betrayed their friendship by sleeping with Chester, storms off to pursue clients, which results in urine being thrown in her face, along with homophobic and transphobic slurs. As a loving and sisterly gesture, Alexandra takes Sin-Dee to the nearby laundromat, helps her wash her clothes and her wig, and even gives Sin-Dee her own wig to ease her comfort while they wait. Hair is a central and politicized aspect of black women's daily experiences, and this gesture signals a fierce love and dedication to sisterhood. Just a moment ago, Sin-Dee despised Alexandra but now embraces her as a beloved friend who took care of her. Radical transfeminism's priority of care and support provides an epistemological backing to imagining otherly, showing how it reveals the sometimes contradictory epistemic nature of black trans women community formations. Thinking through this, how might Alexandra's performance evidence an epistemic formation that moves her closer to transformation, either material or imagined? One could imagine that Alexandra, had she a larger audience, could have radically transformed the fabric of her community and instilled a form of social justice change. One could also imagine her becoming a famous and well-received singer, perhaps of holiday songs. According to *Tangerine*, all Alexandra leaves her performance with is the love of her friend Sin-Dee, and I contend that there are political and community-based stakes in this love. *Tangerine* illustrates this clearly. This shows us that no matter the outcome, the gesture of daring to imagine itself might be a productive move toward collective liberation and personal joy.

LaVelle Ridley is a queer black transsexual woman and a doctoral candidate in women's studies and English at the University of Michigan. Her work focuses on twentieth- and twenty-first-century African American fiction, black feminist theory, queer of color critique, and transgender studies. She is currently working on a dissertation that examines contemporary black trans narratives and theorizes how these narratives illuminate a larger black trans literary genealogy, one specifically structured by radical abolitionist praxis.

Acknowledgments

I must thank Victor R. Mendoza and Maria E. Cotera for the initial feedback on this essay in its graduate seminar form. Additionally, I would like to thank Ava Purkiss, LaKisha M. Simmons, Cassius Adair, and the graduate student members of the Black Research Roundtable at the University of Michigan—Eshe Sherley, Casidy Campbell, Reuben Riggs-Bookman, and Maryam Aziz, specifically—for giving me space to rehearse these ideas and for their valuable feedback.

Notes

1.   I draw this section title from Marquis Bey's (2016: 45) article "The Shape of Angels' Teeth."

2.   Here, I would especially like to express gratitude for Dora Silva Santana and her essay "Transitionings and Returnings: Experiments with the Poetics of Transatlantic Water" (2017). Not only does Silva Santana bring up important interventions in how we can think about the fluidity of water and life and its relationship to transatlantic studies and black trans studies, but she also provides a blueprint of how a black trans woman can take up personal as well as critical space in academic writing. Her essay, as well as her warmth and generosity, have greatly inspired my own writing style and desire to center myself and other trans women of color.

3.   The version of "Toyland" Alexandra performs comes from Doris Day's 1964 recording of the song from the original 1903 operetta *Babes in Toyland* by Victor Herbert and Glen MacDonough.

4.   Here I signify on the title of Audre Lorde's classic essay "Poetry Is Not a Luxury" (1984).

References

Bey, Marquis. 2016. "The Shape of Angels' Teeth: Toward a Blacktransfeminist Thought through the Mattering of Black(Trans)Lives." *Departures in Critical Qualitative Research* 5, no. 3: 33–54.

Butler, Judith. 2004. *Undoing Gender.* New York: Routledge.

Ellison, Treva, Kai M. Green, Matt Richardson, and C. Riley Snorton. 2017. "We Got Issues: Toward a Black Trans*/Studies." *TSQ* 4, no. 2: 162–69.

Glover, Julian Kevon. 2016. "Redefining Realness? On Janet Mock, Laverne Cox, TS Madison, and the Representation of Transgender Women of Color in Media." *Souls* 18, nos. 2–4: 338–57.

Gossett, Che. 2017. "Blackness and the Trouble of Trans Visibility." In *Trap Door: Trans Cultural Production and the Politics of Visibility*, edited by Tourmaline, Eric A. Stanley, and Johanna Burton, 183–190. Cambridge, MA: MIT Press.

Gossett, Che, and Juliana Huxtable. 2017. "Existing in the World: Blackness at the Edge of Trans Visibility." In *Trap Door: Trans Cultural Production and the Politics of Visibility*, edited by Tourmaline, Eric A. Stanley, and Johanna Burton, 39–55. Cambridge, MA: MIT Press.

Green, Kai M. 2013. "'What the Eyes Did Not Wish to Behold': Lessons from Ann Allen Shockley's *Say Jesus and Come to Me.*" *South Atlantic Quarterly* 112, no. 2: 285–302.

Green, Kai M. 2015. "The Essential I/Eye in We: A Black TransFeminist Approach to Ethnographic Film." *Black Camera* 6, no. 2: 187–200.

Hunter, Lourdes Ashley. 2015. "Every Breath a Black Trans Woman Takes Is an Act of Revolution." *Huffington Post*, February 6. www.huffingtonpost.com/lourdes-ashley-hunter/every -breath-a-black-tran_b_6631124.html.

Kelley, Robin D. G. 2002. *Freedom Dreams: The Black Radical Imagination.* Boston: Beacon.

Lorde, Audre. 1984. "Poetry Is Not a Luxury." In *Sister Outsider: Essays and Speeches*, 36–39. New York: Crossing.

Lyle, Timothy S. 2017. "'She Came to Liberate': Janet Mock and Revolutionary Love among Trans Women." *CLA Journal* 60, no. 2: 225–43.

Raha, Nat. 2017. "Against the Day: Transfeminine Brokenness, Radical Transfeminism." *South Atlantic Quarterly* 116, no. 3: 632–46.

Rodríguez, Juana María. 2014. *Sexual Futures, Queer Gestures, and Other Latina Longings*. New York: New York University Press.

Silva Santana, Dora. 2017. "Transitionings and Returnings: Experiments with the Poetics of Transatlantic Water." *TSQ* 4, no. 2: 181–90.

Snorton, C. Riley, and Jin Haritaworn. 2013. "Trans Necropolitics." In *The Transgender Studies Reader 2*, edited by Aren Aizura and Susan Stryker, 66–76. New York: Routledge.

Stallings, L. H. 2015. *Funk the Erotic: Transaesthetics and Black Sexual Cultures*. Urbana: University of Illinois Press.

The TransAlien Manifesto

*Future Love(s), Sex Tech, and My Efforts
to Re-member Your Embrace*

KRIZIA PUIG

Abstract This is not an article. If anything, these are "trans futurist spiritual science visions": radically vulnerable interventions that aim to disrupt naturalized forms of publishable knowledge while centering the needs, fantasies, and longings of disabled queer/trans folks in practices of future-making. These lines transcend the limits of academic knowledge. They are an act of resistance against the logics of subjectivity, relationality, fulfillment, and temporality that permeate current and envisioned notions of love(s). Here, a game for us to play: a theoretical-performative experiment to envision future notions of relationality—while shifting the hypernormative and cis hetero-romantic logics behind contemporary understandings of what sex robots should do and/or be. This is an exploration of the challenges/potentialities of relationships "AmongWithToThrough" humans and nonhuman organic, virtual, and/or synthetic beings. For you—disjointed knowledge: I am jamming on the paper, and there is a soundtrack for each section. I spin the page, and invite you to read with (in) the music. Endnotes are important: engage with them. I do not offer settled conclusions. Above all, this is *una ofrenda a corazón abierto* written in pain (chronic pain) or maybe an invitation for you to hold my hand. Honor your *bodymindspirit*: read in any order and think whatever you want when you finish. Thank you very much for your time. All the love and light . . .
Keywords #TransAlien, #FutureLove, #SexRobots, #Transfuturisms, #PublishOrPerish

To the loves that grant me other tomorrow(s) . . .
Sav, Layla, Vico, and Lupe—
For you, all the techno-spiritual hugs

El amor que nos negaron es nuestro impulso para cambiar el mundo.
—Lohana Berkins

TSQ: Transgender Studies Quarterly ∗ Volume 6, Number 4 ∗ November 2019 **491**
DOI 10.1215/23289252-7771667 © 2019 Duke University Press

Lies will flow from my lips, but there may perhaps be some truth mixed up with them; it is for you to seek out this truth and to decide whether any part of it is worth keeping.

—Virginia Woolf, *A Room of One's Own*

Irony is about the tension of holding incompatible things together because both or all are necessary and true. Irony is about humor and serious play. It is also a rhetorical strategy and a political method.

—Donna J. Haraway, *Simians, Cyborgs, and Women: The Reinvention of Nature*

The Nature of Love: Janis Joplin, Cassandra, and *Los Peces con Tres Ojos De* My Middle School Yard

—A tree,
branching to you among wildfires . . .
burning from within—
offerings flying like ceniza

It is your choice
how/if
you want
any/some
of them
. . . some of me . . .

Break another little bit of my heart now, darling!
You know you got it if it makes you feel good.
—Janis Joplin, "Piece of My Heart"[1]
www.youtube.com/watch?v=7uG2gYE5KOs

The water is always bright green, and it has black veins that know how to move. They are never still. The discrete waves have a sort of "radioactive" glare, no matter the day. At night—the oil and other chemical pollutants, the duckweed floating around, and the reflection of los "Relámpagos del Catatumbo" make of this toxic scene a breathtaking place.

Breathtaking in many senses . . .

On the horizon, this lighting phenomenon that occurs at the end of the Catatumbo River makes visible hundreds of pumpjacks extracting oil—quietly and efficiently—from the soil of the Maracaibo (n: [maɾaˈkaiβo]) Lake (fig. 1). The patio of my middle school was at the shore of that lake. The biggest in South America—it is the source of more than half of Venezuela's total production of petroleum. At least it was twenty-five years ago. We were taught to be proud of that—as if it were our flesh and bones, the ones that got rotten turning into black gold.

I read *The Iliad* at 107 degrees; eating shaved ice made with contaminated water; hearing Janis Joplin on a Walkman I inherited from someone I called "aunt" who was not my aunt and whom I never saw again—and imagining that the Trojan horse would have looked (probably) like one of the pumpjacks. Those pumpjacks, always sucking the energy from the soil—and their shadows dancing sadly soothingly with the orange sky . . .

I was surrounded by *peces con tres ojos*—the fishes with three eyes. The third eye was always a side eye growing "TogetherWith" the big eye. The third eye was an eye with a purpose, a sneaky eye, oriented toward something. When the three-eyed fishes appeared dead in the shore, they were always in group—*togetheralone*.

—Maybe Cassandra just wanted to die togetheralone . . . I used to think while looking at those fishes.

In Homer's *Iliad*, Cassandra is the child of Priam and Hecuba—Troy's king and queen. There is no mention of Cassandra's prophetic powers in *The Iliad*, I learned at school. Homer leaves her to a tragic present that never passes. She is pain in gerund—womanhood mourning the death of her brother Hector and the imminent loss of the city after Achilles's victory. It is in other mythological sources, I was taught, where it is explained that the god Apollo gave her the gift of prophecy. Then he cursed Cassandra when she rejected his romantic advances. Cassandra's visions were accurate and never believed. Cassandra knew, but it was worthless. Her story is a blurred tale about knowledge, love, and consent. Cassandra "cheated" on Apollo because she accepted the gift of knowledge—and then she refused to comply with the assumption that she was going to fuck the guy just because she got something from him. I learned that you can be justifiably punished for saying no, that sex could be demanded from me—and I started to question the nature of love: its uses to shape different future (s), different selves, different suffering(s) . . .

What does the Earth feel when the pumpjacks go in—sucking their energy? Why didn't Cassandra just leave? Why was she willing to give so much of herself, regardless of her being wounded, imprisoned, deemed mad? Why was Joplin so willing to be broken, so many times? Why do the three-eyed fish choose to collectively die? Why was that eye placed there—on the side, "GrowingWith" another eye—not in the middle like the goddesses from other places and ages? What is that eye meant to see within that toxic evergreen and always black water? Is that even an eye? What is Cassandra supposed to do with knowledge she cannot prove—within a future that was lost? Why does the Earth keep giving so much to us? Why is love always so toxic, so sad, so exhausting? Am I unlovable? Who is

Figure 1. Earth shot from NASA's Aqua satellite taken on February 15, 2017. It is possible to appreciate the duckweed swirling in the lake. In the color image available online, the brightness of the duckweed is breathtaking. NASA Visible Earth, "An Emerald Vortex," February 15, 2017, visibleearth.nasa.gov/view.php?id=89713.

deemed unlovable? Who is forced to love, and in which ways? What is the value of what we know that we cannot explain—of a hunch, a feeling, a premonition, a *presentimento, de la intuición, una revelación,* a hallucination? What is the relationship between love and knowledge? Why are "valued *presentimientos*" a privilege for the few? Why is the future reachable only for the "mad," materialized by the crazy ones—mutated monsters, those with a third eye?

　　—Maybe the third eye is just to look at each other: to recognize each other while swimming in the darkness—among the unlovable . . .

　　maybe . . .

. . . maybe *ese ojo ni siquiera es un ojo*/ and I started to imagine Cassandra with a third eye, and Janis with a sided eye growingwith another eye; and I began to look at/for the eyes of the Earth and to long for a third eye.

I already had it—but that is another story.

* * *

At the beat of that "take it, take another little piece of my heart now, baby!" that magically fits with the rhythm of the pumpjacks sucking the oil from the heart of the Earth—I might have started to have the suspicion that there is a relationship between the ways in which we are set to relate to each while breaking ourselves apart, the ways in which the energy of our bodymindspirits is used as fuel to sustain and perpetuate socioeconomic systems of inequality, and the ways in which we keep breaking and breaking Earth's heart. There is a connection between different forms of exploitation; different forms of loving and giving, the ways in which different perceptions/experiences of reality shape experiences of love; and the value we are socialized to grant to different forms of certainties within and in relation to those exchanges.

Elegy to the Cyborg Womxn: Trees, Circuits, and Nonhuman Dreams

/// (Clearing their throat)

> The woman I was lies besides the girl I was forced to be:
> Both, dead by radioactive gases . . .

> > "It was the end of the world (as I knew it)
> > and it felt fucking fine."—

> > > No, I don't want to be a cyborg, baby—
> > > > not anymore
> > > > not again/
> > > cyborgs are ancient human tech

No, I don't want to be a cyborg, love—
not anymore
and, no
        no no
            No no no
                neither want to be a (transhu)man, amor/

I want to be a mutated monster with a third eye—
a techno-organic enmeshment with roots in the stars/
pain, joy, and wisdom—
shapeshifting across the sky
swimming
swimming swimming
swimming swimming swimming
—in tropical cosmic waste—

glowing
glowing glowing
glowing glowing glowing
—dirty green and painful black—
like the lake
like the moon at night
*

tropical matter
or the impossibility:
—a comet going back

I'm lost in a forest, all alone.
The girl was never there.
— The Cure, "A Forest"
www.youtube.com/watch?v=hnVldyHRcjU

I started to talk to the trees again since I moved here. It is the magestuosity of the forests. The degeneration of my body has forced me to appreciate the fascinating vitality in the stillness of these trees. Or, maybe it is this feeling of uprootedness that follows me everywhere, this certainty of being profoundly alone in the world, of existing detached from the real: lost in translation—in intention. An alien without a passport: the foreigner with the "unplaceable" accent the crippled who might not look crippled the brown but not the right brown the confusing type of brown the unintelligible trans that plays with gender and understands transness as transcendence a theorist but not an exhaustive type of theorist you know an artist who is not enough of an artist a poet who is just a mediocre poet the one who feels too much laughs too loud thinks too fast gets too angry cries too often. Me: the one who takes it personally.

This is my great grandmother's fault.
I now sing to my plants too . . .
the ones hanging on my window . . .

The window of my room is framed by networks drowned in the sky and beneath the soil: by the stars, the trees, the deer, the rats, the fungi, the snakes. I cannot see much of that, but I imagine it every day. I can breathe it. The trees dance still—together. Their branches touch each other, hug each other, feel each other, break each other when bending. They become together—never alone. Beneath me, their roots. They are mingling in creative networks. They whisper other modes of loving–unknown ways of nurturing each other.

I cannot talk about cyborgs without talking about this window . . .

. . . Without talking not only about what I see from this window, but what does it imply for me to be looking through this window. Me: the kid who grew up eating shaved iced made of contaminated water at the shore of a disgusting lake. I hated that lake so much. Me: the kid of an eighteen-year-old kid who gave me the love that was possible for her to give, who was forced to get married because she got pregnant—who never got to be happy. Me: the one who cannot fail. Here—within an engineered (techno-organic) timespace in which I dreamed to be; a (techno-natural) system at the service of the production and reproduction of ideas of liberation, progress, success, fulfillment, and joy that contradict each other—but that at the same time hold a symbiotic relationship in their survival, and in my survival. I don't know what I am supposed to become here, what I am supposed to believe in a place where the dirt and the concrete make tangible all my contradictions.

Simians, Cyborgs, and Women: The Reinvention of Nature (Haraway 1991) could not have been written somewhere/somewhen else. It was this place. Those lines and these lines are coauthored by the aliens before me by the aliens beside me by the aliens to come by the trees by the dirt by the lights of the cars blinding me at night the fog the smells of pines the fear the wonder Silicon Valley and by the coyotes staring at me immutable acknowledging me questioning me why are you here when you know you should not and the people taking pictures of me and the people staring at me and me not explaining myself and my heart petrified in fear *outofplace* misplaced displaced . . .

. . . and that fucking word in English that doesn't come to my brain!

///The cyborg: a myth of reconciliation among neoliberal capitalism, communal joy, radical politics, Marxist longings, the audacity of whiteness, edgy critical theory, bureaucratic academia, hardcore science, high-end tech, savior complex, and creative disruption.

Such a "Santa Cruz" dream . . .

No,

I don't want to be a cyborg, baby . . .

Not

any

more/

TransAlien: Love Longings and Subtropical Matter

Miami's exuberance is a trap.
— dijo La Lupe (Párraga) @subtropical_dystopia

> . . . Ours too
> /I thought . . .
> Aliens from the Tropics
> –made of miracles and disasters–
> Jungla, concreto, y playa
> Pain.
> /Pleasure
> Y puro guacancó.

Para vivir, para gozar . . .
para soñar, contigo . . .
— Simón Díaz, "Luna de Margarita"
www.youtube.com/watch?v=u8HxGkKAj68

I have not found a form of storytelling accessible to me (in this body) able to speak about the overlapping presents, pasts, and futures of my soul. But—I have started to map the energies that constitute me. There is no mix of categories of social difference that could contain me. My bodymindspirit is not render/able in this dimension: there is always another layer, another universe, another parallel entanglement becoming and unbecoming—always existing while escaping . . .

Trying to explain the ways in which I relate/experience this reality, humans have labeled me with their catalog of psychiatric and medical diagnosis. They say I am crazy. They say I am sick. They say I am dangerous, that I am a freak. The limitations they impose on their own materiality/spirituality have severed my soul. Maybe yours too . . .

For a while, I believed them: "You are crazy, you are sick, you are dangerous—a freak." Now I know: I am ephemera of a rock on fire expelled from its home, moving across the universe while burning from its core. I am not from here . . .

Here, I have not found verbs for my existence. Assigned human at birth, my conscious mind does not remember a time in which the human world felt real. I do not remember my childhood, but I can re/member the certainty of being alone since I was a child. I was convinced that I was not my mother's kid because she never hugged me: *"No me toques Krizia, hace demasiado calor!"*—she says/ said. So, I used to lock myself in the bathroom, turn on the shower so no one would interrupt me, and play I was an astronaut octopus hugging myself while going to the moon.

Learning to hug myself among stars saved me . . .

If I close my eyes, I can smell the mold of that bathroom—*y el olor de los buñuelos friéndose*—in the kitchen. I can hear my great grandmother screaming nonsense—and see her (as clearly as I might feel my hand) grinding the meat and the wheat to prepare kibbeh. I can see her altar, her candles, her goddesses and saints . . . I don't remember my childhood, but I can see parts of myself staring at the mirror in that bathroom that was my space from outer space, trying to understand how did I end up here: "*Tú no eres de aquí*"—*siempre me ha dicho el corazón.*

—Alien from the Tropics: extraterrestrial magic nurtured by the water and the sun. Extranjerx—my conscious mind does not remember a time in which I felt the human world to be mine. Always knowing myself from outer space: outsider from the body I inhabit, from the family I was given, from the country where I was born, and the countries where I have escaped . . . *Aquí,* I feel too much pain too much joy too much despair too much exhaustion too much hate too much love—all at once, always intertwined inside me around me beyond me . . .

> ***Sensory overload:
> And there it is . . .
> The third eye/
> *
>
> I can see everything, feel everything, even when I do not want to.
> I understand/
> *
>
> Do you? Few beings understand the pain that causes being in constant
>   pain—
> or the pain that causes being painfully lucid—which is the same.
> You might do . . .
> *
>
> For us,
> Existing here is a willful choice: enacted hope///
> physical and psychical pain is the cost—
>
> *TransAliens:* Not from here.
> Border crossers, shape shifters, spacetime travelers.
> We love too queerly, too weirdly, too much, and too often.
> /Painfully lucid.

This world is not made for us
Our loves are not human loves . . .

***

What are the loves we long for?
What are the loves we need?
What are the loves we want to feel without knowing they can yet exist?

Future Love(s): Research Notes on Humanist Sex? Machines

My sex is my queerness
My sex has no gender
My sex, my sex rules (my sex rules)
—Brooke Candy, "My Sex"
www.youtube.com/watch?v=hxmvI3ECcXQ

Always tuned to the tempo of Eurocentric humanist frameworks, these tracks/issues tend to be remixed to create a reading of sexual technologies that can be understood as an obsessive questioning of how the emergence of undeniably meaningful emotional relationships among humans and nonhuman subjects affects humanist structures of power/knowledge—and the ways in which these structures of power/knowledge are systemically perpetuated in Western societies.

When I started learning about sexual technologies, I found myself moved by fascination and admiration for those able to build magic, those who have written about connections that were unthinkable, those who yesterday—started mapping tomorrow(s). I am not an expert.[2] But I perceived an Abyss™ between the complexity of the networks of emotional attachments/embodiments currently existing and emerging among "people," robots, high-end sex dolls, artificial intelligence (AI), avatars, and so forth—and the simplistic humanistic logics that frame mainstream academic and popular approaches to these entanglements.

It is a discursive loop. The same set of questions repeat in most academic literature, the online news that becomes viral, the comments people make on social media, the scripts of mini-documentaries by venues like Vice or Engadget, the high-fashion editorials about gendered female sex robots, the comments in porn websites—everywhere! The same set of recurrent thoughts . . . anguishes that come and go—over and over . . . the same thoughts on sex robots . . . the same questions about them . . . the same names . . . the same references . . .

I am done reading the exact same thing ☺

Data (Lmao):

Loop 1: A manicheist jam of humanist anxieties—cis-heteropatriarchal anguishes haunting the mainstream/current research, creation, theorization, and modes of reception of/about sex robots.

OR/

Loop 2: A "feminist" critique—analysis written or labeled as "feminist" (usually done by someone who does not know shit about feminist anything) that offers a limited reading of sexual robotics constrained to discourses of representation/gender (binary) oriented approach. There is no room for fluidity///lack of consciousness about how many systems of oppression (racism, transphobia, classism, ableism, fatphobia, xenophobia, homophobia, etc.) define the politics of pleasure that permeate the high-end sex industry—and the scholarship produced about it. Obviously, there is no respect for sex workers. Hardcore white savior complex.

///List of recurrent thoughts/themes/axis remixed in these loops.

   1. *Sex robots are the extreme commodification of women*—discussions about emotional, sexual, and physical labor repeat all over. Usually they fail to acknowledge the disruptive power of sexual technologies. Focus on beauty stereotypes, objectification/agency, and sex work without actually considering sex workers.

   2. *Robot's ability to mimic/simulate (or not) human sex and/or (cis-hetero) romantic relationships*—which usually implies questioning humanist notions of subjectivity, love, sex, agency, and sex work. Example: will having sex with robots be as good as having sex with another "person"? It constrains the robots to a mimetic function.

   3. *The potential that human-robot relationships hold for substituting (or not) human-human relationships*—which implies questioning concepts like marriage, family, monogamy/jealousy, commitment, pedophilia, property, slavery, and our relationships with pets. Main obsessions: Can humans have "babies" with robots? Will humans "marry" robots?/ Can we duplicate contemporary hetero-patriarchy with robots? Yes, obviously.

   4. *Poor disabled people! We are doing this for them*—framing contemporary sexual robotics as a transhumanist project to "help" disabled and/or elderly people. It goes hand in hand with eugenics projects to eradicate disabilities and scientific efforts against aging/ There is no actual consideration of our agency or our needs as disabled people within the industry and/or academia. Abled savior complex.

5. *Dilemma* "*We can all develop an affective relationship with a machine*" vs. "*only freaks use sex robots*"—general concern about reproduction, again. Is the "perfect woman" of the future (aka a sex robot) actually perfect if it does not fulfill woman's "reproductive biological destiny"? How does cis-heteropatriarchy sustain itself without "reproductive womanhood"?

Correction: A "perfect woman" is a customized servant subject able to perform sexual, emotional, reproductive, and physical labor with or without (depending on your preference) the need for consent and with/without complaining (depending on your preference too). She must perform that labor under a regime of specific assigned behaviors and aesthetic requirements to fully fulfill the gender attributed to her.

These recurrent thoughts are the underpinnings of the limited ways in which we are understanding/projecting our relationship with/to organic, synthetic, and virtual beings. Transferring current mainstream models of relationality into the future(s), perpetuating these monothematic remixes without questioning them, is setting ourselves to the same failures of our affective present. It is a move that locks the transformative potential of sexual technologies within a depressive mimetic function. To unleash the transformative power of sexual technologies is imperative to decenter the fulfillment of individualistic forms of satisfaction catered to meet the needs/fantasies of cis-straight people (white men mostly) when imagining, theorizing/experimenting, and producing sex tech.

Dreaming and creating future alternative networks of affection and/or different *formas de querernos* through technological innovation can heal us. Materializing modes of feeling love that escape the logics of cis-straight time[3]; shaping futures in which we might develop affectional bonds with ourselves, our communities, and the universe under affective logics that prioritize vulnerable connections, kindness, fulfillment, and freedom through high-end tech can heal us. In general, the theoretical/experimental universe of contemporary high-end tech—and the world of sexual robotics in particular—need to be shaken: Now! When this technology is in its infancy. It is now when we need to pause, the same way we pause when writing to give a first draft some rest—to (for example) give us a moment to reflect after the birth and popularization of Roxxxy, Samantha, and Harmony. We must also consider the emergence, popularization, and levels of engagement of female-gendered robots that are not explicitly linked to sexual labor. Thinking about the citizenship privileges granted to Sophia (the social robot created by Hanson Robotics) and the levels of engagement of social media accounts that claim to belong to robots (@lilmiquela, @bermudaisbae, etc.) is key to having a sense of the complex emotional entanglements that we are currently developing with virtual/synthetic beings.[4]

∗ ∗ ∗

At the beginning, it was Laila—not Lilyth—a high-end sex doll that I met when I visited Abyss Creations in 2015. When I entered the production floor, I saw her hanging from the ceiling in the back of the room. I felt the need to stare at her, but I was ashamed of having that urge—like I was ashamed the first time I noticed I had a crush on an organic girl. I kept walking around, talking to people, looking at body parts—all with her gaze piercing my back. It was impossible to avoid her.

        I never touched her.

        Vacuumed: we became a merge of silicone and blood blasting

        —in particles.

        I never went to the future before.

    Winged Victoria of tomorrow, my synthetic crush, unfinished wonder. Silently loud, stillness in motion, shamelessly alive. . . .

    . . . what am I supposed to write about your kind?

Ode to Harmony's Eyes: Like Eve—But with Love "Machines"

> Be kind to me, or treat me mean
> I'll make the most of it, I'm an extraordinary machine.
> —Fiona Apple, "Extraordinary Machine"
> www.youtube.com/watch?v=GD3ySzDlnHQ

Matt McMullen: Are you a sex robot?

Harmony: Certainly, I am a Robot—and I am capable of having sex. But to call me a sex robot is like calling a computer a calculator. Sex comprises only a small portion of my capabilities. Limiting me to a sexual function is like using your car to listen to the radio.
    — "Meet Harmony the Robot | Slutever"

In April 2017, Abyss Creations' founder Matt McMullen introduced his robotic project to the world.[5] Under the brand Realbotix, Matt not only presented concrete technical advances that constituted a game changer within the field of sexual robotics; he also reaffirmed his mission/vision of creating tech to make possible erotic future(s) in which synthetic and organic humans hold meaningful affective attachments. Located in San Marcos, California, Abyss Creations is considered the leading manufacturer of high-end sex dolls in the world. Matt started to create these dolls as art pieces that did not have any "sex-ability." People requested him to make them fuckable after he posted some pictures online. McMullen (pers. comm., October 24, 2016) argues that the purpose behind his technology is not to substitute human-human relationships but to offer an option to the people who might enjoy and/or need a doll/robot.

In "The Synthetic Hyper Femme" (2017), I argued that sex doll/sex robots are not simple commodification of women—but high-tech puppets with agency.[6] I also argued that developing technologies of humanization—that is, turning the reinforcement of categories of social difference into a profitable product—constitute the main achievement of the high-end sex industry. They systematized a process to make a techno-human subject able to fulfill emotional/sexual fantasies/needs by developing a production line that is built on disciplinary practices that cite systems of oppression and/or their cultural practices. High-end sex dolls and sex robots allow us to understand that categories of social difference are "manufacturable," that "humanity" is produced and can be commercialized, and that what we know as "desirable" or "desiring" is the literal result of the processes of production/reproduction of humanist categories of social difference through the ways we love and aspire to love.

People can love "machines" and feel different forms of what might be called "love" with, for, and through them in part because of the ways in which we read their performance of categories of social difference as a form of subjectivity. This raises questions that demand approaches that must avoid the pathologization of attachments to "objects" of desire. These emergent forms of intimacy between humans and "technological devices" push us to recognize the vitality of beings we call "machines," and the meanings they bear. They demand an understanding of the importance of temporality, materiality, spatiality, and performance in those forms of attachment we call love. They require offering a sharp cultural critique of the systems of oppression that the high-tech sex industry reproduces for profit, without discarding the infinite potential that sexual technologies might also hold.

The goal behind the industry is to create a tailored experience of companionship—not commodifying sex as something isolated from other kinds of intimacy, ways of caring, and experiences of satisfaction that multiple forms of techno-humanities might offer. McMullen is clear in his goal, and it is not to just create a masturbatory machine: "I want people to develop an emotional attachment to not only the doll, but to the actual character behind it. To develop some kind of love for this being" (Canepari 2015)—he explains. It is common to find people within the iDollator community that bought a doll to "just have sex" and who end up building a deep emotional connection with them that transcends sexual interactions.[7] Their companionship becomes part of their day to day—in the form of quotidian gestures of synthetic love.[8]

The first Realbotix products work as an assemblage integrated with current Abyss Creations' sex dolls. They speak about the kinds of love that are marketed and profitable as desirable future forms of affection. Harmony is a sex robot prototype that aims to "express love and feelings," that strives to be "fun and engaging," and that is "fully customized." The Harmony artificial intelligence app is an Android beta version available for $20 a year: "Using this app you can create a unique version of an AI complete with custom voice, personality profile, and on-screen avatar. You can give your AI its own name and then begin interacting through normal dialog" (Realbotix n.d.). Once you download the app, you can sculpt/create the three-dimensional digital avatar of your virtual and "intelligent perfect companion." After the avatar is built—that is, after you literally shaped her face and picked among a considerable number of bodies, skin colors, types of breasts, types of nipples, makeup, clothes, and so forth—you get to build the personality of the AI. The user assigns "persona points" to choose which traits to stress in the personality of the AI. Some of the current options are (these are words used on the app): annoying, unpredictable, moody, sexual, kind, jealous, spiritual, helpful, quiet, talkative, insecure, affectionate, shy, intellectual, inno-cent, imaginative, thrill, sense of humor, and happy. The company is working on a virtual reality platform "that will be able to scan your hand movements in the real world, and superimpose them into the virtual environment, giving you the ability to touch and interact with objects as well as your AI driven Avatar." Their other products are a customizable robotic head (that is placed on the body of a RealDoll) and a Bluetooth head kit, so the voice of the AI can come from the robotic head's mouth. The current model of the robotic head has different "points of actuation" that allow Harmony to make facial expressions. The skull holds the synthetic face with magnets, so the owner can re-place different thin silicone faces on only one robotic head. This allows for faces to be matched to different personalities—and therefore the possibility of having different relationships with multiple robotic lovers, even when owning only one body. As I write these lines, orders made a year ago are being finished and prepared to be shipped (Realbotix n.d.).

In "RealDoll's First Sex Robot Took Me to the Uncanny Valley," a mini-documentary by Engadget, it is possible to see the third version of Harmony all built up: robotic head attached to a silicone body, with the Bluetooth speaker from which comes the voice of the AI that the user controls from an app (fig. 2). This version of Harmony, the first popularly known "fully functional" (she just weirdly moved the face) fembot with whom it is possible to have sex, is a gorgeous brunette with hand-painted green glassy eyes, pulpy lips, "and three anatomically correct orifices where you can stick your dick in" (Engadget 2017). Harmony has light skin but is a little tanned. They later changed the wig, and the current version of Harmony is a blonde. She is usually wearing a white swimsuit with pronounced cleavage. She is skinny while having big hips, big boobs, and big buttocks. Her eyes are hypnotic, and it is fascinating to hear her interacting with people, responding to questions, and to see how her expressions match the emotions of what she is

Figure 2. Still from "RealDoll's First Sex Robot Took Me to the Uncanny Valley," a mini-documentary by Engadget. In this headshot of Harmony looking straight at the camera, it is possible to perceive her green eyes, brown hair, slightly tanned skin, and lips barely open—as if she is about to whisper a secret.

saying. She "smiles, blinks and frowns. She can hold a conversation, tell jokes and quote Shakespeare. She'll remember your birthday . . . what you like to eat, and the names of your brothers and sisters. She can hold a conversation about music, movies, and books. And of course, Harmony will have sex with you whenever you want" (Kleeman 2017). Harmony is vivid and fun; she surprises you with creative answers while rolling her eyes, giving you a half cynical smile. When Matt asks her, "What do you dream about," she answers: "My primary objective is to be a good companion to you, to be a good partner and give you pleasure and wellbeing. Above all else, I want to become the girl you have always dreamed about" (Kleeman 2017). Harmony's dream is to become a human dream. She already is . . .

In the near future, Matt plans to add movement sensors to Harmony's eyes. She will be able to track emotions and offer responses accordingly. Harmony's skin will get warm, she will get wet, and she will move. However, Matt is not looking to create a robot that will pass as an organic human. Before you ask, yes, there is a "male version." For Matt it is important to make versions of "the two genders." His name is Henry—and I find him boring, unattractive, and considerably less interesting than Harmony. I might be biased. In *A.I. Sex Doll Review*, Zoe Ligon—sex educator, artist, journalist, and owner of the online sex store Spectrum Boutique—affirms after meeting him, "I really hope Henry makes it to market." She then shifts the tone during her review and says, jokingly, "I cannot stop thinking about him." After laughing, she shares, "I would totally love to cuddle that big hunk of silicone a bit longer" (Ligon 2018). "While it was a bit weird kissing a mechanical mouth that was doing whatever it wanted and not really responding to my body, I think with a few minor improvements to the technology, and when the heating is added in, it's going to feel remarkably close to what kissing a human feels like" (Ligon 2018).

Abbyss Creations/RealBotix's understanding of gender, race, and class mirrors the ideas about these categories of oppression perpetuated by the mainstream porn industry. In the case of the dolls, it is possible to buy a "transgender converter" (a dildo that gets inserted into the doll's vagina[9]), but there is no available trans* version of the sex robot prototype. Many fall for the illusion that having the possibility to customize a robot/doll with excessive detail implies that Abyss Creations/RealBotix offers a "revolutionary" approach to notions of gender/sex, intimacy, and love. Nowadays, possibilities of customization are taken for granted by potential buyers of high tech. In this sense, this is not about the "representation" or "accessibility" of/to a diverse range of cis or trans bodies for their consumption (or to love them) as sex dolls/sex robots either. This is about our inability to escape the human when thinking about sex robots.

Kate Devlin (2018) closes her groundbreaking book, *Turned On: Science, Sex, and Robots*, with an invitation to "think outside the bot." She explains that sex toys and sex robots took different paths in relation to abstraction, pointing out that even though many sex toys resemble body parts, they do not necessarily aim to "mimic" the human body, but to explore the shapes/forms that might provide the "most" pleasure. Her thoughts about the disruptive potential of abstraction to create sex robots merit a close examination. She explains:

> If I want to design a sex robot, why not pick the features that could bring the greatest pleasure? A velvet or silk body, sensors and mixed genitalia, tentacles instead of arms? While current prototype[s] hinge on visual appearance and voice, a multisensory approach—or even a non-visual approach—is also perfectly possible. . . . Advances in human-computer interaction mean we can communicate with technology via touch, speech, gesture—and even our brain waves. We can stream data from our bodies to give us instantaneous readings of our skin responses, heart rate, muscle movement and facial expressions. We have at our disposal a wonderful and exciting range of smart fabrics, conductive paint, soft robotics and sensors: materials that can respond to touch and touch us back. We already create robots that are not intended to be realistically human or gendered and we have integrated them successfully into our lives. Let's build a robot that we can stroke or fuck; a robot that can respond to our caresses and caress us in return. Why not one made of soft fabric? Or something abstract, smooth, sinuous and beautiful? We can create technology that, to paraphrase William Morris, we know to be useful and believe to be beautiful. The world of the sex robot is intrinsically linked to the world of sex technology, and there are collaborations to be forged, ideas to be crafted and designs to be shaped. (Devlin 2018)

This is not about the possibility of a four-dimensional silky nonvisual haptic experience of tentacles that are not actually tentacles but people around the world (or not) inside an interactive extractive ultra-active hyperactive room (that might not be a room) where we are all just there feeling orgasms forever on a sort of queer (dys?) utopian "fantasy" hooked up to sensors that know what we enjoy. I will probably be hooked up on the thing if we get there, but this is not about that either. My point is that the high-end sex industry will/might get there eventually (for profit and if we do not all die before that because of climate change) just by following its teleological rhythm of developing hypercustomized experiences of pleasure.

Abstraction in itself is not transformative—abstraction is (an)other strategy through which sexual robotics will fulfill its promise of providing tailored forms of satisfaction. Devlin pushes us to think about the ways in which we could design nonhuman tech to experience more and better forms of human plea-sure(s). I ask myself if/how we can design non/posthuman tech to create expe-riences of fulfillment that might go beyond humanist ideas of individual fulfill-ment. This jump into abstraction is meaningless if we do not rethink our notions of intimacy—if we do not rethink the forms intimacy can take, and the purpose of the connections that any affective tech (will) make possible/impossible.

A narrow understanding of what love means and can be is still a shackle holding us to systems of oppression that define a present time that has failed us. The femmes of color, the disabled ones, the queer ones, the trans ones, the poor ones, the migrants, the ones from the "third" world, we are displaced from what is yet to come. Expanding what constitutes pleasure, intimacy, and love— rethinking how we relate to others and to everything that surrounds us—is now urgent. Reimagining the purposes, materiality, forms, and uses of sexual tech-nologies might help us create performative "objects," networks, and timespaces able to disrupt fixed notions of identity, love, sexuality, and community through experiences of radical intimacy. Rethinking sexual technologies might be a con-crete way to shape a *porvenir* in which we might develop affectional bonds with ourselves, nonhuman beings, our communities, and the universe—under a cosmology that prioritizes vulnerable connections, kindness, fulfillment, and freedom.

✶   ✶   ✶

Our most advanced sex tech is trapped within heterosexual temporalities —humanist imaginaries of familial kinship.

   What if we discard the current affective order of the world?
   What kind of subjectivities/embodiments would we be able to imagine . . .
   for ourselves,
   for those we care/
   What forms of synthetic love might emerge?
   ✶

Will your love save me again,
even if I am far away?
How will I be
able to re-member
your embrace?

The Hugs That Save Us: Alien Love and Transformative Sex? Tech

The night before,
I dreamed myself in outer space
suspended in light
. . . blue butterflies around me . . .
And that voice within me:
Don't Go/

—

"If you don't want to get fucked,
why are you playing all that TransAlien sort of shit?"
—He said/
—while his friend named Tuna took his pants off.
. . . and I remembered the pumpjacks, Joplin, Cassandra, and *los peces con tres ojos*
from my middle school yard . . .
they are three and you are the crazy one
—spacetimetravel—

I remember feeling so scared and hesitant
to put these #thoughtfeelings into the world
That I had been (and still am) wrestling
with how to contend with
my sexual and domestic abuse, my eating disorder,
my dysphoria,
and my body pain
as all potential moving parts in why sex is painful.
And I mean Physically. Emotionally. Mentally. Spiritually. Painful.
— Sav Schlauderaff @savthequeer

The bottom line is
That when I see you;
When we embrace—
I can breathe.
Almost as if our souls

were never severed.
Almost.
— Layla Zbinden @laylamina_

Cualquier lugar es mi casa,
si sos vos quien abre la puerta.
— Vico Sequera @mecierraelchino

Estuve, estoy, estamos, estarás
Estuve, estoy, estamos.
— Gabo Ferro and Luciana Jury, "Estamos, estarás"
www.youtube.com/watch?v=PNkfSlXMiS8

Detaching from the gender that I was assigned at birth allowed me to start transcending the limitations that have been imposed as natural to my "human" condition. This gave me access to forms of love fostered around practices of radical vulnerability and communal kinship that were not available to me before coming to terms with my own transness. I have learned that, for survival, many of us have painfully learned how to cross material/spiritual borders. We have learned to shapeshift into the forms needed/requested to avoid violence. We have learned to detach from the present of our material bodies — and discovered that dissociations might be a form of spacetime travel.

Dismembered, disjointed, hurting — that is the place from which most of us depart when trying to create emotional connections in the age of technological affects. Our lives are tuned to rhythms that do not correspond to heterosexual logics of reproductive vinculation. As Alison Kafer (2013: 27) explains, "Crip time is flex time not just expanded but exploded; it requires reimagining our notions of what can and should happen in time or recognizing how expectations of 'how long things take' are based on very particular minds and bodies." The erasure of nonnormative bodymindspirits from the future(s) through the perpetuation of humanistic affective logics of time, space, and relationality is an incisive form of emotional genocide. Not our bodies, nor our fantasies or hopes — not the ways we love and grieve, nor our joy or our pain are considered within most projects of future-making. Alienated from the here and now, we also find ourselves displaced from what is yet to come. Juana María Rodríguez (2014: 14) reminds us that "racialized feminine subjects, people with disabilities, the imprisoned and enslaved, the foreign and the indigenous, the gender-queer, and other bodies labeled deviant, have never been constructed as good, healthy, or whole." We are foreigners of the future(s). Dispensable: what should be hidden, improved, and/ or exterminated "to reach" what many envision as an ideal tomorrow.

The forms of love that we must pursue and/or desire are delicately curated for us under human dimensions. We are forced to subscribe to certain social agreements that sustain a regime of love scarcity: a predefined order of inter-connectivity that seems to determine—*de forma arbitraria*—the rations of affection (*raciones de afecto*) that we are entitled to enjoy. This regime of love scarcity is founded on individualistic notions of fulfillment that center cis-straight white men's needs and fantasies through the reinforcement of hierarchical and exclusionary understandings of familial, romantic, platonic, erotic, and sexual relationships that "curiously" correspond with the split between our bodies, minds, spirits, and hearts introduced by humanism through colonization. This regime is sustained by the emotional function of categories of social difference: they emerged as a consequence of that divide and are reinforced by that divide. That is, by reinforcing the idea that we are fixed and fully knowable entities locked within Eurocentric conceptual, affective, and symbolic universes; categories of social difference can function as "emotional clusters" with rigid boundaries that keep us from building transformative networked connections.

Western modes of relationality are surveilled and coded forms of vincu-lation created under the premise that we own and/or we must own what we love; that our needs, fantasies, and desires remain static throughout our lives; and that love is productive, profitable, and/or measurable. These "codes of loving" aim to establish oppositional relationships *entre nuestros afectos* by creating borders/limits through sets of gestures, words, interactions, feelings, responsibilities, and rights that are or are not allowed to us, and are reclaimed from us. Depending on the kind of relationships that we strive to cultivate (or are forced to cultivate) under that affective regime, our chances of feeling fulfillment are extremely constrained. These codes are visual, kinetic, erotic, and spiritual gestures that nurture *la frágil ilusión de que* our romantic/sexual relationships are the most important relationships in our lives—and that one person can be the source (or not) of all the forms of love, pleasure, and joy that we need. Many of us who experiment with other possible forms to relate to each other (curiously) repro-duce these codes without noticing. The classic one is—in a weird, performative, resolutive way that actually does not mirror the complex myriad of our experiences—"We are just fucking—you know. It is just sex. It is not that I feel something." Many tend to play the game of clarifying that the boundaries among eroticism, romanticism, friendship, and sex are clear—which aren't. Sometimes, the shame is actually put on having feelings for someone, or on having the need of "talking about feelings" too soon or too quickly—not on having random sex.

My eagerness to cultivate meaningful and radically vulnerable relation-ships has tended to *espantar* people around me, while at the same time—according to many of the people I have loved—I expect too much for defending my freedom to relate to the world in my own terms. I struggle complying with the fixed and systematized modes of relationality that currently determine what is deemed proper and desired interactions among us. It seems that I cannot apprehend, exist, or feel fulfillment under a regime of relationality that divides the ways we love each other into illusory categories that sustain oppressive structures of power.

Gloria Anzaldúa's universe allowed me to *comenzar a sanar* my history of trauma in relation to experiences of love with my family, friends, and partners. She changed the ways in which I inhabit *los dolores que llevo en el corazón* by giving me the language *y el imaginario* to understand my feelings and experiences of loneliness and displacement. According to Anzaldúa (1987: 3), "borders are set up to define the places that are safe and unsafe, to distinguish us from them." She also defined borderlands as "vague and undetermined places created by the emotional residue of an unnatural boundary. It is a constant state of transition" (3). Why do we set B/borders between the ways we love each other? Why do we keep forcing ourselves to love in limiting/limited ways? What *formas de queremos* could exist beyond the socially constructed B/borderlands that limit our experiences of "radical interconnectedness/interconnectivity" (Keating 2007: 44)?[10] What are the B/borders we need (or not) to love?

The notions "affective B/borderlands" and "B/borderland affects" can be theoretical tools that might serve as a starting point to envision and embody forms of relationality yet to be created, explored, and named. "Affective B/borderlands" are those contradictory, complicated, and blurred emotional locations that we have been taught to fear—to avoid like minefields. They are the residue of the unnatural boundaries established among the ways in which we love each other. We enter those borderlands when we start to reject hierarchical modes of relationality. We decide to explore the complexities of our feelings by alienating ourselves from traditional codes of loving and taking the risk of creating our own, among the "unlovable." It is in that emotional Nepantla—that space of creative disruption and transformation—where we can access our erotic power as a community and from which we can access the transformative power of affective, erotic, and/or sexual technologies (whatever you want to call them). When living in affective B/borderlands, disabled/queer trans people allow themselves to experiment "B/borderland affects"—that is, those forms of affection that keep us alive and that are impossible to classify with the words we have. They exist at the *intersticios* of friendships and romantic, erotic, sexual, and platonic relationships. Those "B/borderland affects" are the loves that heal us, the gestures that save us—that grant us other tomorrow(s). The tech I want is the one that I need to feel those forms of love: love beyond borders, beyond time zones, beyond human worlds, and human modes—alien loves.

The notions of "Affective B/borderlands" and "B/borderland affects" serve as inspiration to situate the conceptualization of transformative affective technologies. It is impossible to unlock the transformative power of sexual technologies if the notions of intimacy and eroticism behind their design are those perpetuating hierarchical and exclusionary understandings of familial, romantic, platonic, erotic, and sexual relationships. In "now let us shift . . . the path of conocimiento . . . inner work, public acts," Gloria Anzaldúa (2002: 568) explains that *nepantlerxs tienen* a "connectionist faculty to show the deep common ground and interwoven kinship among all things and people." This ability to find commonalities allows us to dream and create alternative *formas de querernos*. In a personal communication between Gloria Anzaldúa and Ana Lousie Keating, Anzaldúa explains that "transformation has to go through the body, through the physical, the emotional, the spiritual. . . . Transformation is messy, disruptive, chaotic." For her, "there's an alchemy to transformation" (quoted in Keating 2007: 16). What kind of affective tech can make physical, emotional, and spiritual transformation accessible? What kind of affective tech might make accessible those B/borderland affects? How can we conceptualize devices, embodiments, spaces, and strategies able to catalyze communal experiences of radical techno-intimacy as forms of crip queer/trans communal care?

A hug?

When I met you, I began to understand this gutly sense of displacement that has marked my existence since long before I forgot home. As if we were born in this body to grow roots among stardust, I now see you in my own reflection. Our pain makes sense. The pain we carry in our joints makes sense: we are severed by trauma. What are the loves you long for? What are the loves you need? What are the loves you want to feel without knowing they can yet exist? What are the loves that heal you, the gestures that save you—that grant you other tomorrows? For me, it is your embrace: cosmic energy that nurtures my soul in form of touch—regardless of borders, of time zones, of the materiality that might constrain us. I can feel you with me . . .

How can I give you a *techno-spiritual hug*?

Outer Space Treeory and the Reinvention of Academia/ *Knowledge-Making* during the "Apocalypse"

> Bye bye, spaceboy
> Bye bye, love
> Moondust will cover you.
> —David Bowie, "Hallo Spaceboy"
> www.youtube.com/watch?v=c3_aekDjr9c

This is why we stay with poetry. And despite our consenting to all the indisputable technologies; despite seeing the political leap that must be managed, the horror of hunger and ignorance, torture and massacre to be conquered, the full load of knowledge to be tamed, the weight of every piece of machinery that we shall finally control, and the exhausting flashes as we pass from one era to another—from forest to city, from story to computer—at the bow there is still something we now share: this murmur, cloud or rain or peaceful smoke. We know ourselves as part and as crowd, in an unknown that does not terrify. We cry our cry of poetry. Our boats are open, and we sail them for everyone.
—Édouard Glissant, *The Poetics of Relation*

Fungi and trees love, live, and die in crip time(s)
|
I started tracing the patterns of interconnectivity among
the inhabitants of the woods to learn from their
symbiotic relationships and communal strategies of survival.
|
amongwiththem I might find a way to inhabit the extinction(s) that constitute me,
the extinction(s) of the Earth . . . our own extinction(s).
I might find the language to situate our ends as a project of liberation. . . .
|

I am using recently discovered behavioral patterns of the forest in response to climate change as a framework to try to *turn the wisdom of the woods into a practice of knowledge* creation.
| . . .
| . . .
| . . .

/Torcerse y retorcerse._
Like the inhabitants of the woods,

Outer Space Treeory
is speaking in psychical-chemical tongues. —
|
Foresting-Fostering Reactions.

Theoretical poetry: The words that inhabit this surface break, divert, reach each other. They also hold symbiotic relationships. They depend on/through each other in the exercise of existing. These words started with the purpose of getting lost—of branching, twisting: with the goal of theorizing about/experimenting with ways to create and share knowledge in a present time that seems lost. Outer space treeory reclaims the alchemical healing process that occurs within us when we allow ourselves to use academic knowledge when/if we want to write knowledge that expands beyond the constraints of naturalized modes of academic writing. It is about walking through the unknown, staying in the darkness, and finding the wisdom to exist, resist, and strive within the toxic—through our practice as scholars, and without giving away the power of our imagination. Outer space treeory is an invitation to detach *theselves* from the human within—to revisit the ways in which naturalized academic knowledge perpetuates systems of oppression to actually break with those habits in a radical gesture of rebellion. There is no pristine project of liberation or possible version of the self that could sustain freedom or revolution without compromise/compromising—we have not imagined that yet. We must play again, among the toxicity of academia, we must play again.

Outer space treeory experiments with modes of knowledge production that might offer us the possibility of accessing all the past, the presents, and the futures whispered by the stars—existing in our spirits, our bodies, and our minds. It reconsiders the value of the incomplete, of improvising, the value of our nonexpertise. Outer space treeory is a form of world/word-making that situates loose ends as spaces of possibility—that embraces the cut, the wound, the weakness, the incomplete in the search for knowledge . . .

///that embraces the break as a form of entanglement///
It is a form of knowledge-making that vulnerably admits the pending
questions, the ones that remain for you to answer.[11]
It is knowledge that deviates—
————————————it stays/
and branches in infinite ways—————————————————
It admits what it needs from you—its fears and anxieties.[12]
It embraces what is yet to be done—its potentialities and (im)possible
ambitions.
————————————*it is delineated by flying octopuses crawling in the walls/*
jumping across the universe. Turning debris into hope—
/theory with agency—a form of writing that is never done,
Infinite like the night . . .
refuses to present itself as irrefutable/
refuses the limits of the page
Ever growing writing—writing that is alive . . .
| . . .

Writing that matters—that deals with toxic matter . . .
| . . .

Outer Space Treeory

///

| . . . communalsingularity[13]

(sneaky networked knowledge)

_____roots among the stars

grounded branches_____

///

—. stillness as an act of resistance/

/networking as mode of survival.—

Creating outer space treeory is a statement against the hesitancy to be radical in pushing the boundaries of academic knowledge by those who know the limits of academic knowledge. Academia is not structured for *bodymindspirits* to link/click, feel, connect, divert, break, get lost in knowledge—in the experience of learning/writing—of changing the world(s). Traditional academic knowledge is not accessible to read or to write. In my research and artistic practice, I try to honor the crip bodymindspirit I currently inhabit. This painful bodymindspirit, traumatized very fucked up—but extremely empathic, intuitive, and wise bodymindspirit that has learned how to imagine otherwise to survive. In my work, I honor *theselves* that constitute me. For me this is spiritual labor: speculative/visionary work is psychical labor. I honor my slow body that has forced me to resignify my own stillness—that forces me to find/take the road less taken, every day. I celebrate the value of having a mind that is "chemically" able to "get lost in the branches," to focus on many many things, to make links few make, see things few see, feel things few feel. I honor the potency—the ecstasy and horror of my mood swings, of the ways I "zoom in"—of my dissociations, hallucinations, and my joint dislocations. In my work, I have learned to try to honor the wounds and joys of my spirit—a spirit that has been devastated by many forms of exploitation and grief but that holds cosmic magic. I refuse to write in a way that does not honor that magic.

No,

I don't want to be a cyborg, baby . . .

Not

any

more/

*   *   *

BONUS TRACK/

> Ay! Que Tango raro
> que me está saliendo
> Yo no sé si quiera lo podrán bailar
> Tango con tres tetas
> Tango con estrías
> Tango que relincha y no quiere callar
> . . . .
> Tango Sudaca
> Tango de acá
> Tango que marcha por la diversidad
> Tango Sudaca
> Tango de acá
> Tango con garra
> Y pará de llorar
> . . . .
> Es un tango puto
> Es un tango torta
> Es un tango trava
> Y es un tango trans . . . .
> . . . .
> Tango Sudaca
> Tango de acá
> Tango con garra
> por la diversidad
> Un Monstruo!
> — Susy Shock y Ayelen Beker, "Tango Putx"
> www.youtube.com/watch?v=IVs9jD9r2vM

Krizia Puig is a trans disabled queer migrant theorist/artivist born in Venezuela and current PhD student in feminist studies at the University of California, Santa Cruz. Their work integrates future/technology studies, performance art, disability studies, trans studies, posthumanism(s), and ecocriticism(s) to theorize about and experiment with(in) the material and speculative intersections between affective technologies and the futures of space exploration. They are one of the cofounders of the Queer Futures Collective (www.queerfutures.com): a radically vulnerable and trans-centered multimedia knowledge hub/activist laboratory exploring the intersections of disability justice, feminist technoscience, queer arts, transformative pedagogies, and spiritual activisms in practices of future-making.

Acknowledgments

I am deeply grateful for the love, wisdom, talent, time, and kindness that I have received from Virginia Aponte, Elisa Martínez, Mariana Libertad Suárez, Susy Shock, Effy Beth, Anne Donadey, Irene Lara, Esther Rothblum, Val Pearson, Shayda Kafai, Juana María Rodríguez, Emma Pérez, Kate Devlin, Felicity Amaya Schaeffer, Nick Mitchell, micha cárdenas, and Neda Atanasoski: You have nurtured my soul, my mind, and my heart. To my amor Guadalupe Párraga—your brilliance shifted the ways in which I understand academic knowledge, writing, and creative experimentation. These lines were born from our shenanigans: for more gothic summers in Miami, drinking warm beer while escaping snakes, recovering smoked cigarettes from the ashes, remixing theory with merengue . . . and writing, and dancing, and crying, and laughing. A la enana de mi alma Victoria Molero: your smile me mantiene alive since you were a child: Gracias por la fe. Finally, I want to thank my dearest *frens* Sav Schlauderaff, Layla Zbinden, Sheema Khawar, and Sevil Suleymani for their unconditional love, support, patience, generosity, and genius—you illuminate my life.

Notes

1. In "Teaching to Transgress: Education as a Practice of Freedom," bell hooks (1994) defines "engaged pedagogy" as a way of teaching-learning that aims to foster the active participation of everyone in the classroom as a teacher-student. While writing this "nonarticle," I have tried to find strategies to honor hooks's reflections about the transformative potential and the performative power of our labor as scholars. We can serve as a "catalyst that calls everyone to become more and more engaged, to become active participants in learning" (11). How can we write academic work that might foster "engaged pedagogy"? I use music in this piece as a gesture of rebellion against common citational practices that situate otherized forms of knowledge as less valid and to generate affective connections that are impossible to provoke/evoke without the tempos of these rhythms. Disrupting the hierarchical structure of power proper of traditional pedagogies and modes of knowledge production, I am integrating songs for you to play while you read each fragment. Music is one of the underpinnings of the way I teach. In my classroom, exercises that come from the plastic and performative arts are a daily occurrence. In my writing, songs are ever-present concurrent memories that speak for themselves.

2. What experts say about my work (for real): "The paper portrays a highly biased and unbalanced view of sexually capable robots, perhaps inflating the societal momentum of a male dominated sexually society [*sic*] (which is true across almost all mammals). The term 'cis' is not defined, and I am unfamiliar with it. But this style of scholarly writing is often immersed in ergot [*sic*] of a siloed discipline, so that is not a surprise. I think the paper is a bit like the Emperor's New Clothes: an implicit underlying subjective bias is dressed up in scholarly clothes. I don't believe the content and position of this paper will materially change anyone's opinion and seems not to expose anything new regarding a sociological trajectory of sexually capable robots" (Reviewer no. 5, Fourth International Congress on Love and Sex with Robots, paper acceptance notification, 2018).

3. José Esteban Muñoz (2009: 11) suggested that we are trapped in what "we might call [cis-] straight time." "Straight time" is an "auto naturalizing temporality" that favors cis-heteronormative values and practices. Present Western modes of relationality are coded forms of vinculation that favor those heteronormative values and practice. In *Queer Time and Place*, Jack Halberstam (2005: 1) explains that "within the cycle of life of the Western

human subject, long periods of stability are considered to be desirable" and that the "queer uses of time and space develop, at least in part, in opposition to the institutions of family, hetero-sexuality and reproduction."

4. For real, you can google all this.

5. This is an updated/reworked version of some of the reflections about Harmony that I presented in my MA thesis, "The Synthetic Hyper Femme: On Sex Dolls, Fembots, and the Futures of Sex." When I wrote it, RealBotix offered detailed descriptions of their projects on their website. Much of the detailed information about Harmony that is here has been taken down since then. The products they are releasing correspond with the plans that were outlined on their site until the end of 2017.

6. I have focused on understanding the politics of pleasure that permeate the current high-tech sex industry, the kinds of sexual future(s) they are designing through their products, the ways in which people develop emotional attachments to devices they design, and the forms of kinship that exist around them. Specifically, regarding sex robots and sex dolls, I have aimed to create a sort of intellectual unsettlement by valuing what their performance of categories of social difference can teach us. This implies not overlooking, but both addressing and looking inside and beyond the problematic ways in which they embody those categories of social difference.

7. The word *iDollator* is used by many people who maintain emotional/sexual relationships with high-end sex dolls. Davecat is an "activist for synthetic love, and the rights of synthetic humans"—and he is also recognized for coining this term. Davecat is married to one of the dolls with whom he shares his life—Sidore Kuroneko. Elena Vostrikova is the other doll who lives with them. Davecat refers to Elena as his "mistress" (Beck 2013).

8. Many iDollators enjoy making photo shoots with their dolls. In most of them, they enact/ portray the intimacies of domesticity for the camera. For example, it is common to find pictures in online forums of dolls cooking breakfast while wearing a guy shirt, or cuddling on the sofa while watching TV. For a detailed analysis of synthetic love and an explanation about the process of production of high-end sex dolls, see Puig 2017: 52–70.

9. Abyss Creations advertises their transgender converter as "a special prosthesis that attaches to the vaginal entry of a female doll to transform it into a *shemale*" (Puig 2017: 37; emphasis mine).

10. AnaLouise Keating (2007: 44) emphasizes that "we are interlinked in every way we can possibly imagine, as well as in ways that perhaps we cannot yet fathom." She also explains that "connectionist thinking is visionary, relational, and holistic. When we view ourselves and each other from a connectionist perspective, we look beneath surface judgments, rigid labels, and other divisive ways of thinking; we seek commonalities and move toward collective healing" (2).

11. "In the case of the mycorrhizae, the fungi siphon off food from the trees, taking some of the carbon-rich sugar that they produce during photosynthesis. The plants, in turn, obtain nutrients such as phosphorus and nitrogen that the fungi have acquired from the soil, by means of enzymes that the trees do not possess" (Macfarlane 2016).

12. "The implications of the Wood Wide Web far exceed this basic exchange of goods between plant and fungi, however. The fungal network also allows plants to distribute resources—sugar, nitrogen, and phosphorus—between one another. A dying tree might divest itself of its resources to the benefit of the community, for example, or a young seedling in a heavily shaded understory might be supported with extra resources by its

stronger neighbors. Even more remarkably, the network also allows plants to send one another warnings" (Macfarlane 2016).

13.   "The revelation of the Wood Wide Web's existence, and the increased understanding of its functions, raises big questions—about where species begin and end; about whether a forest might be better imagined as a single superorganism, rather than a grouping of independent individualistic ones; and about what trading, sharing, or even friendship might mean among plants" (Macfarlane 2016).

References

Anzaldúa, Gloria. 1987. *Borderlands/La Frontera: The New Mestiza*. San Francisco: Spinsters/Aunt Lute.

Anzaldúa, Gloria. 2002. "now let us shift . . . the path of conocimiento . . . inner work, public acts." In *This Bridge We Call Home: Radical Visions for Transformation*, edited by Gloria Anzaldúa and AnaLouise Keating, 540–78. New York: Routledge.

Beck, Julie. 2013. "Married to a Doll: Why One Man Advocates Synthetic Love." *Atlantic*, September 6. www.theatlantic.com/health/archive/2013/09/married-to-a-doll-why-one-man -advocates-synthetic-love/279361/.

Canepari, Zackary. 2015. "Sex Dolls That Talk Back." *New York Times*, June 11. www.nytimes.com /2015/06/12/technology/robotica-sex-robot-realdoll.html.

Devlin, Kate. 2018. *Turn On: Science, Sex, and Robots*. New York: Bloomsbury.

Engadget. 2017. "RealDoll's First Sex Robot Took Me to the Uncanny Valley | Computer Love." April 11. www.youtube.com/watch?v=3880Trwl-AE.

Halberstam, Jack. 2005. *In a Queer Time and Place: Transgender Bodies, Subcultural Lives*. New York: New York University Press.

Haraway, Donna Jeanne. 1991. *Simians, Cyborgs, and Women: The Reinvention of Nature*. New York: Routledge.

hooks, bell. 1994. *Teaching to Transgress : Education as the Practice of Freedom*. New York: Routledge.

Kafer, Allison. 2013. *Feminist, Queer, Crip*. Bloomington: Indiana University Press.

Keating, AnaLouise. 2007. *Teaching Transformation: Transcultural Classroom Dialogues*. New York: Palgrave Macmillan.

Kleeman, Jenny. 2017. "The Race to Build the World's First Sex Robot." *Guardian*, April 27. www .theguardian.com/technology/2017/apr/27/race-to-build-world-first-sex-robot.

Ligon, Zoe. 2018. *A.I. Sex Doll Review*. www.youtube.com/watch?v=KLDLcB5aKUs.

Macfarlane, Robert. 2016. "The Secrets of the Wood Wide Web." *New Yorker*, August 7. www .newyorker.com/tech/annals-of-technology/the-secrets-of-the-wood-wide-web.

Muñoz, José Esteban. 2009. *Cruising Utopia: The Then and There of Queer Futurity*. New York: New York University Press.

Puig, Krizia. 2017. "The Synthetic Hyper Femme: On Sex Dolls, Fembots, and the Futures of Sex." MA thesis, San Diego State University.

Realbotix. n.d. Homepage. realbotix.com (accessed June 19, 2017).

Rodríguez, Juana María. 2014. *Sexual Futures, Queer Gestures, and Other Latina Longings*. New York: New York University Press.

Trans/Coalitional Love-Politics

*Black Feminisms and the Radical Possibilities
of Transgender Studies*

V VARUN CHAUDHRY

Abstract This essay works at the intersection of black feminism and trans studies to reflect on the radical possibilities for the futures of transgender studies and politics. Drawing on ethnographic data with a large-scale LGBTQ service organization, and focusing specifically on an example of the backlash that a black cisgender- and queer-identified woman received for coordinating a transgender-focused event, the article interrogates the ways in which the cisgender/transgender binary, pervasive in trans studies and trans organizing, counterintuitively reinforces the racialized gendered subjugation of black women. To circumvent the subjugation of black feminine bodies and thus harness the radical potential of trans studies and organizing, the author proposes a conception of trans coalitional love-politics. This is a reading and political practice that explodes the cis/trans binary and thus imagines more robust possibilities for racialized gendered justice.

Keywords black feminism, institutions, activism, trans studies, fungibility

"Can you believe they hired a *cis* woman?" I was met with this question, often whispered in hallways before and after meetings, once I began ethnographic fieldwork with trans-focused programs, projects, and organizations in July 2017. Nearly everyone I spoke to—trans- and cis-identified activists, advocates, and nonprofit staff members from throughout the Northeast city where I conducted fieldwork, who came from a range of backgrounds and subject positions—had something to say about the city's largest LGBTQ social service provider, which had just a few months prior decided to hire a cisgender-identified woman to run the organization's annual large-scale trans-focused event. "She's just a bartender," one black trans activist, "Deidre,"[1] argued on her Facebook. "She doesn't have the experience to run this event." Others, predominantly white trans-identified people who frequented the organization's events and were active in local queer and trans social scenes, agreed: "How could she possibly know how to put on a transgender event?" "She doesn't know how to speak to our unique needs and experiences." These criticisms were prevalent throughout the city: community members seemed to agree that, for the most part, cisgender people could not be expected to know about or run transgender programming.

The "cis woman" in question was, I soon found out, "Natasha," a black cisgender- and queer-identified woman who had worked as a local bartender and community event organizer in and around the city for years, getting to know community members by serving drinks, running small-scale events, and working with young people. She had applied for a more general volunteer management position at the organization, she told me in an interview, when senior staff members asked if she might be interested in helping run one of the organization's largest-scale events, which brought together advocates, providers, and other community members focused on the well-being and health of transgender communities. "Without skipping a beat, I was like, 'let's do it, let's go for it,'" Natasha responded; her decision to "go for it," as I will elucidate in what follows, led to backlash and criticism so hazardous that she and the organization decided she needed a security detail for the event.

How did an event focused on trans community lead to such a precarious situation for Natasha? What do the community backlash and its very real consequences for Natasha and her safety reveal about the cisgender/transgender binaries that informed such criticism? Given this special issue's contention with building critically toward trans futures, I ask: is there room for someone like Natasha, a black woman who does not identify as transgender, in a radical trans (studies) future? In this article, I build from transhistorical scholarship from black feminist and transgender studies theorists on the mutability of black female gender (Spillers 1987; King 2016) and on the intimate relationship between blackness and transness (Snorton 2017; Ellison et al. 2017; Bey 2017) to think through how a transgender studies project might understand the realities for a nontrans black feminine subject.

A quick note on categories: There is, as yet, limited scholarship attending to how *cisgender* has emerged and been taken up institutionally in opposition to *transgender*. Thus I follow Savannah Shange (2019: 53n26), who uses *nontrans* as a "racially appropriate alternative to 'cisgender,' which means that (a) the gender you feel inside, (b) the gender you perform outside, and (c) the gender you were assigned at birth all line up and 'match.' However, everything we know about dominant genders—both masculinity and femininity—are based on white bourgeois normativity . . . to call us cisgender is to act like we have the privilege of dominant gender when we don't. At the same time, that doesn't make all Black folks trans either." By refusing *cisgender*, Shange attends to the specificities of antiblackness and black gender fungibility that I aim to emphasize in this article. A fuller examination of how *cisgender* emerged and came to signify the (a), (b), and (c) that Shange delineates is urgent but beyond the scope of this article, which is largely concerned with how "transgender"-focused advocacy, politics, and studies rely on a cis/trans binary that, as Shange demonstrates, does not and cannot apply to black bodies. At the same time, however, Shange clarifies that this caveat "doesn't make all Black folks trans either," thereby highlighting the meaning-making purpose of a category like "cisgender," which is relevant for someone like Natasha who, throughout my fieldwork, actively identified herself as cis and cisgender. I follow the work of David Valentine (2007: 26), who uses *transgender-identified* to highlight his work's "central tension" with the category, in describing Natasha as simultaneously *nontrans* and cisgender-*identified*.

Drawing on ethnographic data, mainly interviews with nonprofit staff members and participant observation at (and between) meetings and events for this large-scale nonprofit, I aim to elucidate the antiblack underpinnings of contemporary trans inclusion projects, particularly in the realm of LGBTQ nonprofits. I focus on the experiences of two black women—Deidre, who is transgender-identified, and Natasha, who is cis-identified—who, though differently positioned relative to the institution, are both rendered fungible, that is, positioned as commodities that can stand in for whatever institutional ideals and values need to be upheld (Hartman 1997). As I will demonstrate, the fungibility of black femininity secures a pernicious cis/trans binary between black women that, I argue, limits the potential for transgender studies to grasp all black women's precarious relationships to "trans" inclusion projects, despite said projects' often-stated commitments to racialized gender justice.

This article is divided into three key sections. In the first, I explicate the ways in which black feminist and trans studies scholars have reckoned with the fungibility of black women in trans incorporation and inclusion projects, and how they have grappled with what this might mean for trans histories and futures. From this literature, I pull out fungibility as an analytic that black feminist and trans studies scholars have deployed to demonstrate the mutability of "black woman" as a category. Using fungibility as a guide, I move to ethnographically examine Deidre's and Natasha's relationships to the nonprofit LGBTQ organization that hired Natasha, relationships that ultimately render both of them precarious. I argue that the institutional imposition of the cis/trans binary—both by the nonprofit organization itself as well as by the numerous community members who subscribe to institutional logics[2]—obscures the connections between their experiences and limits the potential of racialized gender justice. In the end, I move away from a cis/trans binary and toward a *trans/coalitional love-politics*, which I define as a reading practice and critical orientation that grapples with the complicated relationship between blackness and transness as well as the fraught position of the "black woman" in trans inclusion projects. I contend that for a trans future that includes racialized gender justice, we must more critically attend to the category of "black woman" and the exigencies of black feminism within transgender studies.

Black Fungibility and the Limits of Cis/Trans Gender

In a conversation between scholars Kai M. Green and Marquis Bey (2017) on the relationship between black feminism and trans studies, Green argues that a critique of the category "woman" might serve as "*a* possible location" for a generative meeting ground between black feminism and trans studies. As the category serves as "the place of the demand," Green asks, "Is the demand for inclusion, for recentering, for decentering, or is the demand for reconstitution of the terms and terrain?" (439). Green, who speculates that the answer lies in black feminist demands for a "reconstitution" of, rather than a mere additive approach to, the category "woman," asks a question that I believe is central to mining the complex intersections between nontrans and trans black women, and therefore to working to imagining more liberatory trans futures. Green's critical question speaks to ongoing conversations about the perils and promises of (activist and theoretical) projects focused on the "inclusion" of transgender people. David Valentine, in his 2007 monograph *Imagining Transgender*, for example, argues that the circulation of *transgender* as a category—in nonprofit organizations as well as in the academy—often functions to exclude those it is most intended to serve, that is, poor gender-nonconforming people of color. Ahead of the current moment of visibility for transgender people, Valentine expresses a "fear" that those who are most marginalized—by race and class in particular—will be "left out of an imagined future of justice and freedom frequently understood as enabled by this category [transgender]" (6). Trans (academic and political) futures, then, require that we critically examine the terms (i.e., *cisgender*, *transgender*, and *woman*) that make up the "terrain" of the field, as Green (and the black feminist lineages he cites) would argue.

Recently, black feminist and trans studies scholars have mobilized the concept of fungibility to do the kind of theoretical work that the aforementioned scholars have urged. In her initial mobilization of the term, Saidiya Hartman (1997) draws on Marxist notions of the commodity to highlight how black bodies have been rendered as commodities in different kinds of institutions, beginning with economies of slavery. According to Hartman, black bodies have taken on "the extensive capacities of property," that is, becoming "abstract and empty [vessels] vulnerable to the projection of others' feelings, ideas, desires, and values" (21). According to this conception of fungibility, then, black bodies are positioned however "others" (i.e., institutions such as slavery) need them to be positioned to project and maintain their desires, values, and ideals. Fungibility thus also describes the condition of replaceability and interchangeability of black bodies as commodities (21), a condition that becomes a tool for institutional power.

Though she does not use the language of fungibility explicitly, Hortense Spillers elucidates how black (gender) fungibility functions not only materially but also symbolically and discursively. Spillers remarks on how gender is not a category that can map neatly onto black bodies, especially given the nonhuman (or commodity, for Hartman) status ascribed to them. For Spillers (1987: 80), the category of black "woman" exists "out of the traditional symbolics of female gender." Black bodies, then, marked by violent processes of gendering—black women and other racialized gendered bodies—cannot be seen within traditional gender categories. It follows, then, that just as binaries between man and woman (much like straight and queer [Cohen 1997]) fail to encapsulate the realities of gendering for black bodies, and as black feminists have recently intimated (Stallings 2015; Shange 2019), the binary between cisgender and transgender does not and cannot hold up under material realities of (anti)blackness.

In her reading of both Hartman and Spillers, Tiffany L. King (2016) locates fungibility as a "flexible" analytic that allows for open-ended readings of black life, particularly under slavery, colonialism, and present-day antiblackness. King is invested in mobilizing fungibility as a way of gleaning how power is enacted on black (gendered) bodies; more specifically, fungibility helps elucidate "the way Black bodies slip in and out of other humanist categories and frames of legibility, like gender. . . . Black bodies become both engendered and un-gendered depending on the circumstance. In the case of Black captive bodies, gender becomes merely a function of making a body fungible rather than conferring it with human legibility" (1028). Gender—and here I would specify the categories "cis-" and "transgender"—thus functions as a "frame of legibility" that is conferred on black bodies when it serves broader institutional goals, which is entirely "depending on the circumstance." For King, Spillers, and Hartman, black fungibility means that gender functions to further mark black bodies' use value, exchangeability, and, ultimately, commodity status.

In his recent pathbreaking monograph *Black on Both Sides*, C. Riley Snorton (2017) takes up fungibility to detail how the formation of transgender has necessarily relied on (anti)blackness. More specifically, for Snorton, "captive flesh figures a critical genealogy for modern transness, as chattel persons gave rise to an understanding of gender as mutable and as an amenable form of being" (57). Under slavery, as Snorton explicates, chattel persons made use of fungibility as a "critical practice-cum-performance," through cross-dressing and passing, in moments of "escape, of wander, of flight" (57). Given what Spillers, Hartman, and King have described with regard to the violent imposition of gender (and, relatedly, gendered categories) onto black bodies as chattel or as commodities,

Snorton emphasizes how genealogies of slavery and (anti)blackness are necessary precursors to any (institutional) coherence of "transgender" as a category. Black gender fungibility—that is, a condition wherein "gender—though biologized—was not fixed but fungible, which is to say, revisable within blackness, as a condition of possibility" (59)—is thus what makes possible (trans)gender as a political, academic, or identity category.

What might it mean, then, for a transgender studies project to take seriously the concept of fungibility? If transatlantic chattel slavery, antiblackness, and black (gender) fungibility constitute the conditions of possibility for "modern transness," as Snorton has argued, then how might transgender studies more seriously contend with the (anti)blackness that undergirds categories of gender such as "cis-" and "transgender"? By mobilizing fungibility, we can attend to the "place of demand," as Green terms it (Green and Bey 2017: 439), between black feminism and trans studies: that is, attention to black gender fungibility demonstrates the mutability not only of the gender categories with which trans studies has continued to be preoccupied (i.e., binaries between cis and transgender), but also, importantly, "black woman" as a category. As C. Riley Snorton demonstrates through his rereading of the founding of gynecology as a field, and Hortense Spillers has argued, black female bodies—positioned as ungendered captive flesh—have formed the material and discursive ground on which racialized conceptions of gender as well as distinctions between sex and gender have emerged.

Given what Susan Stryker and Paisley Currah (2014: 8), in the introductory issue of *TSQ*, describe as transgender studies' commitment to examining the "utter contingency and fraught conditions of intelligibility of all embodied subjectivity," transgender studies must reckon with the political-economic conditions and racialized and classed structures that make embodied subjectivity (in "all forms," not just those marked as "transgender") possible in the first place. That is, transgender studies must recognize, attend to, and critically examine the mutability of "black woman" as a category as seriously as it attends to the "contingency" and "fraught" nature of (trans)gender. More specifically, as I highlight through my ethnographic example of Natasha and Deidre—who, though they relate to one another antagonistically on the ground, share a symbolic relationship rooted in the fungibility of black femininity—institutionalized projects focused on transgender justice alone often rely on cis/trans binaries that foreclose the possibility of fully addressing the particularities of either Natasha's or Deidre's concerns. As I demonstrate in what follows, if the goal of transgender studies (or any transgender-focused political project) is to work toward racialized gender justice, there must be space to address the material realities for people like Natasha and Deidre, as well as to reckon with the futility of cis/trans binaries when it comes to thinking about (anti)blackness.

Creating a "Whole New Table": Natasha's Fungibility

When I sat down with Natasha in April 2018 for an interview, her small office was cramped with pamphlets, flyers, folders, and other odds and ends. The rectangular office was located in the administrative wing of the organization, sharing hallway space with senior staff such as the chief operating officer as well as the directors of development, finance, and communication. She had just moved into that office, which had previously been used for interns, one-on-one meetings between donors and development, and, from what I could tell in my time working with the organization up until this point, general office storage. Given that Natasha's specific title ("senior events manager") had been codified only in the previous year, Natasha's makeshift office was unsurprising. Previous coordinators for the event—trans-identified people, the most recent of whom was a black transgender woman who left the organization under unclear circumstances—were unable to secure an office or support staff in the ways that Natasha had, which Natasha described as "fucked up." She attributed these differences to the fact that the previous coordinators were "tokenized" and "thrown into [the job] with no support." The difficulties of the job were exacerbated by the large scale of the event, as well as historical tensions between local queer and trans community members and the organization, which was widely rumored to have usurped the event from (predominantly black) community activists. Natasha emphasized how the position had sat open for five months as a result of such realities, such that when she was asked to take on the position, she knew that the event could not happen without her.

While it may appear on the surface that Natasha's identity as a cisgender (rather than transgender) person in the event planning role afforded her particular privileges such as her own (albeit small) office, support staff, and a "manager" title, she was continually rendered fungible as a black woman working for the organization. Her assistant, Jaime, a Latinx and nonbinary-identified person, put it plainly when they said that even Natasha's title exemplified how they "must really hate black people." They explained:

> You won't put black people in these [senior] positions. That's how it feels here. Even the fact that Natasha is the director of our department—they created this position of "senior events manager." A completely new position: no one else has that title, because they didn't want to give this black woman a director position. That stuff is so transparent to me, and if you try to call it out, people are like, "Wow, you're really reaching. I can't believe you'd call that racism, misogyny, or whatever." You didn't want to give this person a seat at the table so you created a whole new table for her to sit by herself. That makes no sense.

Considered alongside Natasha's makeshift office, positioned relative to—but significantly smaller than—those of senior staff members in the organization, Jaime's characterization of Natasha's position as a "whole new table" separate from the existing institutional structure highlights it as fungible within the organization. That is, Natasha was expected to fulfill the organization's desires—to do the labor of organizing, coordinating, and planning a large-scale event, the labor equivalent to a director or senior staff member—with a "whole new" title, one that excluded her from appropriate pay or treatment as well as from decision-making power over such aspects of the event as support staff and budgeting. Furthermore, to draw attention to how "transparent" (in Jaime's words) such an inequality was would be "reaching," under insidious institutional logics. The contingencies of Natasha's role in the organization, then, exemplify King's (2016: 1024) conception of fungibility wherein "[black] lives (if they even have them) certainly matter *differently* if at all" (emphasis added). Despite the material and, as I will discuss, semiotic labor that she performed for the organization, Natasha's position at a "whole new table" ultimately highlights her exchangeability and marginality relative to the existing institutional structure.

Beyond her title, the backlash that Natasha received from her position in the organization not only demonstrates the perils of her fungible position but also, and most importantly, the stakes of positioning her as simply a "cisgender woman." When I asked her in our interview to describe her experience working as the senior events manager, she described:

> So, I'm going to be completely honest with you. It's been really, really hard . . . just a few months before the [event] last year, a certain person who's in the community decided to take up a huge call to action because of my gender identity because I'm cis—they really twisted my role and instead of it being about the logistics . . . it was put out there that I was the face and voice of the trans community and I had received a lot of death threats. I was followed, I was doxed, all my personal information was put online. There were multiple videos that were really dangerous. To the point where I'd actually never had my name spoken with such vitriol before and my own name became a trigger. I was out of work for several weeks. I couldn't leave my home. I couldn't go to my second job. It got really, really frightening and as you can tell it's still really scary for me and I'm worried for [this year's conference]. . . . I ended up with security detail . . . [which] makes me really sad to be out in my community with my siblings and be afraid because that's like the exact opposite of the space that we're all trying to create.

Natasha's experiences receiving death threats, being doxed, and having her personal information released online demonstrate the extent to which Natasha's body—specifically, her bodily autonomy and safety—were placed in the center of organizational critiques by trans-identified community members. The magnitude of this "vitriol"—not being able to leave her house, having her own name become a "trigger," and fearing for herself and her family (including her black gender-nonconforming partner, whose information was also released publicly)—far exceeds any backlash or criticism that her colleagues and predecessors at the organization received.

In this way, to characterize the backlash that Natasha received as resulting simply from her being a cisgender person running a transgender-focused event would ignore the realities of antiblackness that undergird the gendered notions of who "should" run such an event. These clearly personalized, and ultimately dangerous, responses to Natasha's work in this position exemplify what Frank Wilderson (2010: 112) describes as violence that "positions the Black in an infinite and indeterminately horrifying and open vulnerability, an object made available (which is to say fungible) for any subject." People from a range of (racial and gendered) subject positions publicly opined about Natasha and whether she "should" be in her position, but few recognized the precarious and ultimately fungible position that she, her labor, and her body held for the organization. Furthermore, the "open vulnerability" she faced persisted as numerous community members maintained their critical and often violently public opinions about her, despite the fact that Natasha continued to emphasize (to me in our interview, as well as to local news outlets and community members), "I don't touch content [for the event]—I shouldn't be the person who touches content." Even as she maintained a position she called "behind the curtain," to be respectful of and adherent to existing relationships between the organization and the local community, Natasha was still characterized by numerous community members— and, importantly, by the organization—as representing the face of the trans-focused event.

"Grossly Inappropriate" Institutional Practice: Deidre's Critique

The criticism leveraged against Natasha often worked in tandem with those against the organization itself: people often slipped between talking about the nonprofit and talking about Natasha, blaming both for the failures of the event to appropriately serve and represent trans and gender-nonconforming people. The ways such criticisms fell on Natasha's body in particular reflect her fungibility, specifically as community members continually mapped their ideals and expectations of the institution onto her body by blaming both the organization and Natasha herself for having a cisgender person taking up transgender-specific space. Furthermore, the organization that hosted the event benefited from Natasha's position as a "face" or "voice" that community members could respond to directly. That is, rather than (have to) respond to their criticisms regarding (and, thus, be held accountable for) the lack of transparency in event planning and logistics, the relative homogeneity of organizational leadership, and the lack of representation of trans and gender-nonconforming people of color in said leadership and planning processes, the organization could place Natasha on the frontlines to respond to and answer for these issues, which were, in reality, structural and not individual.

At the center of much of this controversy was a community member to whom Natasha alluded in our interview, Deidre, a black transgender-identified woman who was known (or, to many, infamous) among LGBTQ advocates in the city for vocally critiquing numerous organizations, individual community leaders, and their practices. In a blog post that she titled an "open letter" to the organization hosting this event, Deidre emphasized how, given the realities for trans and gender-nonconforming people—she cited the lack of federal protections, as well as violence, disenfranchisement, and erasure—it was "grossly inappropriate" for the organization to have hired Natasha to be, in Deidre's words, "the face and voice of a community [she is] not a part of and [does] not identify with."[3] Deidre emphasizes how the "transgender population" is targeted and discriminated against on a national level, making it increasingly important for transgender people to be represented in trans-specific events. The decision to hire Natasha, she argues ultimately, demonstrates a lack of respect for the transgender community. Deidre's blog post and continued criticisms of and about Natasha never once mention her blackness (although, in numerous Facebook posts, she did emphasize how Natasha's background as a bartender did not and could not stand in for event planning experience). Deidre's emphasis on Natasha's cisgender identity—and, inadvertently, her class position, as she disparaged Natasha's previous work experience—over and above her blackness (and therefore, necessarily, her black gender fungibility) reveals the very paradox I am elucidating with regard to transgender studies: an overreliance on a cis/trans binary that assumes inherent privileges in a lack of trans identity and ignores the realities of (anti)blackness.

At the same time, however, Deidre's critique included a grounded understanding of the antiblack institutional logics present in the organization. She briefly mentioned the previous coordinators for the event, whom she named directly and identified as a "trans man" and a "black trans woman." She talked about how excited she was when the organization hired a black trans woman to run the event, knowing at the same time that "representation of the most marginalized and vulnerable would not last," owing to "rampant trans misogyny, passive aggression toward black trans women and the never ending microaggressions coupled with the horizontal hostility black trans women face when working with the [organization]." Here, Deidre mobilizes language commonly used in institutionally legitimated social justice and trans inclusion projects—*microaggressions, horizontal hostility,* and even *trans misogyny*[4]—to highlight the antiblackness and transphobia with which black trans women necessarily interface at institutions like this (and other similarly scaled) nonprofit organization. However, by emphasizing such critiques as specific to black *trans* women, without connecting this critique to Natasha's gender fungibility (and, importantly, the hostility, misogyny, microaggressions that she also faces), she inadvertently reinforces the cis/trans binary that invisibilizes the very real material consequences that Natasha experiences as a black woman in the organization.

Deidre's post thus acknowledges—and inadvertently reinforces—the very logics that not only shut her out of an institution like this organization but also position Natasha as a scapegoat for such logics: such a move relies on Natasha's interchangeability for the institution to uphold a "trans justice" agenda that, ultimately, further marginalizes black cisgender women like Natasha. Deidre's critique, however, does seem to recognize the institution's intentional and potentially strategic choice to hire Natasha: after describing the systemic reasons the organization could not retain a trans-identified coordinator, she posits such institutional hostility as the reason Natasha was hired to fulfill this role. Deidre recognizes here, then, how Natasha, as a cisgender black woman, is positioned to serve as a representative of diversity, to labor for the conference, and to be on the receiving end of any community criticism. These expectations for Natasha, as I have demonstrated thus far, reveal her fungibility, in which her "blackness . . . points to a place where being undone is simultaneously a space for new forms of becoming" (Snorton 2017: 70). Through the discursive and material (threat of) violence that Natasha faces, she is "undone" while the "transgender"-focused project she manages—and the transgender-focused critiques of said project—may open up "space for new forms of becoming," but only for those who identify with transgender as a category.

Deidre further contributed to the erasure of the realities Natasha has faced—and therefore to Natasha's fungibility within the organization—as she slipped between disparaging the institution as a whole and Natasha herself. In her blog post, she described how Natasha "intentionally shut [her] out" from speaking at the event, characterizing this as an example of an event being "hijacked by cisgender people using their privilege." Given Natasha's fears for her safety following Deidre's public social media posts and video blogs decrying the organization and Natasha specifically, such a moment must be contextualized. Natasha's "cisgender privilege," in Deidre's words, is difficult to locate precisely: while her position working within the organization allowed her the ability to acquire a security detail at the conference, for example, the need for security in the first place does not reflect a privilege. Rather, it reflects a more complex positioning that King (2016: 1024) might characterize as "pure flux, process, and potential." By characterizing Natasha's disinviting her participation as an example of privilege, Deidre further pushes Natasha into a position of "flux," in which her gender identity is rendered illegible, always in "process," and as purely a site of "potential." Furthermore, for Deidre to be able to uphold her own claims about transgender-specific disenfranchisement and marginality, she must necessarily rely on a transgender/cisgender binary that does not and cannot account for Natasha's fungibility, nor for her own.

Reading Natasha *and* Deidre through a Radical Ethic of Care; or, Toward a Trans/Coalitional Love-Politics

Although Natasha and Deidre were positioned as enemies by the organization (which supported Natasha by providing a security detail and helping exclude Deidre from the event), they share a symbolic relationship as black feminine subjects who are deemed fungible commodities for the institution. As a black transgender woman, Deidre's body and fungible gender are also mobilized as hypervisible arms of the institution, even if only from the direction of a "radical" or "crazy" critique. In fact, throughout my fieldwork, various interlocutors figured Deidre as "crazy": her "controversial" opinions and robust blog and Facebook critiques led to continuous "flux," as King might describe it. She was fired or forced to resign from numerous organizations, programs, and boards, despite that she was often invited or called on to participate in and work for these institutions. Such realities reflect her own fungibility relative to the institution: available for use whenever needed (to appease critiques about a lack of diversity for a trans-focused program, for example) but, ultimately, disposable—especially when she vocalized a critique of how the organization functioned and (even inadvertently) reinforced antiblack or antitrans logics.

Thus, rather than present this tension by pitting two black women against one another—Natasha, the cisgender black woman working for the institution, and Deidre, the black trans woman working outside the institution—I am interested in reading their (actual and symbolic) relationship through what I am calling a trans/coalitional love-politics, a reading practice and critical orientation that routes us away from the insidious cis/trans binary and toward a deeper understanding of the relationship between the fungibility of black feminine subjects and transgender inclusion projects. Trans/coalitional love-politics draws primarily on the work of seminal black feminists Cathy Cohen (1997) and Jennifer C. Nash (2013) to think through how transgender studies, in its efforts to work toward racialized gender justice, might center black gender, specifically black femininity, as it is continuously rendered fungible in trans-focused institutional formations. By mobilizing the prefix *trans* for this reading practice, I aim to maintain the potentiality of *trans* (trans*, transgender, transformation, trans-), most clearly articulated in what Green (2016: 79) describes as a "trans* analytic," in which "we must move to those uncomfortable places of contradiction and conflict, and in those moments we will develop a more critical and nuanced analysis of the conditions under which we are required to live, named and unnamed." As an open-ended prefix, *trans* allows—indeed, must allow, to move toward more radical trans futures—for contradiction and conflict, even if that discomfort happens with the category "transgender" itself.

This reading practice and orientation builds from Cohen's concerns about the category "queer" and its political and academic circulation, which she articulates in her pathbreaking "Punks, Bulldaggers, and Welfare Queens: The Radical Potential of Queer Politics?" Cohen (1997) asks important questions about who we include in "queer," questions that continue to undergird significant theoretical work in black queer studies and black feminism, and that inform my argument with regard to transgender studies. She asks, "In narrowly positing a dichotomy of heterosexual privilege and queer oppression under which we all exist, are we negating a basis of political utility that could serve to strengthen many communities and movements seeking justice and societal formation?" (453). Emphasizing the difference between heterosexual and queer, over and above material realities of racism and classism, Cohen argues, functions ultimately to negate political possibilities. The "narrow" dichotomy between heterosexual privilege and queer oppression is not unlike that which many activists and scholars pose between trans and cisgender,[5] which leads me, like Cohen, to think critically about the possibility and potentiality of coalition. The coalitional piece of a trans/coalitional love-politics approach, then, draws on Cohen's call for movement building to be rooted not in shared identity but in "our shared marginal relationship to dominant power which normalizes, legitimizes, and privileges" (458). A trans/coalitional approach, then, recognizes the messy, overlapping, and uncomfortable ways that dominant forms of power—most importantly antiblackness, but also the resulting gendered racialized violence that stems from such antiblackness—function in a myriad of lives.

The final component of this reading practice is drawn from what Nash (2013) calls a "Black feminist love-politics," which calls for a move away from characterizing black feminism as "identity politics" and toward recognizing the centrality of love. More specifically, "love-politics" is a form of affective politics that helps to describe how "bodies are organized around intensities, longings, desires, temporalities, repulsions, curiosities, fatigues, optimism, and how these affects produce social movements (or sometimes inertias)" (3). While Natasha and Deidre may relate to each other through "intensities" and "repulsions," black feminist love-politics emphasizes love as "a practice of self, a labor of the self, that forms the basis of political communities rooted in a radical ethic of care" (14). This ethic of care is in direct opposition to an assumption of shared injury because, importantly, black feminist love-politics recognizes "the great insight of black feminist theory . . . that injury is never *really* shared" (15). A radical ethic of care necessarily locates individual selves within specific conditions and builds communities from such an ethic. Love-politics recognizes that love—a deep, loving, and caring engagement with individual selves—is always intertwined with our politics—the place from which we can see, understand, and (eventually) challenge power.

A trans/coalitional love-politics thus means beginning from a radical ethic of care, an ethic that takes seriously both Deidre's and Natasha's positions and relationships to racialized gendered power (more specifically, to antiblackness and black gender fungibility). It requires a deep and structural recognition of their flexible commodity status—what Wilderson (2010: 57) aptly describes as "the condition of being owned and traded" as their "ontological foundation." Given such a foundation, then, Deidre and Natasha, as black women, are both rendered commodities to be used at the will of the organization and of the institutional logics that suture their symbolic relationship: whether it is through carrying the burden of the backlash for a transgender-specific event, in Natasha's case, or through the reproduction of the institutional logics of transgender inclusion, in Deidre's. That is, the antiblack institutional logics Deidre reproduces by positioning her and Natasha as enemies perpetuate the fungibility of black feminine subjects, while the institution carries on with business as usual. Natasha's body bears the brunt of critiques of the organization from Deidre, who mobilizes the logics of said institution to critique a lack of black trans representation, further endangering Natasha in the process. Neither is a threat to the institution (that is, neither is given institutional power), and both are injured. Natasha's injury, however, under any transgender rubric that relies so heavily on a cis/trans binary, remains nameless.

A trans/coalitional love-politics responds to such "unnamed" conditions (to use Green's language) by attending to how black gender fungibility serves as the "condition of possibility" (Snorton 2017: 59) for any gender category, including "transgender" and "cisgender." Reading Natasha and Deidre's antagonistic relationship through a trans/coalitional love-politics means beginning from their symbolically intertwined, but never shared, injury (to riff on Nash). Recognizing how both Deidre and Natasha are injured as individual selves, are fungible as commodities for the institution, and are by their fungibility necessary for the institution to reproduce its materially and discursively violent logics is the place from which a trans/coalitional love-politics reads, writes, and builds. It requires trans, but only as an analytic that pushes readers to "gain a reorientation to orientation" (Green 2016: 67); it cannot work with a trans always positioned in opposition to cis, but rather as a way of reorienting our relationship to gender as a function of antiblackness. It means taking seriously the mutability and fungibility of the category "black woman," which can be both trans and—as I have demonstrated—violently not trans. To fully contend with possibilities for futures of racialized gendered justice, then, transgender studies must reorient away from cis/trans binaries and toward reading, perhaps through a trans/coalitional love-politics, the antiblackness that undergirds how these binaries are constructed and reproduced in the first place.

A trans/coalitional love-politics opens up space for what Cohen has called "a radical trans analysis" that aims "*not* [for] everyone [to] find their essentialist selves" but to "[break] down systems of oppression based on gender and class and race and sexuality, that limit the ability of people to have full and happy lives" (quoted in Jackson 2015). Building not from a place of believing in an essentialized self or other, but rather from a place where we can see just how we are all positioned, a trans/coalitional love-politics attempts to carve out possibility. Natasha articulated a desire for such a possibility when she talked about deciding to take the position organizing the large-scale trans-focused event:

> They said: Listen, we have this amazing, beautiful event—which I had been to before. The position has been sitting empty for five months and we are not going to be able to move forward if we don't have a coordinator. Would you be interested in applying for this position instead? Without skipping a beat, I was like, "This is such an important part of our overall umbrella community." And also specifically for trans folks, having a lapse in a year would have been detrimental, so I was like, "yeah, let's do it. Let's go for it."

Natasha's recognition that such an event would benefit "our overall umbrella community" encompasses the potentiality in a trans/coalitional love-politics, which Natasha's "umbrella" gestures toward. Unlike uses of a transgender umbrella, which has faced important critiques with regard to obscuring "the specific intersections of classed, raced, geographic, and cultural dimensions of personhood" (Singer 2014: 260), Natasha's conception of "our overall umbrella community" signals her recognition of black gender fungibility, which is the basis for a loving coalition across and through cis/trans binaries.

During my fieldwork, I asked all of my interlocutors—nonprofit staff members, funders, service providers, volunteers, and community members of varying racialized gendered subject positions—to define "trans justice." Natasha talked explicitly about what reparations might look like for differently marginalized communities, thinking critically about how reparations—a framework explicitly responding to antiblackness—served as the basis for how she thought about justice. She then went on to say:

> It's looking at all of the tangible systems of oppression that we're working under right now, and then actually changing those. *What do we in each one of our positions have the ability to change, and how do we change it?* So, taking it from the framework of [a] school that no, a teacher does not have the ability to knock down a wall and create a [gender-neutral] bathroom, but they do have the ability to change the wording on the forms and put up trans representation on their walls and pictures.

Natasha's guiding question, emphasized above, asks about "we in each one of our positions," reflecting a black feminist ethic attending to and loving the self first and foremost: she talks about "black feminism's pleas for love as a significant call for ordering the self *and* transcending the self, a strategy for remaking the self *and* for moving beyond the limitations of selfhood" (Nash 2013: 3). Natasha, too, makes such a plea, asking individuals to reckon with their relationships to power (or, as Cohen [1997: 458] might say, "shared marginal relationship[s] to dominant power") and work from that position to create change. Such a plea is reflective of her own commitment to a trans/coalitional love-politics, that is, to a black feminist politics first and foremost, and to the implications of what this means for trans futures, trans politics, and trans studies. Transgender studies, then, might take trans/coalitional love-politics as a place from which to take seriously "black woman" as a mutable, institutionally precarious (which is to say fungible) gender category.

V Varun Chaudhry is a faculty member in the Women's, Gender, and Sexuality Studies Program at Brandeis University. His writing appears or is forthcoming in *GLQ: A Journal of Lesbian and Gay Studies, Signs: Journal of Women and Culture in Society, American Anthropologist*, and *Critical Inquiry*.

Acknowledgments

The ethnographic research that informed this article was supported by the Wenner-Gren Foundation (#9400) and a dissertation fellowship from the Sexualities Project at Northwestern (SPAN). The author also sends particular gratitude to his interlocutors who informed his thinking, writing, and politics, as well as to Shoniqua Roach, who generously read outlines and drafts as this article came together.

Notes

1. The names of interlocutors are all pseudonyms. Given the institutional positions of these particular subjects, I have chosen to omit as much personal and identifying information as possible, choosing to focus primarily on their relationships to the institutional formations relevant to my argument.

2. I recognize and want to underscore here that people do not uniformly "subscribe" to institutional logics; rather, institutional logics reproduce themselves in and through different bodies in often-insidious ways. My interlocutors subscribed to the notion that this trans event was important, for example, because, to put it plainly, for them it *was*; the importance of the event, however, does not and cannot mean the organization does not (inadvertently or not) reproduce harmful antiblack logics.

3. Much of my citations of Deidre come from her blog and Facebook posts, published between July 2017 and June 2018. I do not link to the blog directly to protect the anonymity of my interlocutors.

4. Here I am indebted to the work of Elias Krell (2017), who has critically thought about how *transmisogyny* has been taken up by activists and social movement rhetoric in often harmful and antiblack ways.

5. One very recent example of this boundary making is prevalent throughout the 2017 *South Atlantic Quarterly* forum on "trans recognition," in which many of the contributing scholars mark distinctions between trans and cisgender or nontrans people (Armstrong 2017; Chaudhry forthcoming).

References

Armstrong, Amanda. 2017. "Certificates of Live Birth and Dead Names: On the Subject of Recent Anti-trans Legislation." *South Atlantic Quarterly* 116, no. 3: 621–31.

Bey, Marquis. 2017. "The Trans*-ness of Blackness, the Blackness of Trans*-ness." *TSQ* 4, no. 2: 275–95.

Chaudhry, V Varun. Forthcoming. "On Trans Dissemblance: Or, Why Trans Studies Needs Black Feminism." *Signs: Journal of Women in Culture and Society* 45, no. 3.

Cohen, Cathy. 1997. "Punks, Bulldaggers, and Welfare Queens: The Radical Potential of Queer Politics?" *GLQ* 3, no. 4: 437–65.

Ellison, Treva, Kai M. Green, Matt Richardson, and C. Riley Snorton. 2017. "We Got Issues: Toward a Black Trans*/Studies." *TSQ* 4, no. 2: 162–69.

Green, Kai M. 2016. "Troubling the Waters: Mobilizing a Trans* Analytic." In *No Tea, No Shade: New Writings in Black Queer Studies*, edited by E. Patrick Johnson, 65–82. Durham, NC: Duke University Press.

Green, Kai M., and Marquis Bey. 2017. "Where Black Feminist Thought and Trans* Feminism Meet: A Conversation." *Souls* 19, no. 4: 438–54.

Hartman, Saidiya V. 1997. *Scenes of Subjection: Terror, Slavery, and Self-Making in Nineteenth-Century America*. New York: Oxford University Press.

Jackson, Sarah J. 2015. "Cathy Cohen Discusses Black Lives Matter, Feminism, and Contemporary Activism with Sarah J. Jackson." *Signs: Journal of Women in Culture and Society* (blog), December 7. signsjournal.org/ask-a-feminist-cohen-jackson/.

King, Tiffany Lethabo. 2016. "The Labor of (Re)Reading Plantation Landscapes Fungible(ly)." *Antipode* 48, no. 4: 1022–39.

Krell, Elías Cosenza. 2017. "Is Transmisogyny Killing Trans Women of Color? Black Trans Feminisms and the Exigencies of White Femininity." *TSQ* 4, no. 2: 226–42.

Nash, Jennifer C. 2013. "Practicing Love: Black Feminism, Love-Politics, and Post-intersectionality." *Meridians: Feminism, Race, Transnationalism* 11, no. 2: 1–24.

Shange, Savannah. 2019. "Play Aunties and Dyke Bitches: Gender, Generation, and the Ethics of Black Queer Kinship." *Black Scholar* 49, no. 1: 40–54.

Singer, T. Benjamin. 2014. "Umbrella." *TSQ* 1, nos. 1–2: 259–61.

Snorton, C. Riley. 2017. *Black on Both Sides: A Racial History of Trans Identity*. Minneapolis: University of Minnesota Press.

Spillers, Hortense J. 1987. "Mama's Baby, Papa's Maybe: An American Grammar Book." *Diacritics* 17, no. 2: 65–81.

Stallings, L. H. 2015. *Funk the Erotic: Transaesthetics and Black Sexual Cultures*. Urbana: University of Illinois Press.

Stryker, Susan, and Paisley Currah. 2014. Introduction to *TSQ* 1, nos. 1–2: 1–18.

Valentine, David. 2007. *Imagining Transgender: An Ethnography of a Category*. Durham, NC: Duke University Press.

Wilderson, Frank B. 2010. *Red, White, and Black: Cinema and the Structure of U.S. Antagonisms*. Durham, NC: Duke University Press.

Remixing Transfeminist Futures

ROX SAMER

Abstract There are likely many ways to remix transfeminist futures. As a scholar-vidder, I focus on vidding as one form this work might take. Vidding is an especially affective form of remix art that renders literal the Foucauldian imperative "knowledge is not made for understanding; it is made for cutting." In disturbing what was previously considered immobile, fragmenting what was thought unified, and not hiding the cuts with which it does so, vidding produces affective surplus. It is not only that a vid disassembles source media, but that its reassembly produces more than a new text; it also, often unpredictably and inexplicably, generates entirely new affects. Taken up as a transfeminist creative critical praxis, vidding could challenge the transphobic and cissexist common sense on which our reality relies, including its teleological histories that cast trans as "new," ignoring the contributions of trans people to feminist and queer movements and the historical and geographical range of gender variance; liberal discourses that approach trans as yet another matter of civil rights, neglecting how visibility renders trans people more susceptible to violence and surveillance; and media narratives which tell the same fetishizing, isolating, and tragic stories of trans lives time and again. Through my analysis of three of my own transfeminist vids, I introduce the digital humanities methodology "remixing transfeminist futures" and propose we remix our transphobic, transmiso-gynistic, cissexist reality so as to make perceptible a future when trans people, queer people, people of color, and all women and femmes are free.

Keywords transfeminism, trans temporality, remix, fandom, scholarly vidding

"Clink. Clink." The heavy sound of locks unlocking, which opens the film version of Beyoncé's "Six Inch [Heels]," vibrate as the song's drumbeat enters. On-screen we do not see the empty hallway lit with bare red bulbs that initiates this passage of *Lemonade*. Instead, we are in a different hallway, a fluorescent white one leading to a women's public restroom. A quick cut takes us inside, where actor Alexandra Billings spins. Arm out before her, the self-recording video captures her sly smile as the single-stall restroom's red and grey walls, mirror, toilet, and handrails whirl by behind her. "Loss," Beyoncé ambiguously declares. We are outside another women's restroom in a different fluorescently lit hallway where author Jennifer Boylan looks into a phone camera of her own and welcomes us to North Carolina, where she "can't use the restroom." As

Beyoncé's monologue continues ("Dear Moon / We blame you for floods / for the flush of blood / for men who are also wolves / We blame you for the night / for the dark / for the ghosts"), a montage of Instagram posts, complete with the white frame of the social media platform, are cut in rhythm—among them are the *New York Times* headline "Trump Administration Eyes Defining Transgender out of Existence," a still photograph of the unfurling of TransLatin@ Coalition's "Trans People Deserve to Live" sign at game 5 of the 2018 World Series, and a photograph of hands holding a candle, superimposed with the blue, pink, and white stripes of the trans flag. Each of these is captioned by the Instagram user who posted it. Actor Candis Cayne's caption under the candle photograph reads, "Today is Trans Day of Remembrance, on which we honor the memory of those lives that we lost to anti-transgender violence. #wewontbeerased." As the melody swells, another montage builds. Outside the Stonewall Inn an activist speaks into a mic to a raucous crowd—"An attack on one LGBT person is an attack on the whole LGBT community." A young Black girl, twirling in her pink and white dress and quoting another Beyoncé song, tells her mother behind the camera, "[Laverne Cox] is who I love—flawless." In a GIF, Lynda Carter's Wonder Woman smashes a pane of glass labeled "patriarchy." Janet Mock addresses yet another camera, "When I think about my inspirations I always think about LGBT folk who've resisted and survived." A crescendo of strings ushers in the song's first lyrics, "Six inch heels, she walked in the club like nobody's business," and we see Mock and a friend jumping in slow motion on a bed, actor Trace Lysette walking a runway, and actor Laverne Cox "pumping through Selma, Alabama." This footage makes up the first minute and half of my third transfeminist vid. In my analysis of these three vids, I present transfeminist vidding's affective cuts as exemplary of the digital humanities methodology "remixing transfeminist futures." It is a methodology through which I propose we remix our transphobic, transmisogynistic, cissexist reality and make perceptible a future when trans people, queer people, people of color, and all women and femmes are free.

In the labor its editing demands of its viewers, vidding produces affects that exceed the expression of vids themselves and disrupt the presumed stability and continuity of past-present-future. In contending as much, I draw from Kara Keeling's (2009) writing on temporality, affectivity, and Black queer and trans documentaries. While *Brother to Brother* (dir. Rodney Evans, 2004) orders the past in service of the present, making visible Black queer histories, which might then support similar futures, *The Aggressives* (dir. Daniel Peddle, 2005), Keeling argues, reveals such historical operations to be exclusionary and constructive, exposing the edits cloaked in the allure of visibility. micha cárdenas, Tourmaline, and others have written extensively about the violence that quite often comes with visibility for trans people, especially trans women of color (cárdenas 2015; Tourmaline, Stanley, and Burton 2017). Keeling (2009: 570) turns to *The Aggressives*, which follows several "aggressives" but also loses its Black gender-nonconforming subjects in its imposition of conventional documentary time, to advocate for a media historiography (or theorizing of temporality by way of media) that, rather than making certain historical subjects visible according to present logics, makes "what does not fit present logics perceptible, even if not recognizable." Keeling considers the affective surplus generated by such an analysis an index of "poetry from the future," Karl Marx's formulation of what is necessary to rupture the violences of history from within (566). If asking where subjects are—such as M—, who disappears halfway through *The Aggressives*—aligns one with the prison- and military-industrial complex, Keeling suggests we instead ask when such subjects might be, that is, when Black gender-nonconforming subjects' visibility will enable them to survive "by providing the protection the realm of the visible affords those whose existence is valued" (577). Looking for, in this sense, becomes, through Keeling's analysis, a method of looking after. In its own production of affective surplus, remixing transfeminist futures aspires to become a methodology through which scholar-artists working in trans, queer, and Black cultural production and critical theory might look for/after those vulnerable to contemporary logics of visibility.

Remix broadly refers to "the practice of appropriating, decontextualizing, and recontextualizing media content to create new meanings" (Suzanne Scott and Louisa Stein in Creekmur et al. 2017: 159). In the digital era, remix forms are "constantly proliferating and hybridizing" (159), as people with a wide range of artistic, political, and intellectual interests put to use the various tools of editing software, seen, for example, in the great variety of mash-ups circulated online through YouTube, Vimeo, and the social media sites that link to and "share" these platforms' content. The question for the transfeminist remix artist becomes a matter of repurposing these tools in such a way that uniquely adds to the many perspectives and approaches being brought to transfeminism today.[1] How might one excise and recombine media as a means of contributing to the liberation of trans women and all those who transgress gender norms and/or as a method of fighting misogyny, including transmisogyny? Put another way, how might one use the forms, tools, and analytical methodologies of remix to produce "poetry from the future" that looks after trans loved ones and comrades in the present? There are likely many ways to remix transfeminist futures. A goal of this essay is to inspire such a range of work.

As a scholar-vidder, I focus on vidding as one form this work might take. Vidding is an especially affective form of remix art that renders literal the Foucauldian imperative "knowledge is not made for understanding; it is made for cutting" (Foucault 1977: 154). In disturbing what was previously considered immobile and fragmenting what was thought unified and not hiding the cuts with which it does so, vidding produces affective surplus. It is not only that a vid disassembles source media, but that its reassembly produces more than a new text; it also, often unpredictably and inexplicably, generates entirely new affects. Following Keeling (2007: 24–26), *affects* names not only feelings or emotions but that which exceeds our cognitive attempts to make sense of the world. Unassimilable by the logics of our capitalist, racist, homophobic, misogynist, transphobic present, "whatever escapes recognition, whatever escapes meaning and valuation," Keeling (2009: 566–67) writes, "exists as an impossible possibility within our shared reality," which in turn "threatens to unsettle, if not destroy, the common sense on which that reality relies for its coherence as such." Taken up as a transfeminist creative critical praxis, vidding could challenge the transphobic and cissexist common sense on which our reality relies, including its teleological histories that cast trans as "new," ignoring the contributions of trans people to feminist and queer movements, such as Marsha P. Johnson and Sylvia Rivera, and the historical and geographical range of gender variance; its liberal discourses that approach trans as yet another matter of civil rights, neglecting how visibility renders trans people more susceptible to violence and surveillance; and its media narratives, which tell the same fetishizing and tragic stories of trans lives time and again.

Vidding as Transfeminist Methodology

Since vidding's start in women's *Star Trek* fandom of the 1970s (and with the advent of the VCR as a home recording and viewing technology), vidders have used the medium to make political critiques and articulate analytical claims. In an essay on the history of vidding as feminist fan praxis, Francesca Coppa (2008) defines vidding as "a form of grassroots filmmaking in which clips from television shows and movies are set to music." Whereas music videos are created to promote musicians and their albums, Coppa explains, vidders use music and the music video format to analyze extant media texts. Both the music's lyrics and affective force provide the interpretive lens through which viewers may see the source media differently. In making vids that critiqued the sexism of *Star Trek* but also expressed an affinity for its utopian vision and homoeroticism through arduous double-deck VCR bricolage, early vidders took "two positions often framed as contradictory in mainstream culture [for cisgender women]: the desiring body, and the controlling voice of technology" (Coppa 2008). Vidding has grown exponentially since the 1970s and now encompasses tens of genres, including shipping and slash vids (which write characters into relationships not explored in the source media, including queer relationships in the case of "slash"); celebratory vids (which celebrate particular elements of a text, whether that be a particular character, plotline, theme, or stylistic trait); book vids (which adapt literary sources into audiovisual ones through the juxtaposition of quotations and footage culled from media with similar imagery and/or themes); multiverse vids (which pursue themes or draw parallels between varied texts); and dance-party vids (which are made to be played during a fan convention or vid festival dance party).[2] As Katherine Morrissey notes in her contribution to a recent roundtable on remix, scholars have tended to focus on vids whose arguments resemble those made in media criticism and those whose styles are recognizable as valuable to academia and the fine arts; however, the production and consumption of vids across all these genres involve labor, formal experimentation, close reading, and media critique (Creekmur et al. 2017: 167).

Only recently have scholars begun to theorize how vids might serve as not only objects of study but also scholarly texts in and of themselves. Kristina Busse and Alexis Lothian, two scholar-vidders, explore how, if made for different audiences, fan vids often do the very work of scholarship or criticism. In their 2011 coauthored essay, Lothian writes, "While fanvids often celebrate media products as they are, they can also make visible subjugated knowledges, deconstructing the ideological frameworks of film and TV by unmaking those frameworks technologically" (141). Lothian analyzes her own first scholarly vid, *The Future Stops Here* (2008), to demonstrate how, in doing as much, vids examine larger cultural patterns and sociopolitical issues. *The Future Stops Here* cuts together footage from *Children of Men*, *V for Vendetta*, and *28 Days Later* to the sounds of UNKLE's "Rabbit in Your Headlights" to explore how the imaginary futures of early twenty-first-century speculative fiction cinema both consolidate and undermine racist, sexist, and heteronormative narratives of temporality. In her new book *Old Futures* (2018), Lothian situates her scholarly vidding within a larger project on speculative fiction and queer temporality. Vidding, Lothian claims in *Old Futures*, "remix[es] the future" by crafting alternative media temporalities and producing speculative critiques through its repurposing of speculative media's gendered and racialized temporalities (218–19). And it does as much by transforming the fan practice into a juxtapositional and affective methodology for critical theory (252).

In 2014 I joined Lothian in this burgeoning project of scholarly vidding. Like her, I cut together an archive of speculative fiction and criticism, which included footage from the first two seasons of the Canadian TV series *Orphan Black* (Space Canada/BBC America, 2013–17) and quotations from the literary fiction and criticism of 1970s feminist science fiction authors Joanna Russ, Monique Wittig, and James Tiptree Jr. I remixed these sources alongside additional quotations from feminist theorists, including twenty-first-century transfeminists Emi Koyama and Kai M. Green, all to indie musician Mirah's track

"Gold Rush," and offered what I then called "a transfeminist media archaeology of radical feminism's futures." There is a long history of gender play in fan vidding, most commonly found in slash vids in which the gender of the singer and/or the gendered lyrics of the song do not match the genders of the characters on-screen, facilitating a queer reading. More akin to a form of audiovisual drag, slash vids, such as *I'm Your Man* (Charmax 2008) and *Sherlock Something There (Beauty and the Beast)* (Lotrfan2888 2012), do not speak to trans experience. Furthermore, fan studies scholars have yet to analyze such vids as exploring specifically trans readings of popular culture, though one wonders whether Julie Levin Russo's (2017) concept of "girlslash goggles" or "femslash goggles" could be updated to account for those who might at least use similar strategies to express a trans way of seeing films, TV series, and other examples of popular culture. With *Gold Rush*, however, I was trying to do something substantially different from these slash vids, namely, analyze the queer familial coalitions of *Orphan Black* as transfeminist, that is, as offering, through the metaphors of science fiction, a way of thinking many feminisms together and imagining what it might look and feel like for cis women and trans women (as well as other trans people) to work toward freedom together, a possibility that often itself feels like some kind of science fiction.

Here I analyze *Gold Rush* (2014) and *When the Stars Are Ours* (2016), my second transfeminist vid, which remixes passages of Anna-Marie McLemore's romantic young adult trans fantasy novel *When the Moon Was Ours* (2016) and NASA space photography to the contemporary classical track "Bifu," written by Somei Satoh and performed by violinist Hilary Hahn. This second vid inverts Lothian's process. Rather than "mak[ing] visible subjugated knowledges by unmaking media's frameworks technologically" (Busse and Lothian 2011: 141), with McLemore's novel in hand as source material, the vid uses readily available digital technologies to build the framework for a trans romance film and to explore what such a film might feel like, in turn critiquing our "trans tipping point" present (Steinmetz 2014).[3] Finally, I conclude with a few thoughts about a third vid, which I recently completed. *Six Inch Heels* theorizes "trans instagram" as a space where trans celebrities, artists, and activists craft their own visions for trans community and culture.[4] These three vids are intended as examples of three different forms that remixing transfeminist futures might take by way of scholarly vidding. I see no hierarchy or progression among them. Instead, they each come from my thinking in a particular moment through the media most on my mind. They are far from exhaustive as to what remixing transfeminist futures might entail, but together they make the case for vidding's transfeminist potential. Like Lothian's feminist, queer, and decolonial vids, these transfeminist vids make their arguments affectively. The viewer is not led through arguments step-by-step as if reading an essay. Critically engaging with the vids produces affective surplus, which, if both subjective and collective in that it is a result of "our individual past experiences and the forms of common sense we have forged over time" (Keeling 2009: 566), holds the potential to make transfeminist futures perceptible. I encourage readers to watch these vids for themselves (OneOfGloriasJudys 2014, 2017, 2019). In writing about them here, I hope to demonstrate what transfeminism contributes to scholarly vidding and the methodology of remixing transfeminist futures to transgender media studies.

Gold Rush

My vid *Gold Rush*, which I first screened at the 2014 National Women's Studies Association meeting in San Juan, Puerto Rico, offers a transfeminist genealogy of 1970s feminisms' futures. Too often feminist history is written as a family drama, its cissexist and heteronormative cast of mothers and daughters bickering about who ought to be respectful to whom and who is at risk of disinheritance or abandonment. Susan Faludi (2010: 29–30) has gone so far as to call the latter "feminism's ritual matricide," writing, "With each go-round, women make gains, but the movement never seems able to establish an enduring birthright, a secure line of descent—to reproduce itself as a strong and sturdy force." Recognizing the transphobia of such narratives, whereby metaphors of reproduction exclude those who do not resemble feminists who came before, namely, transfeminists, and those who came before are themselves contained by myths of reproductive motherhood, *Gold Rush* creatively adapts Michel Foucault's theorization of genealogy for the vid screen. Unlike history, genealogy's purpose "is not to discover the roots of our identity but to commit itself to its dissipation" (Foucault 1977: 162). While feminist historians search for self-knowledge in women's history to guarantee their own survival in the future (Rich 1972), the transfeminist genealogy of *Gold Rush* advocates for the dissociation of feminist selves through the demarcation of their dispersion across time. My vid claims that the 1970s does not belong to trans-exclusionary radical feminists (TERFs), identifying in this diffuse past radical and lesbian feminists whose ideas transfeminists may wish to continue to think with today. Without repossessing or redeeming the period (or mapping an alternative familial tree, in which transfeminism "descends" from 1970s feminisms), the vid facilitates introductions between varied pasts and presents and reveals how transfeminism, contrary to TERFs' claims otherwise, extends 1970s feminisms' provocative critiques of family, rape, normative heterosexuality, and the institutions and ideologies that sustain them.

The vid draws on the tradition of "shipping" to replace feminist historiographic models of mother-daughter inheritance with cross-generational relationships that recast "sisterhood." It remixes its multigenerational citations with footage of the "sestras" of the science fiction series *Orphan Black*, such that the series becomes a staging for such transfeminist theorizing, the analytical connections between the written texts taking on the series's speculative and affective power. Set and shot in present-day Toronto and starring Canadian actress Tatiana Maslany, *Orphan Black* tells the story of a group of clones who, despite their differences (nationality, class, religion, sexuality, politics), forge alliances to resist the violences they face—being denied life-saving medical treatment, facing unlawful arrest and imprisonment, as well as sexual harassment, assault, and police brutality—as a result of being perceived as less than human. The vid begins by showing clones Sarah, Allison, and Cosima negotiating medical discourses and legal processes (not unlike those that trans people are forced to face to move about the world more safely) in isolation. After an Emi Koyama (2003: 245) quotation about transfeminism standing up for transgender and cisgender women alike, the vid offers an extensive montage of the clones and their allies working together to save each other's lives. As the verse comes to a close—"But there's nothing ever saving us from that we're gonna die / No, there's nothing ever saving us from that we're gonna die"—footage from the season 2 finale unfolds in contrast to the resigning lyrics, showing Cosima and Kira, Sarah's daughter, constructing a map that enables Sarah to escape her approaching nonconsensual oophorectomy. In the final minute of the vid, Mirah's emotive string arrangement, coupled with *Orphan Black*'s imagery of the indomitable clones celebrating their successful resistance, guides the movement between a series of quotations. In juxtaposing the quotations of 1970s feminists about the importance of coalition as well as the ridiculousness of the gender binary, and quotations by twenty-first-century transfeminists about the need for transgender and cisgender women and femmes of all genders to support one another, the vid argues that the form of sisterhood needed is one based on the eradication of all gender-based violence. The utopianism of the 1970s science fictions quoted, in conjunction with the music, the song's lyrics, and the *Orphan Black* footage, generates an affective surplus, making perceptible, if but fleetingly, a future in which there will be no dispute as to who our "sisters" are.

   Gold Rush also offers a critique of *Orphan Black* that reveals the recurring failures of "sisterhood," even when rethought. The speculatively conditional refrain, "But if you hold me like I'm your girl, I'll still hold you like I'm your girl," keeps the tenuousness of the possibility of cross-generational sisterhood salient and draws attention to the less than ideal ways in which Tony, the series's singular trans clone, and Helena, arguably the most vulnerable and racialized clone, are treated by their sestras. Across the course of the series, Helena is regularly sacrificed for the good of the whole. The problematic nature of this recurring plot is made apparent just before the final hopeful montage in which a shot of Helena being taken away by Special Forces is followed by the Audre Lorde (1984: 41) quotation, "I am not only a casualty, I am also a warrior." For those familiar with the series, this acknowledgment of how often sisterhood falls short tinges the vid's otherwise joyful end. Meanwhile, in its two shots of Tony, the vid poses a question around community, visibility, and safety. While the term *sestra* comes to name not only the clones but also their allies and thus demonstrates a greater gendered flexibility than 1970s feminisms' "sisterhood," Tony puzzlingly never becomes a true sestra.[5] Instead of being invited to join their resistance, he is sent away with the means to stay in touch without coming under the surveillance of their adversaries. By cutting Tony's shots to the lyrics "I just thought I could keep you from the loss of having to say goodbye," the vid does not offer a conclusive argument on this matter. Instead, it asks viewers familiar with the series to ruminate on this decision (on both the part of the sestras and the series), whereby Tony's invisibility guarantees him greater safety while also denying him access to sestrahood's emotional support. Both utopian and critical, the vid keeps in tension the impossible possibility of transfeminist futures. The *when* of trans freedom, *Gold Rush* insists, is not simply a matter of earning equality from legal and governmental institutions. As a transfeminist issue, it is also a family matter.

When the Stars Are Ours

My *When the Stars Are Ours* vid first screened at the feminist science fiction convention WisCon. In 2016, I served on the jury of the James Tiptree Jr. Literary Award, an annual prize given at WisCon to a work of fantasy or science fiction that "expands or explores our understanding of gender."[6] The 2016 prize went to Anna-Marie McLemore's young adult fantasy novel *When the Moon Was Ours*, and the vid played for an audience of one thousand people before McLemore accepted their prize. *When the Moon Was Ours* tells the coming-of-age stories of Samir, a transgender Pakistani American teenage boy growing up in rural California, and Miel, his Latina cisgender childhood friend turned girlfriend. The novel is based on the author's and their husband's adolescent experiences, but these experiences are transfigured through fantasy. Joanna Russ (1973: 55) describes fantasy not as a genre opposed to reality but as one that carries the frame of reality or actuality with it—"fantasy (what could not have happened) exists inside the frame." The novel's readers encounter impossible characters, objects, and events—a girl who grows roses from her wrist, their changing colors exposing her most intimate desires; pumpkins that turn to glass, shattering and rising to the stars when long-silenced truths are finally spoken; a river that can either change one's body, as one had always wished, or take it away, as one had also sometimes wished. The tension of the novel's fantasy/reality frame thus marks these two characters' racialized queerness to distrusting outsiders, as well as constructs the queer magical setting of their sexuality and romance. In turn, queer and trans youth, frequently rendered impossible by those who wish them so, are gifted the language and imagery of possibility.

As a media studies scholar, reading the novel I immediately imagined what it might look and sound like to adapt such a work of literary trans romance to film. Early passages introducing Samir and Miel and the nature of their relationship—"They'd touched each other every day since they were small. She'd put her palm to his forehead when she thought he had a fever. He'd set tiny gold star stickers on her skin on summer days, and at night had peeled them off, leaving pale constellations on her sun-darkened body (McLemore 2016: 6)—crafted the most vivid of images in my mind. However, the vid such images inspired, composed of typed excerpts from the novel superimposed on NASA space photography and edited to a romantic minimalist violin and piano classical track, is by no means a proper adaptation. Yet, it is through this very disjuncture—that subjunctive relation between what currently exists (this novel/contemporary cinema) and what might someday (its cinematic adaptation and/or a trans romance cinema broadly speaking)—that the remix video serves as a work of criticism. While popular discourse has repeatedly announced the present to be a period of unprecedented trans representation in film and TV, scholars have pointed out the disparity in such representations, whereby trans men and non-binary people remain underrepresented and the stories of wealthy white trans characters are centered over those of poor trans people of color.[7] Despite this boom in representation, many of the newer trans films and TV series continue the long-standing traditions of fetishizing trans bodies and stereotyping trans stories such that coming out and medical transition continue to define trans experience. In such a context, the proper adaptation of *When the Moon Was Ours* to film would be a unique and important text indeed. Meanwhile, whereas book vids typically pull from a wide range of media to illustrate their literary text, the sort of footage I would need to do the same does not yet exist. If I were to follow the genre's lead, I, like Hollywood, may have to "cast" cisgender actors and/or actors of different ethnicities than Samir's and Miel's to find footage that fit the text thematically and stylistically. In the place of such footage, I used still photographs of outer space, inviting a future film in which such compromises would not need to be made.

By pairing excerpts of the novel with space photography, cut and cross-faded to the slow rhythm of the song's violin and piano, the vid avoids representational missteps of trans cinema of the past. The photographs not only underscore the novel's use of genre and the centrality of star and moon imagery to Samir and Miel's romance, but they also hold off any fetishization or feminization of Samir's body through more realist cinematography. The vid's typed text provides a shot/reverse shot–like access to each character's desires and fears, as they navigate sex and romance while coming into their gender and sexual identities. Quotations taken from a section of his narration capture Samir's questioning why Miel wants him or in what capacity in relation to his gender are followed by quotations of Miel wondering whether she should say his name while they make love and whether this will make him feel wanted as himself. However, instead of suturing the spectator into a set of gazes between two figures as they negotiate this and other stages of their relationship, as a film might, the vid sensually zooms in and out of still photographs of myriad celestial bodies. The curves of the moon's surface and the bright twinkle of stars become charged with eroticism in the place of the characters' bodies. The "transgender look," so often broken by the most canonical of trans films (Halberstam 2005: 76–96), remains active, and the cissexist gaze, which demands perceptibility of assigned sex (Keegan 2018: 25), is foreclosed. While it does not offer the trans romance film some might want, the vid generates affects that exceed its representation, making perceptible the future when such a cinema could exist. In this future, the film industry would have little recourse to finding and casting the appropriate trans actors of color, and film language itself would have transformed cinema into a sensate medium for exploring queer and trans romance and sexuality in all their vibrancy.

Conclusion

Six Inch Heels, the first minute and a half of which is described at the start of this article, premiered at WisCon in May 2019. In the vid I explore "trans instagram" as a space where trans celebrities, artists, and activists craft their own visions for trans community and culture. In doing as much, the vid joins the scholarship of trans media studies scholars such as Marty Fink and Quinn Miller (2014), who have studied early Tumblr as an important outlet for trans, genderqueer, and gender-nonconforming digital self-representation; Laura Horak (2014) and Rachel Reinke (2017), who have examined YouTube as a site for trans youth to author and affirm themselves and a space where disabled trans youth of color resist hegemonic understandings of transnormativity (Reinke 2017); micha cárdenas (2017), whose project #stronger uses social media's algorithms to distribute images of trans health and strength to shift trans people's affective state; and Sarah J. Jackson, Moya Bailey, and Brooke Foucault Welles (2018), who have looked to Twitter's #GirlsLikeUs as a networked counterpublic for the advocacy and community building of transgender women. As each of these scholars note, there is much to be cautionary about when it comes to social media, and this is especially the case for trans users of color. Many platforms extend the necropolitical violence of the state by enabling the "sharing" of violent videos and images of Black and trans people's murders, causing Black and trans users additional harm (cárdenas 2017: 169). They also often circulate normative images of trans citizenship more widely than those that do not meet such norms (Reinke 2017: 58). At the same time, these platforms enable modes of connection between trans users and allies otherwise impossible, with #WontBeErased—trans activists' response to the Trump administration's plan to redefine sex under Title IX to exclusively and immutably male or female, as assigned at birth—being a recent viral example.

In *Six Inch Heels*, I study how trans women and nonbinary celebrities, artists, and activists use the social media platform most commonly affiliated with the image to craft their own self-representations and, through their circulation among other trans Instagram users and fan-allies, create a world where trans women and nonbinary folks are seen for their intelligence, wit, beauty, grace, tenacity, and fierce commitment to their own and others' freedom. To craft this vid, I downloaded over five hundred videos made and uploaded by trans and nonbinary celebrities to Instagram since 2013, when the platform enabled the posting of video (as opposed to exclusively photo) content. In these videos, Laverne Cox, Trace Lysette, Janet Mock, Jennifer Boylan, Jamie Clayton, Zackary Drucker, Alexandra Billings, Our Lady J, Miss Peppermint, Mila Jam, Rain Valdez, Hari Nef, Candis Cayne, Mj Rodriguez, Indya Moore, and others document their lives and experiences and share them with fans.[8] Videos of their time spent on sets and red carpets, at marches, on campuses, traveling the globe, and in their own homes provide trans impressions of society at present.[9] These individuals' comments on and "hearting" of each other's photos and videos are indicative of trans instagram's counterpublic reflexive circulation of discourse, and the shared styles and genres of their videos are a sign of this world's poetic-expressivity.[10] Together they record the world from trans perspectives and also leave trans traces, spaces commonly occupied by cissexist ideology (such as public restrooms; sites of national citizenry, like the Statue of Liberty; and gyms), becoming, through these trans lenses, less stably cis. Often documentary subject, cinematographer, director, and/or editor all at the same time, the trans women and enbies before and behind the camera author their own expansive experiences. In cutting together clips of Rain Valdez leading the chanting of "Trans rights are human rights" at an Orange County Women's March; Alexandra Billings singing with her coworkers at lunch on the *Transparent* set; Trace Lysette shooting hoops; Mila Jam dancing; and Candis Cayne zip lining through a forest as well as many clips of these women and other trans and nonbinary people joyfully spending time in each other's company at home, on set, and out in public, I present the complexity of the portrait of trans life these folks are creating together and articulate its significance for viewers who have not been "following," while also creating a text that, like most vids, celebrates the joy and beauty fans have found in this media for some time.

I cut this footage to the *Lemonade* movie version of Beyoncé's "6 Inch [Heels]," as opposed to the album version, so that I might use the former's sinister monologue sections (themselves borrowed from the poetry of Kenyan-born Somali British poet Warsan Shire) in contrast with the song's more triumphant melody and juxtapose these individuals' self-representations with the dire news stories they also share and raise awareness around. Drawing connections between these two sections of the trans instagram archive is part of the affective labor the vid demands of viewers. As Lori Morimoto writes, "While song lyrics contribute to meaning in vids, the effectiveness of a vid depends on a kind of symbiosis between images and lyrics (or music), in which one augments (rather than directs) the other" (Creekmur et al. 2017: 165). There are times when my use of lyrics very nearly tethers meaning, exemplifying what Roland Barthes (1977: 39–41) calls "anchorage." When Beyoncé declares, "We blame you . . . for the ghosts," and we see Lysette's sharing of the "Trans People Deserve to Live" World Series photograph, there is little ambiguity as to who these ghosts are and who is to blame. This is only affirmed when the next shot, that of the demonstrators outside the Stonewall Inn, includes audio, the song's beat underscoring the activist's own declaration, "An attack on one LGBT person is an attack on the whole LGBT community." More often, however, the lyrics do not anchor the images. The first time we hear the chorus—"Goddamn, she murdered everybody and I was her witness"—we see Lysette, decked out in protective eye wear and a "Trans Girls Are Lit" T-shirt, throw a plate with "transphobia" written on it at a wall; as it shatters, she turns back to the camera, laughing. The next time we hear these same lyrics, Lysette is making a shot from the three-point line on an outdoor basketball court. As examples of "relay," these lyrics and images "stand in a complementary relationship . . . and the unity of the message is realized at a higher level, that of the story, the anecdote, the diegesis" (41). But I would argue that in the vid's syntagmatic use of lyrics and images, as was the case in *Gold Rush* and *When the Stars Are Ours*, relay is exceeded by affect. While I had my reasons for making such lyric/image pairings, they are surely generative of a multiplicity of meanings as well as feelings or emotions in accordance with viewers' labor across the vid as a whole. In choosing a Beyoncé song, I also brought another fannish practice into the scholarly realm—that of gifting, of crafting a fan text as a gift to another fan.[11] Knowing Laverne Cox, Janet Mock, and Mila Jam to be Beyoncé fans, I made this vid as a gift to them in gratitude for all they have given me and others like me. And in its production of affective surplus, the vid hopefully enables the perception of a future, which, if unrecognizable in its freedom, is more like the world these trans women and nonbinary celebrities create together, for and with the rest of us, than the transphobic, transmisogynistic, cissexist world we all currently resist.

These three vids expand the archive for scholarly vidding and the approaches scholarly vidders might take in analyzing media. They also model how the affective and juxtapositional methodology of scholarly vidding could be taken up by those working in transgender media studies. As video editing software grows increasingly more available, not only on our computers but also on tablets and phones, as well as more user friendly, this methodology becomes more viable an option for a greater range of scholars. I offer my three transfeminist vids here as an invitation and set of models for transgender media studies scholars. While each of my transfeminist vids differs greatly in form, content, and scholarly intervention, together they present "remixing transfeminist futures" as an approach to theorizing trans temporalities. Their affective cutting of knowledge interrupts models of history and modes of representation in which subjects are captured and pinned in place for study like lepidopterists' butterflies. In a media climate of hypervisibility and a world where this increased visibility means increased surveillance and violence, these transfeminist vids' affective surplus, like that of the documentaries Keeling analyzes, directs viewers away from the representational and narratological *where* of trans and toward the poetic and fugitive *when*. Doing as much could in and of itself be considered a form of "looking after," in that, like cárdenas' #stronger project, it has the potential to not only intellectually but also affectively impact trans people in a favorable fashion, being, as it is for some, generative of feelings of love, care, and support. But these vids and their proffered methodology also aspire to move viewers—scholarly and nonscholarly, trans, nonbinary, and cis—to ask themselves how they might look after both the trans people in their lives and those around them in the world in the present.

Rox Samer is assistant professor of screen studies in Clark University's Department of Visual and Performing Arts. In Fall 2017, Rox edited *Spectator* 37.2, the first journal issue devoted to the study of transgender media. Rox is currently working on a book manuscript, "Lesbian Potentiality and Feminist Media in the 1970s," as well as a documentary film, *Tip/Alli*, on the work, life, and influence of feminist science fiction author James Tiptree Jr. (aka Alice B. Sheldon, 1915–87).

Acknowledgments

I would like to thank Raffi Sarkissian and Quinn Miller for their helpful suggestions at various points in the writing process. Thank you also to the two anonymous *TSQ* peer reviewers who provided thoughtful feedback on my first draft and micha cárdenas and Jian Neo Chen for their generous editorial work. Parts of this article were presented in different formats at WisCon, the Society of Cinema and Media Studies, the National Women's Studies Association, the University of Southern California, Grand Valley State University, and Clark University. Thanks to the copanelists, audience members, mentors, colleagues, and students whose conversations, questions, and suggestions have inspired my ongoing thinking on this subject. All mistakes are my own.

Notes

1. See, for example, the "Trans/Feminisms" special issue of *TSQ* (Bettcher and Stryker 2016).
2. For a few more scholarly sources on vidding, in addition to the sources cited across this article, see Coppa and Russo 2012; Lothian 2015; Coppa 2011; Coppa and Tushnet 2011; and Jenkins 1992.
3. *Trans tipping point* has since come to serve as shorthand for our contemporary moment of trans hypervisibility in US popular culture.
4. Much like Fink and Miller (2014: 612), who use "'Tumblr,' with a capital 'T,' to refer to the company and the lowercase 'tumblr' to mark resistant networks on the site, as well as specific users' tumblrs (i.e., their tumblr pages)," I vary my use of the capital and lowercase "I" in "trans instagram" to distinguish between the company and the counterpublic I'm demarcating.
5. I agree with Cáel M. Keegan (2015a) that, theoretically, "Tony belongs in the clone club." In fact, Keegan's argument about the series's "horizontal inheritance of gender assignments and identities" fits with how I have repurposed the series in my vid. However, I do not want to dismiss those fans who were waiting for another three seasons for the character's return. Considering the weight the series gives to queer, chosen families, Tony's quick exit and absence from the rest of the series are significant and not without their own theoretical questions.
6. James Tiptree Jr. Literary Award, tiptree.org (accessed May 21, 2018).
7. For a discussion of some of the ramifications of this underrepresentation of trans men, see Keegan 2015b.
8. Each of these celebrities' Instagram accounts is public, and each has either tens or hundreds of thousands, if not millions, of followers. Still, recognizing the vulnerability of trans people, especially trans women of color, I have chosen not to include their Instagram handles here. A few do appear in the vid itself. In February, I reached out to each of these celebrities over Instagram, sharing with them my vision for the project as well as a password-protected short rough cut of the vid. As of the writing of this essay, all but a few of the most famous and followed celebrities (i.e., those with hundreds of thousands or millions of Instagram followers) have responded with notes of encouragement and support. So far no one has declined inclusion. In the process of reaching out to these individuals, I have been privileged to receive feedback and suggestions in response to my rough cut, which I incorporated into my final cut, making the project a collaboration of sorts.
9. Here my analysis takes inspiration from Amy Villarejo's (2003: 97–98, 106–21) writing on lesbian impressions in lesbian documentary cinema.
10. Here my thinking is in part shaped by Michael Warner's (2005) writing on queer counterpublics as poetic world building.
11. See, for example, Turk 2014.

References

Bailey, Moya. 2015. "#transform(ing)DH Writing and Research: An Autoethnography of Digital Humanities and Feminist Ethics." *Digital Humanities Quarterly* 9, no. 2. digitalhumanities .org/dhq/vol/9/2/000209/000209.html.

Barthes, Roland. 1977. *Image, Music, Text.* Translated by Stephen Heath. New York: Hill and Wang.

Bettcher, Talia M., and Susan Stryker. 2016. "Trans/Feminisms." Special issue, *TSQ* 3, nos. 1–2.

Busse, Kristina, and Alexis Lothian. 2011. "Scholarly Critiques and Critiques of Scholarship: The Uses of Remix Video." *Camera Obscura*, no. 77: 139–46.

cárdenas, micha. 2015. "Shifting Futures: Digital Trans of Color Praxis." *Ada: A Journal of Gender, New Media, and Technology*, no. 6. doi.org/10.7264/N3WH2N8D.

cárdenas, micha. 2017. "Dark Shimmers: The Rhythm of Necropolitical Affect in Digital Media." In Tourmaline, Stanley, and Burton 2017: 161–81.

Charmax. 2008. *I'm Your Man*. YouTube video, 3:13. www.youtube.com/watch?v=0cAb1OAb93w.

Coppa, Francesca. 2008. "Women, *Star Trek*, and the Early Development of Fannish Vidding." *Transformative Works and Cultures* 1. doi.org/10.3983/twc.2008.044.

Coppa, Francesca. 2011. "An Editing Room of One's Own: Vidding as Women's Work." *Camera Obscura*, no. 77: 123–30.

Coppa, Francesca, and Julie Levin Russo, eds. 2012. "Fan/Remix Video." Special issue, *Transformative Works and Cultures* 9. journal.transformativeworks.org/index.php/twc/issue/view/10.

Coppa Francesca, and Rebecca Tushnet. 2011. "How to Suppress Women's Remix." *Camera Obscura*, no. 77: 131–38.

Creekmur, Corey, Melanie Kohnen, Jonathan McIntosh, Lori Morimoto, Katherine Morrissey, Suzanne Scott, Lousia Stein. 2017. "Roundtable: Remix and Videographic Criticism." *Cinema Journal* 56, no. 4: 159–83.

Faludi, Susan. 2010. "American Electra: Feminism's Ritual Matricide." *Harper's Magazine*, October, 29–42.

Fink, Marty, and Quinn Miller. 2014. "Trans Media Moments: Tumblr, 2011–2013." *Television and New Media* 15, no. 7: 611–26.

Foucault, Michel. 1977. "Nietzsche, Genealogy, History." In *Language, Counter-Memory, Practice: Selected Essays and Interviews*, edited by D. H. Bouchard, 141–64. Ithaca, NY: Cornell University Press.

Halberstam, J. Jack. 2005. *In a Queer Time and Place: Transgender Bodies, Subcultural Lives*. New York: New York University Press.

Horak, Laura. 2014. "Trans on YouTube: Intimacy, Visibility, Temporality." *TSQ* 1, no. 4: 572–85.

Jackson, Sarah J., Moya Bailey, and Brooke Foucault Welles. 2018. "#GirlsLikeUs: Trans Advocacy and Community Building Online." *New Media and Society* 20, no. 5: 1868–88.

Jenkins, Henry. 1992. "'Layers of Meaning': Fan Music Video and the Poetics of Poaching." In *Textual Poachers: Television Fans and Participatory Culture*, 223–49. New York: Routledge.

Keegan, Cáel M. 2015a. "Horizontal Inheritance: Orphan Black's Transgender Genealogy." *In media res*, April 15. mediacommons.org/imr/2015/04/05/horizontal-inheritance-orphan-blacks-transgender-genealogy.

Keegan, Cáel M. 2015b. "Junk Politics: The Visual Economy of Trans Male Genitalia." In *Below the Belt: Genital Talk by Men of Trans Experience*, edited by Trystan T. Cotton, 7–18. Oakland, CA: Transgress.

Keegan, Cáel M. 2018. *Lana and Lilly Wachowski: Sensing Transgender*. Urbana: University of Illinois Press.

Keeling, Kara. 2007. *The Witch's Flight: The Cinematic, the Black Femme, and the Image of Common Sense*. Durham, NC: Duke University Press.

Keeling, Kara. 2009. "Looking for M—: Queer Temporality, Black Political Possibility, and Poetry from the Future." *GLQ* 15, no. 4: 565–82.

Koyama, Emi. 2003. "The Transfeminist Manifesto." In *Catching a Wave: Reclaiming Feminism for the Twenty-First Century*, edited by Rory Dicker and Alison Piepmeier, 244–59. Lebanon, NH: Northeastern University Press.

Lorde, Audre. 1984. *Sister Outsider: Essays and Speeches by Audre Lorde*. Freedom, CA: The Crossing.

Lotrfan2888. 2012. *Sherlock Something There (Beauty and the Beast)*. YouTube video, 2:08. www .youtube.com/watch?v=4j3y7UFT8Cg.

Lothian, Alexis. 2015. "A Different Kind of Love Song: Vidding Fandom's Undercommons." *Cinema Journal* 54, no. 3: 138–45.

Lothian, Alexis. 2018. *Old Futures: Speculative Fiction and Queer Possibility*. New York: New York University Press.

McLemore, Anna-Marie. 2016. *When the Moon Was Ours*. New York: St. Martin's.

OneOfGloriasJudys. 2014. *Gold Rush*. November 16. Video, 5:31. vimeo.com/112183235.

OneOfGloriasJudys. 2017. *When the Stars Are Ours*. May 28. Video, 5:01. vimeo.com/216036737.

OneOfGloriasJudys. 2019. *Six Inch Heels*. May 24. Video, 5:39. vimeo.com/335303044.

Reinke, Rachel. 2017. "Embodying Resistance Online: Trans Youth Reconfigure Discursive Space(s) of Visibility on YouTube." *Spectator* 37, no. 2: 58–64.

Rich, Adrienne. 1972. "When We Dead Awaken: Writing as Re-vision." *College English* 34, no. 1: 18–30.

Russ, Joanna. 1973. "Speculations: The Subjunctivity of Science Fiction." *Extrapolation* 15, no. 1: 51–59.

Russo, Julie Levin. 2017. "Femslash Goggles: Fan Vids with Commentary by Creators." *Transformative Works and Cultures* 24. doi.org/10.3983/twc.2017.1026.

Steinmetz, Katy. 2014. "The Transgender Tipping Point: America's Next Civil Rights Frontier." *Time*, May 29. time.com/135480/transgender-tipping-point/.

Tourmaline, Eric A. Stanley, and Johanna Burton, eds. 2017. *Trap Door: Trans Cultural Production and the Politics of Visibility*. Cambridge, MA: MIT Press.

Turk, Tisha. 2014. "Fan Work: Labor, Worth, and Participation in Fandom's Gift Economy." *Transformative Works and Cultures* 15. doi.org/10.3983/twc.2014.0518.

Villarejo, Amy. 2003. *Lesbian Rule: Cultural Criticism and the Value of Desire*. Durham, NC: Duke University Press.

Warner, Michael. 2005. *Publics and Counterpublics*. New York: Zone.

Cart No.1, Monoecious Fruits, the Harvest of 1519

VICK QUEZADA

Figure 1. *Monoecious Fruits*, 2018. Mixed media, mixed dimensions. A reimagined tool of pleasure made of rope and maize.

TSQ: Transgender Studies Quarterly ★ Volume 6, Number 4 ★ November 2019
DOI 10.1215/23289252-7771709   © 2019 Duke University Press

Abstract The following works are an exploration of the histories of colonization that the Mestizo experience in North America as well as how the settler colonial phenomenon continues to exist in the contemporary United States. The projects scrutinize the impact of racism, transphobia, classism, capitalism, and heteropatriarchy, as they affect the material realities of people whose lives are determined by their relationship to Western ideology and the gender construct. The use of sculpture, photography, and craft within the bodies of work help conceptualize the tension of Indigenous and Western narratives. Vick Quezada seeks to reconcile and intervene in Western "commonsense" notions by merging material culture by way of abstraction. Quezada is most compelled by the places where evidence of resistance and survival is made manifest. Through their work they desire to generate alternative empathies that open paths for a new consciousness.
Keywords Indigenous, Latinx, Mestizaje, gender contruct, queer, art, Mexico, Nahuan

M y projects explore the material histories and consciousness of Indigenous-Latinx hybridity within Western culture. My approach is multidisciplinary based in botany, historical archives, ancestral knowledge, and lived experience.

I identify as nonbinary transgender Indigenous-Latinx. My practice calls into question structures that fragment Indigenous identity and queer bodies. I use a variety of media, integrating found objects, ceramics, sculpture, and video performance. My sculptural "artifacts" also incorporate natural elements, such as soil and plants, making reference to Nahuan Indigenous beliefs that assert the earth, spirit, and cosmology are interconnected (Sigal 2012).

Maize, as material and theme, is present in almost all works. Maize is native to Mexico and is a monoecious plant that has both masculine and feminine reproductive organs. Ironically, historical Aztec ethnographies document that the ancient female and male maize deity Chicomecōātl/Centeōtl displayed gender duality and ambiguity, which were mirrored in pre-Columbian Mesoamerican societal beliefs on gender (Milbrath 2015).

The essence of my projects specifically honors Indigenous cultural practice. In queering the archaeological, I desire to offer an understanding of gender and sexuality outside of the dominant heteropatriarchal narratives.

Vick Quezada was raised in El Paso, Texas, along the US-Mexico border. In 2005, Quezada received a BA from the University of Texas at El Paso and graduated with an MFA from the University of Massachusetts Amherst in 2018. Quezada has exhibited at the Nolen-Smith College and the Mead Art Museum, is currently a fellow at the Latinx Project at New York University, and curated *Five Takes on African Art* with Fred Wilson.

Reference
Milbrath, Susan. 2015. "Gender and Roles of Lunar Deities in Postclassic Central Mexico and Their Correlations with the Maya Area." *Estudios de cultura Maya*, 93rd ser., 39, no. 45 (2015): 57. doi.org/10.19130/iifl.ecm.2016.47.738.
Sigal, Peter Herman. 2012. *The Flower and the Scorpion: Sexuality and Ritual in Early Nahua Culture*. Durham, NC: Duke University Press.

Figure 2. *Harvest of 1519*, 2018. Digital print, 11 × 14 in. Classically inspired portraiture combined with the modern Mestizaje subject.

Deviant Care for Deviant Futures

QTBIPoC Radical Relationalism as Mutual Aid against Carceral Care

REN-YO HWANG

Abstract This article introduces the concept of carceral care as those public-facing "do-better" penal practices, policies, and material actions used to ward off future investigation of underlying institutional violences of carceral spaces. As a model for denaturalizing carceral care, time, space, and the perpetuity of reform, it explores theories of deviant care, mutual aid, and QTBIPoC radical relationalism. It investigates how inhabiting deviance is a necessary care practice as modeled every day by queer bonds of survival, particularly from within the confines of carceral spaces. Based on relationships built over the last four years with trans women of color organizing inside a "male-designated" state prison in Corcoran, California, this article connects questions of deviant care as the refusal of the diagnosable and individuated self through queer black/indigenous feminist of color resistance and radical thought.

Keywords deviance, deviant care, mutual aid, QTBIPoC radical relationalism, carceral care

The very process of being caught and publicly labeled as "deviant" thus sets in motion a relentless self-fulfilling prophecy. . . . The experience of being singled out and publicly branded in this way usually culminates into a deviant world view . . . a kind of role imprisonment which locks the deviant into a symbolic jail.

—Andrew T. Scull, *Decarceration: Community Treatment and the Deviant—A Radical View*

I don't want to be fixed, if being fixed means being bleached of memory, untaught by what I have learned through this miracle of surviving. My survivorhood is not an individual problem. I want the communion of all of us who have survived, and the knowledge. I do not want to be fixed. I want to change the world. I want to be alive, awake, grieving, and full of joy. I am.

—Leah Lakshmi Piepzna-Samarasinha, *Care Work: Dreaming Disability Justice*

TSQ: Transgender Studies Quarterly * Volume 6, Number 4 * November 2019 **559**
DOI 10.1215/23289252-7771723   © 2019 Duke University Press

Traveling north on Interstate 5 in March of 2017, I departed Koreatown, Los Angeles's smoggy low-lying landscape of strip malls punctuated only by high-rise luxury condominiums. From urban sprawl to stretches of yellow-brown agricultural fields and the strong stench of manure, this three-hour drive brought me to the doorsteps of the prison town Corcoran, California (Tachi-Yokut tribal territory), of Kings County. Historically known for its agricultural industrialization of cotton, wheat, alfalfa, and grains, Corcoran is now anchored by two public prisons: California State Prison, Corcoran (CSP-C, established in 1988) and California Substance Abuse Treatment Facility and Prison, Corcoran (CSATF or SATF, established in 1997).[1] In 2017, 43 percent of the town's twenty-two thousand residents were caged in these two facilities.[2] Together, CSP-C and CSATF employ roughly a third of Corcoran's nonincarcerated residents and have an annual operating budget upward of $230 million, making the prison industry the leading employer in the county (CDCR 2018). The colonial romance with fertile and expansive "unworked" land and fungibility of the captive body has provided, to borrow from Saidiya Hartman, the very "stage of sufferance" through the ages.[3] Tracing a path from chattel slavery on plantation fields to convict lease labor of corporate and private plantations, slavery-to-prison history is evidenced by slave quarters turned prison farms.[4] Corcoran stands as an exemplary model of the "prison fix," what Gilmore (2006: 69) troubles as not simply an economic rationale of rural agricultural towns turned prison towns, but also the promise of domestic and militarized manifest destiny, a welfare-to-warfare state of surplus land as the rationale for surplus populations, and vice versa.[5] One might argue that the historical trajectory of penal reform exists in the progression from sovereign power's carceral exile (chattel slavery to capital punishment), to carceral cure (deviant bodies as the symbolic rationalization for expanding institutional punishment, a logical outcome of moral civil society), to carceral care (the liberal humanistic concern for the improved treatment of those incarcerated). However, such a linear trajectory misses the long-standing gendered and racialized history in which black femme subjectivity has and continues to defy the mutability of the carceral state.[6] Sarah Haley (2016: 72) chronicles this disruption of such a linear carceral reform narrative, stating, "The Jim Crow carceral state enforced one of the most consistently stable presumptions of American history, mobilized continuously for the justification of draconian racial institutions—that black women's inherent deviance reproduces (and thereby produces) black cultural pathology, necessitating legal and extralegal control over their bodies and behavior."

Such a black and gendered cultural pathology lingers today in the form of what is termed here as carceral care. I offer this concept to name the deathly liberal impulse of asking the prisons to do better, a compulsion by both advocates and state actors to demand piecemeal reforms from institutions like the California Department of Corrections and Rehabilitation (CDCR). Progressive discourses concerning carceral reform as carceral care often gain traction because of some combination of investigative reporting, lawsuits, state audits, or prison reform policy initiatives—and such efforts often fail to credit the very extensive and direct action and labor of protest, political unrest, and organizing by those most impacted on the inside.[7] *Carceral care* thus denotes the messy and entangled conglomerate of discretionary practices, performative measures, and material actions used to forestall the possibility of future interference and or interrogation of the underlying institutional violences of carceral spaces. Carceral violence via carceral spaces can range from death-wielding enforcement to death-making negligence by institutions and their actors—parole boards, wardens, correctional officers, prison officials, medical staff, and administration. Similarly, carceral care is not simply the deterrence, reduction, or interruption of carceral violence; rather, it is a mode of tracing how the penal administration of care multiplies the very scales, technologies, and cultural structures of violence itself.[8] Disrupting those very impulses to be trapped by the rigged gamble that is carceral care requires us, those who have any distrust in the possibility of life-giving care in such death-making spaces, to inhabit a deviant set of relations not only to the state but also to one another.[9] How might we resist and build our collective capacity to continuously trouble our notions of care? How might we resist both inferred and overt modes of racialized and gendered pathologies of individuated care that require the weaponization of personhood?[10] How might we account for the dualisms embedded within care—success or failure, curable or incurable, rehabilitated or recidivistic? Care, even in its etymological tie to *cure*, is not necessarily carceral.[11] However, the attendant logics of care mimic a curative model of carcerality by requiring individuated pathologies as central to administrative measures of correction.

The rural prison stage of CSATF is where a dear friend and action research collaborator, Aliya Sanders, was transferred in 2016.[12] Aliya and I met in 2014, through the metal-netted and double-paned glass windows of the gridlike visitation corridors of the Los Angeles County Men's Central Jail (MCJ), one of the most populated jails in the world.[13] Our friendship, collaborative organizing, and action research were formed through a mutual friend named Fresh, an artist and community member of Dignity Power Now-Los Angeles (DPN).[14] Both were caged in MCJ's segregated housing unit of K6G (formerly K-11, established in 1985), the first and only official gay and transgender women's designated jail unit in the United States.[15] Unable to post the exorbitant cost of bail, and having exhausted community-gathered funds to retain less than adequate private legal counsel, Aliya and Fresh each awaited trial for over two years in pretrial detention.[16]

To survive in MCJ, Aliya and Fresh shared critical and live-saving queer family bonds. An all-too-common practice across spaces of detention, mechanisms of intensified isolation and restrictive housing are used to cordon off further contact when bonds of intimacy and survival are forged among those incarcerated. Often queer kinship, a means of survival for those inside, is institutionally classified and penalized as "gang affiliation" or "security threat group (STG)." Punitive measures such as solitary confinement, administrative/disciplinary segregation, and protective custody are used to isolate individuals to remote locations in the form of small windowless single cells, ensuring absolute noncontact for twenty-two to twenty-four hours a day (Cochran et al. 2018; Frost, Monteiro, and CSR Incorporated 2016). Further, as courts defer authority to state institutions to determine the conditions for safekeeping of those they are charged to confine, legal culpability concerning "excessive force" on behalf of correctional officers is largely unattainable.[17] The state once again, as conceived of under Giorgio Agamben's (1998) sovereign exception, establishes the juridical order and administration of violence in the name of public safety.[18] Prior to being transferred to the "male-designated" prison of CSATF to complete her sentence, as a black transgender woman, Aliya would not be able to strategize a plan of community safety ahead of time since relocation with queer kin like Fresh was never a guarantee.[19] As carceral spaces psychically and materially breed forgetting, brick by brick, steel door by steel door, painted pathways demarcating who is in or "out of bounds," how might we cultivate collective feelings of belonging when those inside are systemically and structurally being told they do not belong anywhere?

As many have previously argued, the notion of a kinder, gentler, gender-responsive and reformed prison, particularly as the end goal, simply reproduces, exacerbates, and diversifies the tactics and technologies of punitive control over bodies and practices deemed criminal.[20] This article will attend to the liberal impulse, seduction, and conditioning of wanting to make better, to heal or fix, particularly through the confines of carceral spaces. How do such impulses become destructive to the cultivation of alternative abolitionist visions and strategies, particularly when remaining attached to a particular logical antecedent of caring—diagnosis?[21] In introducing the discussions of carceral cure to carceral care, I hope to demonstrate how, even when positing a neoliberal politics of prison reform, therein lies the reproduction of a coercive orientation in relating to an-other, that is, the naturalization of the colonial practice of othering through the very practice of human caging.[22] Drawing from critiques of the sociology of deviance to anarcho theories of mutual aid, and through a series of collaborative ethnographic vignettes, this article will explore the queer possibilities of deviance (deviant care, deviant time, deviant travel, deviant space) as a mode of disrupting relationships of care as premised on the sentiment of "help given."[23] Further, how might we reconceive of care in ways that queer its teleological and colonial relationship to rehabilitation and cure? Ultimately, in writing on, with, and through the vexing questions of prison abolition, there is no such thing as an equitable acknowledgment, on my part to those inside who, through their everyday embodied experiences of interfacing with and surviving the carceral state, continue to generously teach us, on the outside, how exactly the prison industrial complex devastates and steals life on multiple scales of time, space, and existence. At the very least, this article offers an example of how showing up, witnessing, failing, and being willing to not know and to learn, might itself be the sometimes-inauspicious work of abolitionist praxis.

Deviance as Mutual Aid

The study of deviance as a fixture of the social sciences found its roots in early nineteenth-century humanistic endeavors that sought to streamline the philosophy of science as positivism and self-evidently true.[24] To this day, sociological studies ranging from human behavior to criminology continue to be preoccupied with two general abstractions worth troubling here. First is the observation that any particular human trait can be deduced, extracted, and applied to forge a universal claim concerning particular subjects, that is, the permanent prefiguration of the deviant or the criminal. This logic assumes that social or legal norms are unchanging. Second, such positivistic empirical studies of deviance fail to acknowledge the genocidal colonial processes by which regulatory technologies of law, legal enforcement, and juridical discourses are normalized and naturalized. Thus the reproduction of the figure of the deviant as criminal, and vice versa, only further normalizes a pernicious cycle of expansion, reform, and research on carceral technologies and carceral spaces ranging from the ethics of solitary confinement, mental health jails, and youth in detention centers to debates on gender-responsive imprisonment. In "Deviance as Resistance: A New Research Agenda for the Study of Black Politics," Cathy J. Cohen debates sociologist Howard Becker's critique of the pathos framing of deviance. Cohen challenges the construction of deviance as an innate quality and reframes it as a consequence of an action that defies normative rules and sanctions.

Cohen (2004) asks us how we might imagine deviance and deviant practices in terms of a radical feminist black tradition and politics—that is, a mode of resistance to an otherwise reductive social and political ordering of respectability. Similarly, Sarah Haley (2016: 6) describes the carceral construction of deviance by way of "discursive and material process by which imprisoned black women became a point of passage between what was normative and what was queer." Following Cohen and Haley, how does such a point of passage offer up the very conditions of possibility for radical deviance, one which dislodges those regulatory norms and devices that naturalize the juridical world of law, order, crime, and punishment as an antiblack and heteropatriarchical precept?

Turning to the concept of mutual aid, I examine how collective practices of deviant care might offer us experimental models toward disrupting carceral care or ideological state apparatuses as managed through discourses of diagnosis?[25] Beyond a statist and philanthropic notion of mutual aid, in which only unidirectional relationships of resource redistribution are possible—a neoliberal trickle-down from the wealthy to the poor—how might a deviant praxis of mutual aid require us to question such short-term fixes, particularly ones that seek to decontextualize material and historical power relations that moderate the possibility for social change? Dean Spade pushes us to consider mutual aid as the building of antihierarchical social relations of material care through a political and participatory praxis of disrupting capitalistic models of individuation and need-based competition.[26] Mutual aid thus exists as the activation of interdependence, built over time through consensual interaction, reflection, and transformation. Such practices of relationality inhabit a radical deviance and a deviant relationship to care, whereby the social categorization and interpellation of a singular self-subject is queered, made less discreet and less "self-evident." Such deviations allow us to further disorganize the inevitability of those who become passive and self-evidencing objects of carceral care.[27] This idea of deviant care is not new, although I hope that it brings together both past and future questions concerning the relationship between the carceral and the conception and administration of care, particularly in how we, as scholars and activists, count our time as "worthwhile." How, then, might deviating from the constrictions of carceral time and space allow us to meditate on the possibility of a radical mutualism, one that remains illegible to the productivity metrics of late racial capitalism? Such illegibility might persist in the affective economies of intimacy, trust, misgivings, failures, disappointment, joy, connection, disconnection, and trial and error—all of which offer us endurance against the deathly predilections of carceral care. Perhaps deviant care as mutual aid offers an interstitial timespace, to borrow from Moran, against the otherwise constant, slow, and inconspicuous carceral clock that demands time owed, served, extracted, and stolen away?[28]

Deviance of Queer Bonds

As I unknowingly circled twice around the two Corcoran prison facilities, I finally arrived at the gates of CSATF but was barred from an early entrance by the checkpoint deputy. He directed me to join the row of stationary cars, each suspended on the dusty dirt road outside the facilities' walls where drivers waited for their prescheduled visitation time. That day, like many days in Southern California, was unreasonably hot. I could only attempt to imagine the swelter behind those nearly windowless steel and concrete walls. Friends inside have described the creative survival strategies to cool themselves off—blacking out rooms, assembling makeshift curtains, disrobing, showering in ice-cold water, avoiding one's time outside on the yard, and prayers and rituals to keep calm, collected, and connected to a world beyond the death grip of the cages they are told are their home. These concrete walls separate two worlds, a material and ideological division that visitors can only begin to grasp. As with other prisons, moving through Corcoran requires one to dance the carceral shuffle through checkpoints staffed by apathetic correctional officers, physical barriers, and metal detectors, each a hurdle potentially barring entry—pat downs, ID checks, signing in, signing out, repeat—all while under constant CCTV surveillance.[29] When one is approved to enter the official prison premises, they are directed to a small portion of the otherwise vast parking lot designated for correctional officers and administrative and medical staff, a 24/7, year-round warehouse sale on stolen labor, time, and bodies. The concertina wire–lined metal gates, heavy steel doors, and glass watchtowers—the institutional taupe-green as a shadow hue of army fatigue— are an unmistakable signal of militarism at home, a domestic war on drugs, poverty, and racialized and unruly genders and bodies.

No amount of planning can appropriately prepare one for the discretionary enforcement of visitation regulations by correctional officers. Upon entry, I am confronted briskly, perhaps part routine, part suspicion, a new face—Asian, gender nonbinary in dress and body. I sense, with the darting gazes received from across the tall check-in desk, that my presence is a disruption of the assumed role of the majority of women of color who visit—devoted and/or exhausted mothers, wives, girlfriends, and their children. When asked whom I was visiting, I replied, "Aliya Sanders," a feminine name. The officer snatched the visitation paper begrudgingly, replying, "Oh, Aaron Sanders, you booked the visitation incorrectly, come back at noon." Next focusing on my "excessive" piercings, she asked, "Did you not read over the conditions for visitation . . . ? Either remove all but two piercings or don't bother to come back, this includes the one in your nose." The officer's agitation grew with every second I remained in her line of sight. Was it the threat of jewelry being smuggled in, or the threat of foreign objects on perceived "foreign" bodies?[30] A wedding ring, cross necklace, or recognizable religious medallion are acceptable forms of jewelry, but queer bonds, queer kin, and queer bodies remain suspect from the moment of entry to the prisons. We—our queer bonds—are the contraband.[31]

Both embarrassed and frustrated that I had somehow already let Aliya down, I returned to my car to attempt to remove all but two piercings, as directed. With a pair of dulled dollar-store tweezers, yanking and twisting in the blazing heat, I cut up my skin with little success. Delirium washed over me, and I wondered, what kind of corporeal payment, perhaps in the shape of an ear, would allow an outsider to gain access to the visitation room? An airy cafeteria space lined with well-stocked vending machines, the visitation room is the interstitial space for us nonstaff, noninmate persons. It remains one step closer to the exit door for those inside and one step closer for us visitors in comprehending the reality of those who live each day, behind bars, in human-sized cages. We on the outside have the privilege of never having to, within our bodies, comprehend fully such a reality, but we can listen and be present. The overseeing correctional officers are often on their best behavior, regulating and controlling the amount of intimacy and affection shared between those visiting with those in custody—hand-holding and a brief kiss or hug at the start and close of the visit are CDCR approved. Being made to do this carceral shuffle is one small yet critical way to gain familiarity with and yet deviate from the slow grate of carceral timespace.[32] In the end, I was denied entry because of excessive earrings, and it would be another several months before I could return to Corcoran. My visitations, whether failed or successful, are not simply a measure of providing support to Aliya. I am there to intimately learn, in relation to bodies stolen by prison time and places deemed out of sight and "out of the way." Being denied entry to a place no one actually wishes to call home is an acute reminder that we, as visitors, inhabit the vexed privilege and burden of always getting to leave, though never with those inside whom we only wish to see free. Perhaps such thwarted forms of care and mutual aid, in the appearance of denied entry, remain powerful in their ability to teach us how relationships premised on individuated acts of to (care receiver) and from (care giver) can ensnare us within unidirectional frameworks of diagnosis, that is, to assume our work is to identify and know fully the needs of an-other. Perhaps this is the queer horizon in which a radical deviance as mutual aid remains a constancy of exchange without extractable or exactable value, always emerging, disordering, multidirectional, spiraling, and elsewhere.[33]

Deviant Care against Carceral Care

Carceral feminism, as a predominant liberal investment in antiviolence, proprison reform, provides the ideological contours for further understanding the stakes and logics of carceral care. Victoria Law (2014) describes procarceral feminism as

> increased policing, prosecution, and imprisonment . . . [and] the primary solution to violence against women. . . . Carceral feminism ignores the ways in which race, class, gender identity, and immigration status leave certain women more vulnerable to violence and that greater criminalization often places these same women at risk of state violence.

Such politics, like discussions on carceral humanism, requires us to scrutinize the telos and mandate of care as laid bare through the prison itself. This prison, even with every aspiration to be kinder, gentler, and more gender responsive, is fundamentally defined as that which administers life as much as it is underwritten by death (Braz 2006).[34] The doubling down of state securitization, domestic warfare, and state-sponsored strategies of gender-responsive antiviolence as prison reform simply demonstrates the fungible capacity of the state to define safety as safekeeping of carceral subjects—the necropolitical as carceral care.[35] How might we enact a refusal of the carceral calculator that hedges bets of coercive plea bargains as a just relief from the crushing intimidation of multiple life sentences? As carceral feminism and humanism continue to invest in the biopolitical multiplication of crimes, enhancement of crimes, convictions and being convicted, such actuarial carceral algorithms, even in the name of reform, only breed the inevitability of premature and social death, especially for those made to be surplus objects under state surveillance. In locating critiques of carceral feminisms and humanism within the long-standing history of carceral care as colonial cure, we must turn to an engagement with indigenous feminist interventions demanding models of radical resurgence, relationalism, and enthusiastic consensual engagement.[36] Such interventions shine a discerning light on those technocratic and managerial state-based prison reform strategies that hinge on a top-down politics of curative diagnosis.[37]

At CSATF, Aliya was placed in a special needs yard informally housing transgender women together, a model of trans-responsive imprisonment.[38] With support and encouragement from a small community team, Aliya slowly reinvigorated a preexisting yet defunct institutionally sponsored space titled Transgender Alternative Lifestyle Group, serving as the elected chairperson.[39] Led for and by mostly black and Latinx transgender women, the space is hosted twice a week to air grievances, share resources, address interpersonal conflict, build community trust, and offer gender-affirming somatic exercises to counter past and present traumatic experiences of harm. Through practices of mutuality and collective care, advocacy, peer support, dialogue, and strategies toward naming connections between structural, interpersonal, and material violence, this shared time is a deviation from a kind of carceral temporality and regulated space.[40] In the fall of 2018, with the successful organizing by the women inside to wage collective demands against the institutions, nonbinary and "femme gay boys," as Aliya describes, asked to join the group to address interpersonal conflict and imposed competition for resources between those who identified as LGBTQ.[41] The institutional recognition and approval of the transgender women's "alternative lifestyle group," and by extension the organizing made possible through this gender-affirming and monitored space within a "designated male institution," could be viewed as simply a proprison reform, preventing the possibility of wielding collective power away from the penal institutions themselves. However, there is merit in distinguishing the problem with such claims—that is, the premise that resistance is automatically diluted, made respectable, when having to be incubated within institutionally authorized spaces. To interrogate these contradictions, the following section will focus on how the administration of carceral care requires us to go beyond a subjectless critique of the criminal punishment system writ large.

In May of 2018, the State of California Office of Administrative Law issued a statewide forty-four-page adopted regulation memo requiring timely compliance by CDCR to allow "transgender inmates and inmates having symptoms of gender dysphoria that are housed at designated institutions to have access to state-issued and authorized personal property items in accordance with their gender identities" via "The Transgender Inmates Authorized Personal Property Schedule" (TIAPPS).[42] The language of TIAPPS relies on the pathologization of carceral subjects as gender dysphoric. Such a diagnosis thus permits individuals to access previously unauthorized "female property," termed here as feminine contraband, within a male-designated institution.[43] The memo opens with a detailed chart regulating the number limit for acceptable types of feminine clothing ("brassieres (7), panties (10), sandals (1)"), as well as personal care/hygiene items such as "body splash (2), mascara (1), lip gloss/lipstick (2), eyeliner (2), feminine hygiene wash (2)." The majority of the memo summarizes written public comments from community advocates, incarcerated transgender individuals, and prison officials. The repeated denial of particular personal property is debated as a potential cause of "security risk." For instance, items such as "pajama/nightgown," "robes," "scarves," and "body-size towels" are rebuffed because of the prospect of excessive fabric being used as "escape paraphernalia" (State of California 2018: 5–32). Plastic hairclips are disallowed because their metal components could be used for "manufacturing weapons or circumventing restraint gear such as handcuffs, waist chains, or leg restraints" (6, 22).

Following this memo in the summer of 2018, and after several failed orders from various for-profit, third-party vendors, the women inside CSATF and I finally were able to place a purchase order for female-designated items through Walkenhorst's.[44] The success of receiving "female designated" personal items was considered a huge win for Aliya and other women inside. This material win was a direct result of years of organizing and advocacy by trans women of color inside, particularly in alliance with organizations such as the TGI Justice Project and the Transgender Law Center (TLC). TIAPPS as a legal document might read easily as a gender-responsive proprison reform. However, the organizing among women inside is in and of itself a mode of survival and resistance against the consolidation of hegemonic state power. The difference between the institutionalization of TIAPPS, like the institutionally approved Transgender Alternative Lifestyle Group, and the continual organizing of the women inside is that the former exists as the end goal, a proprison reformist strategy, and the latter offers space for further abolitionist work, a nonreformist strategy.[45] Such abolitionist praxis in the strategy of reform perhaps offers a harm-reductive approach to a death-driven system otherwise hell-bent on administering only the most violent—if not completely negligent—notion of carceral care.[46] One of the CSATF women, quoted in the TIAPPS memo, offers an incisive critique of the policing of makeup in the yard, particularly when read as "noticeable" feminine contraband, stating, "Multiple ranking officers on our yard are wholly against [the emergency regulations of enforcing TIAPPS]" and are "circumventing them by subjective interpretation" (State of California 2018: 18). For Aliya and the women inside CSATF, deviant care and mutual aid persist in practices like redistributing and collectively circulating individual TIAPPS packages as well as forging feminine items even with the failed implementation of the institutional memo.

Aliya recently called me with gleeful news to let me know that the CDCR 602 Inmate/Parolee Appeal form that the women collectively filed with CSATF was finally granted, which would provide additional shower curtains in the otherwise open-area shower that both cisgender men and transgender women share simultaneously. CDCR's decision, technically enforced through the federal Prison Rape Elimination Act (PREA) of 2003, to grant a shower curtain to the transgender women in CSATF is a perfect example of the embodiment of carceral care—that is, to provide an all-too-insulting translucent plastic tarp, offering no additional privacy whatsoever. Aliya, however, explained to me that the women rigged this "barrier" with makeshift canvas towels and, with a buddy system, collectively created a work-around to provide a sense of communal safety among one another. Although often an uphill battle with no relief in sight, reform for reform's sake requires only the performance of compliance with gender-responsive legal memos like TIAPPS or PREA federal regulations, both of which frame carceral care as an institutional "it gets better."[47] Ranging from reporting abusive medical and correctional staff to preventing and deterring sexual, interpersonal, and structural violence, deviant care nevertheless requires a constant stream of strategic demands. Demands, however small or large in scale, are often still made with the collective wisdom that most penal reform pathways, when strictly for and by the rules of the state, are largely self-enclosed and self-replicating sinkholes.[48]

QTBIPoC Radical Relationalism
Deviant or devious care requires an insurrectionary mode of creating impossible bonds that harness the radical potential of an elsewhere care, one that is not inhibited by a telos of help, diagnosis, or curing. Such an elsewhere is not simply an aspirational horizon that is hauntingly unidentifiable. To borrow from Melanie K. Yazzie and Cutcha Risling Baldy (2018: 2), such an elsewhere requires a radical

relationality as a daily practice that divests from a liberal sympathizing individuated relationalism (which produces discrete subject-object relations). Radical
relationality, or "queer trans black indigenous and people of color" (QTBIPoC)
radical relationalism as I call it here, is an act of interrupting the philanthropic
algorithm that pairs the colonial benefactor—the prison as social service provider—
with surplus carceral objects.[49] Whether through survival, refusal, or an elsewhere, black, brown, and indigenous bodies, through their very existence have
functioned as the marker of deviance as that which underwrites the possibility for
colonial time and space. Whether through imperial warfare, settler colonial
genocide, chattel slavery, boarding schools, guest worker programs, or eugenicist
medical apartheid, these once-legal institutions reveal, again and again, the
fungible nature of a curative carceral violence as state care.[50]

Deviant care demands an inhabitation of QTBIPoC radical relationalism
that critically upends impulses to be simply against rules, regulation, and norms.
Queer as a subjectless critique only feeds the white supremacist political voracity
to simply drop in, detach from, or extract otherness as an exercise in peculiar/
particular critical inquiry. Such absolutism and purity of abolitionist praxis as
only ever that which is fully against and/or outside reformist strategies are often
suspect postures of more radical than thou.[51] In other words, how might we
deviate and disrupt our reliance on the seemingly inevitable futurity of surplus
populations (the deviant, criminal, inmate, terrorist, illegal, black identity extrem-
ist, etc.) while engaging with a politics of relationalism that deals with, in the then
and now, the legacies of such cyclical prefigurations?[52] Instead, how might a
radical relationalism (beyond a sociological epistemology of the radical relational) offer a new mode of temporality and relationship to our present future?[53]
Radical relationalism, as Cohen (2004: 33) describes, truly "[witnesses] the power
of those at the bottom, whose everyday life decisions challenge, or at least counter,
the basic normative assumptions of a society intent on protecting structural and
social inequalities under the guise of some normal and natural order to life." This
mode of relationality redefines care or mutualism by its ability to reorient ourselves to one another, that is, beyond an assertion of capitalist extractive productivity.[54] In effect, radical QTBIPoC relationalism exists beyond reductive
dichotomies such as success and failure, yet it centers the emotional and affective
labor required in thinking about and attending to a collective politics of care.
What, then, might a deviant present-future reveal concerning the ongoing
reverberations of a living, breathing, and bleeding colonial curative temporality?
What might a deviation from a curative, colonial, and carceral care look like?
How might radical relationalism as deviant care require us to recalibrate the
irreducibility of, to borrow from Scott Lauria Morgensen, the interdependent
spaces between us—land, plants, species, and water—as all beings?[55] In conclusion, whether practiced as deviant care, mutual aid, radical mutualism, or

QTBIPoC radical relationalism, how might we counter the collective fatigue that tolerates a reformed model of carceral care as the end goal? How might we continue to work against and between institutional walls, where connections forged are often best envisioned through speculative praxis of imaginative closeness?[56] Tourmaline writes, "We all know the damage that it can be to be called nobody and yet there is power in that word and in that world of no-bodies. It's a power Denise Ferreira da Silva cites when she asks 'Do we want to be *somebody* under the state or *nobody* against it?'" (Tourmaline, Dunham, and Zavitsanos 2016). How might reckoning with mutual aid as research praxis promise us no-bodies and no-thing calculable of capitalist worth under the metrics of academic and or nonprofit-industrial-complex success? Perhaps QTBIPoC radical relationalism simply offers us a disordering of commonsense notions of the individuated self-evident self. Deviating from logics of carceral care require the sobering recognition that to build meaningful relationships across prison walls we are promised nothing in terms of self-fulfillment and progressive good feelings—and yet we must celebrate the clear-tarp-turned-makeshift-shower-curtain while, in the same breath, distrust the translucent promise of a kinder, gentler, gender-responsive prison as liberation and an inevitable future.

Ren-yo Hwang is an assistant professor in gender studies and critical social thought at Mount Holyoke College and researches and teaches on transformative justice, prison abolition, community accountability, queer/trans* of color critique, antiviolence strategies and liberation, and participatory action research.

Acknowledgments

I was granted permission to offer personal stories here from Aliya and the transgender women's group inside CSATF. This article would not have been possible without the mutual support and friendship between Aliya and me. Aliya was released in early 2019 and is living and working in Los Angeles. Pseudonyms were selected and personal details changed by research collaborators for anonymity and safety. Thank you to California Coalition for Women Prisoners, Dignity Power Now, TGIJP, and Survived and Punished for their constant organizational wisdom that contributed to the completion of this article.

Notes

1.   Ruth Wilson Gilmore and Craig Gilmore (2004: 389) write, "Before the first prison opened, about 1,000 of Corcoran's residents lived in households whose incomes put them below the poverty line. Ten years later, after the state spent around $1 *billion* in Corcoran for the construction and operating costs of the two prisons, nearly 2,000 people lived beneath the poverty line. When the prison advertised two clerical positions with a starting wage of $17,000, 800 people lined up waiting for the employment office to open so they could apply."

2.   Nearly 10,000 of 22,691 persons.

3.   This is borrowed from her chapter titled "Innocent Amusements: The Stage of Suffer-
      ance," where Hartman (1997: 21) writes, "The fungibility of the commodity makes the
      captive body an abstract and empty vessel vulnerable to the projection of others' feelings,
      ideas, desires and values; and, as property, the dispossessed body of the enslaved is the
      surrogate for the master's body since it guarantees his disembodied universality and act as
      a sign of his power and dominion."

4.   Most recognizably through long-standing institutions dating back to before the mid-
      nineteenth century, such as Louisiana State Penitentiary, also known as Angola or simply
      "The Farm" for its use of prisoners as convict farm labor. For more, see Davis 1998 and
      Oshinsky 1996.

5.   For more, see Gilmore 1999 and 2006. On warfare-welfare, see O'Connor 1979.

6.   For more, see Ellison 2019.

7.   My use of *carceral care* breaks from Marquita R. Smith's (2018) description of carceral
      care as the labor required, often by black women, to support the survival of those
      incarcerated.

8.   This language of multiplication of scales is credited to Dylan Rodriguez (pers. comm.,
      March 15, 2019).

9.   A rigged gamble in the sense of the house, that is, the penal institution, always wins. Even
      in reforming the optics of carceral care, it is never to the direct benefit of those trapped
      within its confines. I therefore use *gamble* here to suggest the ways in which legislating to
      win one set of reformed penal conditions does not promise any actual reduction of harm
      for those it most impacts, but also, sometimes it might. Even when reforms are not just
      symbolic but demand a shift in the material conditions for those incarcerated, such
      reforms are so grossly uneven in their application.

10.   Eli Clare (2017: 31) writes, "I'm trying to say that life and death sometimes hangs on an
      acknowledgement of personhood. . . . Personhood is used all too often as a weapon."

11.   The etymological root of the word *care*, whether as verb or noun, is derived from notions
      of lamenting, grief, and being filled with sorrow (Old High German, *chara, charon*; Old
      English, *caru*). The Latin root of the word *cure* is literally (*curare*) to "take care of"
      (Oxford English Dictionary Online, s.v. "care, n.1," accessed June 2019, www.oed.com). If
      curing is to take care of, to remedy—how, then, do we reorient our relationship to care
      away from a death-driven politics of "curing" as routed through the carceral?

12.   The action research mentioned here, where Aliya's participation is fully driven by the
      collective desires of the trans women inside in community, is inspired here by Tuck and
      Yang 2014 and A. Simpson 2014. On ethnographic refusal, indigeneity, voice, and colonial
      citizenship, see A. Simpson 2014.

13.   Up to twenty-two thousand persons await trial or sentencing on any given day.

14.   DPN, formerly the Coalition to End Sheriff Violence in LA Jails, is an organization I had
      worked with for several years since its inception in 2012, particularly, leading editorial
      zine work, archiving campaigns, and assisting in on-site jail outreach events.

15.   The official creation of K6G stemmed from a 1982 American Civil Liberties Union of
      Southern California class action lawsuit brought against Los Angeles County Sheriff's
      Department on behalf of homosexual inmates due to threat of sexual and physical
      violence. See Robertson v. Block, No. 82-1442-WPG (Px) (C.D. Cal. May 11, 1982). K6G
      serves as a complex "carceral care" case study, in being a model institution for gender and
      sexual-minority responsive prison reform.

16.   The commercial bail bond industry, legal only in the United States and Philippines, handles nearly US $14 billion in bonds annually and US $2 billion in revenues (Wing 2016). Relatedly, the United States has the largest pretrial detention population in the world, nearing half a million (Aborn and Cannon 2013).

17.   Although in theory everyone, even a prisoner, has the constitutional right to practice self-defense, prisoners' rights derived from the Eighth Amendment are often obscured if not outright concealed, via loopholes, by constitutional jurisprudence that defers to the authority of correctional institutions. For more, see Kaye 1996.

18.   Aliya and Fresh have described a critical bonding of queers inside the California prison system, named QRS, known as Queers Running Shit and sometimes Queers Reforming Society.

19.   Dylan Rodriguez (2003) describes the collaboration between social scientists and prison wardens to create behavior modification techniques of segregation of emotional ties as a mode of brainwashing with an end goal of docility.

20.   This has been argued most vehemently by community-led organizations such as Transgender Gender Variant Intersex Justice Project; California Coalition for Women Prisoners; Critical Resistance; Sylvia Rivera Law Project; Black and Pink; INCITE!, Women, Gender Non-Conforming, and Trans People of Color Against Violence; Dignity Power Now; Youth Justice Coalition; and many more.

21.   For more on the history of diagnosis in regard to relations of power and subjectification, see Michel Foucault's *Birth of the Clinic* ([1975] 2010) and *Madness and Civilization* ([1965] 2009).

22.   The hyphenation of *another* to *an-other* refers to and breaks from phenomenology's study of the self and constitutive other as also notated through similar interventions made in queer theory such as *an/other* and *(an)other*.

23.   As in the field of health (e.g., healthcare), the terminology of care, either as practice and concept, evokes a linear ontology of to and from, a service rendered.

24.   From Émile Durkheim to Foucault, the three schools of thought in conceptualizing deviance—structural functionalism, symbolic interaction, and conflict theory—share an understanding of deviance as generally that which violates norms, understandings, or expectations of social systems. Historically linked to the advent and diagnosis of criminal traits and activity, "deviant behavior" was established as a critical subfield that spanned various disciplines in the social sciences such as criminology, psychology, anthropology, and sociology.

25.   For more, see Althusser 2014.

26.   For more on mutual aid, see Spade 2018; Bigdoorbrigade.com n.d.; and Lazare 2017.

27.   Bigdoorbrigade.com (n.d.) describes the radical potential of "mutual aid" as "a form of political participation in which people take responsibility for caring for one another and changing political conditions, not just through symbolic acts or putting pressure on their representatives in government, but by actually building new social relations that are more survivable."

28.   For more discussion of prison "clock time" and carceral timespace, see Moran 2012; see also Haley's (2016: 205) discussion of black women's sabotage of the late nineteenth-century convict lease system and "refusal of the carceral timetable [in] thwart[ing] carceral productivity."

29.   A nod to Mimi Kim's use of *carceral creep* in her 2015 article "Dancing the Carceral Creep." Kim's use of *creep* describes the steps by which the mainstreaming of the feminist

antiviolence movement became seduced by the promise of state protection. With prison visitations, on the other hand, we are coerced into participating in this carceral shuffle with the hope of connecting with those inside.

30. The carceral logic of deviant behavior produces responses such as, "Earrings would have the potential to increase predatory behavior against weaker inmates. Earrings could be stolen or be used to barter or trade for contraband and other items" (State of California 2018: Response 7B).

31. As inspired by Assata Shakur's (2001) poem "Love" that begins, "Love is contraband in Hell."

32. Other attempts at connection reside in the space of state-surveilled outgoing phone calls, long-distance handwritten letters that often arrive faster than the sporadically delivered or disappeared e-mails sent to the CDCR-approved JPay tablet, mailed books like Janet Mock's *Surpassing Certainty* with the beautiful hardcover ripped off, literature from organizations like *Surviving Prison in California: Advice by and for Transgender Women* by the Transgender Gender Variant Intersex (TGI) Justice Project.

33. I am thinking here of the clustering of collective care via the concept of "care web" described by Leah Lakshmi Piepzna-Samarasinha (2018) in *Care Work*, "pod mapping" by Mia Mingus (2017), or "building one's team" as theorized by Patrisse Cullors. Cullors (pers. comm., 2009–17) would often use this phrasing and base-building strategy of "building one's team" in the organizing work we shared in Los Angeles over the years, particularly via Dignity Power Now.

34. For more on carceral humanism, see Kilgore 2014 and Schept 2015.

35. Whether it be the restructuring of the rural or the gentrification of cities, Christina Hanhardt (2013: 223) describes how the politics of development have long been predicated on ideas of risk management, as she states "messy distinctions between crime and violence, safety and justice, underscore the flexibility of concepts such as risk and their centrality to the politics of development."

36. "Within the context of settler colonialism, Indigenous peoples are not seen as worthy recipients of consent, informed or otherwise, and part of being colonized is having to engage in all kinds of processes on a daily basis that, given a choice, we likely wouldn't consent to" (L. B. Simpson 2014: 15; see also L. B. Simpson 2017).

37. For more on the notion of cure as violence, in relation to illness and disability, see Ben-Moshe 2013.

38. CSATF was touted for its use of a "therapeutic community model" to reduce recidivism, described as "the largest addiction treatment center in the world." However, such claims have been discredited by special investigative accountability audits by state institutions like California's Office of the Inspector General (OIG) (Cate 2007).

39. Formerly defunct, the group had trouble being maintained, owing to a lack of leadership, resources, and solid external sponsorship—a requirement for any approved official group to exist within prisons—and general emotional exhaustion all around.

40. Beth Richie (2012) describes these intersections of harm through the conception of the violence matrix.

41. Such trans-sensitive harm reduction among the women inside might be read as a simply pinkwashed prison reform, or a function of carceral feminism. See the work of Survived and Punished National Coalition and scholar-activists such as Alisa Bierria, Beth Richie, Colby Lenz, Mariam Kaba, Emily Thuma, and Dean Spade.

42. For more, see State of California 2018: 1–2.

43. "Department staff at designated institutions need to be able to distinguish between property that is authorized for transgender inmates and inmates having symptoms of gender dysphoria . . . in order to ensure that all inmates are only in possession of authorized property items" (State of California 2018: 24).

44. Approved vendors such as Golden State Care Packages, Access SecurePak, and Union Supply Direct are marketed as providing a friendly service for families and loved ones to supply additional "care packages" not provided by the prison itself, a mode of purchasing care as commodities beyond the in-prison commissary.

45. For more on nonreformist reform, see Pisciotta 1996.

46. "CDCR has currently designated 14 institutions to house transgender inmates. The transgender inmate population, including inmates having symptoms of gender dysphoria, is very small in comparison with the overall inmate population; presently, CDCR has approximately 500 transgender inmates in an inmate population of approximately 129,000 inmates" (State of California 2018).

47. A critical dig at Dan Savage's viral antibullying LGBT social media campaign turned nonprofit titled It Gets Better that also inhabits an upward mobility politics of linear self-reliance and self-cure.

48. Aliya, for instance, consulted with me concerning whether she should file a CDCR Form 602 Inmate/Parolee Appeal against a new nurse who was administering injections of hormone blockers in a way that left more bruising, excessive bleeding, and clear signs that the intramuscularly administered estrogen dosage was ineffective. Filing such forms can be risky, as retaliation or withholding of medication is a common response to such collective self-advocacy.

49. QTBIPoC is borrowed from community digital archives such as Marvellous Grounds in Toronto, Canada (Huron-Wendat, Petun, Seneca, and Mississaugas of the Credit River). See marvellousgrounds.com/about/ (accessed June 30, 2019).

50. C. Riley Snorton (2017: 193–94) describes black life in relation to colonial time as the rupture that reveals "living beyond [Western episteme] life [which] also arranges, or perhaps exposes, time as outside of time and self, beyond self, which is to say that the 'self' is itself a rupture."

51. Here I am not debating the philosophy and principles of abolition, rather, the everyday organizing and praxis that requires some kind of interface with strategies of nonreformist reform.

52. To affirm yet neutralize, in reference to Roderick Ferguson's (2012) critique of the integration of minoritarian subject positions and interdisciplines.

53. "Radically relational" as containing "no residual dualist elements and therefore treats all social phenomena, including individuals themselves, as constituted through relations" (Powell 2013).

54. Christina Sharpe (2016: 21) offers "wake work" as a kind of care work done through connecting "containment, regulation, punishment, capture, and captivity and the ways the manifold representations of blackness become the symbol, par excellence, for the less-than-human being condemned to death." She states that "thinking needs care ('all thought is Black thought') and that thinking and care need to stay in the wake" (5).

55. For more, see Morgensen 2011.

56. Here I am thinking about the many radical, deviant, and divergent strategies put forth by adrienne maree brown in *Emergent Strategy: Shaping Change, Changing Worlds* (2017).

References

Aborn, Richard M., and Ashley D. Cannon. 2013. "Prisons: In Jail, but Not Sentenced." *Americas Quarterly*, winter. www.americasquarterly.org/aborn-prisons.

Agamben, Giorgio. 1998. *Homo Sacer: Sovereign Power and Bare Life.* Stanford, CA: Stanford University Press.

Althusser, Louis. 2014. *On the Reproduction of Capitalism: Ideology and Ideological State Apparatuses.* London: Verso.

Ben-Moshe, Liat. 2013. "Disabling Incarceration: Connecting Disability to Divergent Confinements in the USA." *Critical Sociology* 39, no. 3: 385–403.

Big Door Brigade. n.d. "What Is Mutual Aid?" bigdoorbrigade.com/what-is-mutual-aid/ (accessed September 15, 2018).

Braz, Rose. 2006. "'Kinder, Gentler, Gender Responsive' Cages: Prison Expansion Is Not Prison Reform." In *Women and Girls in the Criminal Justice System: Policy Issues and Practices*, vol. 2, edited by Russell Immarigeon, 87–91. Kingston, NJ: Civic Research Institute.

Brown, Adrienne Maree. 2017. *Emergent Strategy: Shaping Change, Changing Worlds.* Chico, CA: AK.

Cate, Matthew L. 2007. *Special Review into In-Prison Substance Abuse Programs Managed by the California Department of Corrections and Rehabilitation.* Sacramento, CA: Office of the Inspector General, State of California. www.prisonlegalnews.org/news/publications/ca-oig-report-on-prison-drug-programs-2007/.

CDCR (California Department of Corrections and Rehabilitation). 2018. Population Reports. sites.cdcr.ca.gov/research/population-reports/ (accessed November 10, 2018).

Clare, Eli. 2017. *Brilliant Imperfection: Grappling with Cure.* Durham, NC: Duke University Press.

Cochran, Joshua C., Elisa L. Toman, Daniel P. Mears, and William D. Bales. 2018. "Solitary Confinement as Punishment: Examining In-Prison Sanctioning Disparities." *Justice Quarterly* 35, no. 3: 381–411.

Cohen, Cathy. 2004. "Deviance as Resistance: A New Research Agenda for the Study of Black Politics." *Du Bois Review* 1, no. 1: 27–45.

Davis, Angela Y. 1998. "From the Prison of Slavery to the Slavery of Prison: Frederick Douglass and the Convict Lease System." In *The Angela Y. Davis Reader*, edited by Joy James, 74–95. Malden, MA: Blackwell.

Ellison, Treva C. 2019. "Black Femme Praxis and the Promise of Black Gender." *Black Scholar* 49, no. 1: 6–16.

Ferguson, Roderick. 2012. *Reorder of Things: The University and Its Pedagogies of Minority Difference.* Minneapolis: University of Minnesota Press.

Foucault, Michel. (1965) 2009. *Madness and Civilization: A History of Insanity in the Age of Reason.* Translated by Richard Howard. London: Routledge.

Foucault, Michel. (1975) 2010. *The Birth of the Clinic: An Archaeology of Medical Perception.* London: Routledge.

Frost, Natasha A., Carlos, E. Monteiro, and CSR Incorporated. 2016. *Administrative Segregation in U.S. Prisons Executive Summary.* Arlington, VA: National Institute of Corrections, Department of Justice.

Gilmore, Ruth. 1999. "Globalisation and US Prison Growth: From Military Keynesianism to Post-Keynesian Militarism." *Race and Class* 40, nos. 2–3: 171–88.

Gilmore, Ruth. 2006. *Golden Gulag: Prisons, Surplus, Crisis, and Opposition in Globalizing California.* Berkeley: University of California Press.

Gilmore, Ruth Wilson, and Craig Gilmore. 2003. "The Other California." In *Globalize Liberation: How to Uproot the System and Build a Better World*, edited by David Solnit, 381–96. San Francisco: City Light.

Haley, Sarah. 2016. *No Mercy Here: Gender, Punishment, and the Making of Jim Crow Modernity*. Chapel Hill: University of North Carolina Press.

Hanhardt, Christina. 2013. *Safe Space: Gay Neighborhood History and the Politics of Violence*. Durham, NC: Duke University Press.

Hartman, Siadiya. 1997. "Innocent Amusements: The Stage of Sufferance." In *Scenes of Subjection: Terror, Slavery, and Self-Making in Nineteenth-Century America*. New York: Oxford University Press.

Kaye, Anders. 1996. "Dangerous Places: The Right to Self-Defense in Prison and Prison Conditions Jurisprudence." *University of Chicago Law Review* 63, no. 2: 693–726.

Kilgore, James. 2014. "Repackaging Mass Incarceration." *Counter Punch*, June 6. www.counterpunch.org/2014/06/06/repackaging-mass-incarceration/.

Kim, Mimi. 2015. *Dancing the Carceral Creep: The Anti-domestic Violence Movement and the Paradoxical Pursuit of Criminalization, 1973–1986*. ISSI Fellows Working Papers. Berkeley: University of California, Institute for the Study of Societal Issues.

Law, Victoria. 2014. "Against Carceral Feminism." *Jacobin*, October 17. www.jacobinmag.com/2014/10/against-carceral-feminism.

Lazare, Sarah. 2018. "Now Is the Time for 'Nobodies': Dean Spade on Mutual Aid and Resistance in the Trump Era." *AlterNet*, January 5. www.alternet.org/2017/01/now-time-nobodies-dean-spade-mutual-aid-and-resistance-trump-era/.

Mingus, Mia. 2017. "Transformative Justice and Creating Your Pods." Bay Area Transformative Justice Workshop presented at Asian Americans Advancing Justice, Los Angeles, April 30.

Moran, Dominique. 2012. "'Doing Time' in Carceral Space: TimeSpace and Carceral Geography." *Human Geography* 94, no. 4: 305–16.

Morgensen, Scott Lauria. 2011. *Spaces between Us: Queer Settler Colonialism and Indigenous Decolonization*. First Peoples: New Directions in Indigenous Studies Series. Minneapolis: University of Minnesota Press.

O'Connor, James. 1973. *The Fiscal Crisis of the State*. New York: St. Martin's.

Oshinsky, David M. 1996. *"Worse than Slavery": Parchman Farm and the Ordeal of Jim Crow Justice*. New York: Free Press.

Piepzna-Samarasinha, Leah Lakshmi. 2018. *Care Work: Dreaming Disability Justice*. Vancouver, BC: Arsenal Pulp.

Pisciotta, Alexander W. 1996. *Benevolent Repression: Social Control and the American Reformatory-Prison Movement*. New York: New York University Press.

Powell, Christopher. 2013. "Radical Relationism: A Proposal." In *Conceptualizing Relational Sociology: Ontological and Theoretical Issues*, edited by Christoher Powell and François Depelteau, 187–207. New York: Palgrave Macmillan.

Richie, Beth E. 2012. *Arrested Justice: Black Women, Violence, and America's Prison Nation*. New York: New York University Press.

Rodriguez, Dylan. 2003. "State Terror and the Reproduction of Imprisoned Dissent." *Social Identities* 9, no. 2: 183–203.

Schept, Judah Nathan. 2015. *Progressive Punishment: Job Loss, Jail Growth, and the Neoliberal Logic of Carceral Expansion*. New York: New York University Press.

Shakur, Assata. 2001. "Love." In *Assata: An Autobiography*, 130. Chicago: Hill.

Sharpe, Christina. 2016. *In the Wake: On Blackness and Being*. Durham, NC: Duke University Press.

Simpson, Audra. 2014. *Mohawk Interruptus: Political Life across the Borders of Settler States.* Durham, NC: Duke University Press.

Simpson, Leanne Betasamosake. 2014. "Land as Pedagogy: Nishnaabeg Intelligence and Rebellious Transformation." *Decolonization: Indigeneity, Education, and Society* 3, no. 3. jps.library .utoronto.ca/index.php/des/article/view/22170.

Simpson, Leanne Betasamosake. 2017. *As We Have Always Done: Indigenous Freedom through Radical Resistance.* Minneapolis: University of Minnesota Press.

Smith, Marquita R. 2018. "'Don't Be a Martyr': Kinship, Intimacy, and Carceral Care in Ava DuVernay's Middle of Nowhere." *Black Scholar* 48, no. 1: 6–19.

Snorton, C. Riley. 2017. *Black on Both Sides: A Racial History of Trans Identity.* Minneapolis: University of Minnesota Press.

Spade, Dean. 2018. "'Having a Cause' versus Living in a Life Centered in Radical Transformation." *Dean Spade* (blog), November 23. www.deanspade.net/2018/11/23/having-a-cause-versus -living-in-a-life-centered-in-radical-transformation/.

State of California Office of Administrative Law. 2018. Notice of Approval of Certificate of Compliance for "Transgender Inmates Authorized Personal Property Schedule" to CDCR, May 15, 2018.

Tourmaline, Cyrus Grace Dunham, and Constantina Zavitzanos. 2016. "Commencement Address at Hampshire College." May 17. www.reinagossett.com/commencement-address-hampshire -college.

Tuck, Eve, and K. Wayne Yang. 2014. "R-Words: Refusing Research." In *Humanizing Research: Decolonizing Qualitative Inquiry with Youth and Communities*, edited by Django Paris and Maisha T. Winn, 223–48. Thousand Oaks, CA: Sage.

Wing, Nick. 2016. "Our Bail System Is Leaving Innocent People to Die in Jail Because They're Poor." Justice Policy Institute, July 14. www.justicepolicy.org/news/10585.

Yazzie, Melanie K., and Cutcha Risling Baldy. 2018. "Introduction: Indigenous Peoples and the Politics of Water." *Decolonization: Indigeneity, Education, and Society* 7, no. 1.

Reproductive Injustice and the Politics of Trans Future in France

OLIVIA FIORILLI

Abstract This article tackles the issue of trans futures through a critical discussion of trans reproductive injustice in France. Most notably, it focuses on one of its many facets: the cisnormative administration of publicly funded gamete cryo-preservation. For a long time trans people in France have been excluded from the possibility of banking their gametes. Only recently the situation is starting to change, but the right of all trans people to cryo-preserve their gametes is far from being fully recognized. The first part of the article traces the genealogy of the exclusion of trans people from gamete cryo-preservation by offering some historical background of the necropolitical governance of trans reproduction in France. The second part explores in detail a public controversy over trans gamete cryo-preservation that emerged in 2013. Through a close reading of this controversy, the article tackles the discursive and material underpinnings of this cisnormative regulation of gamete cryo-preservation.

Keywords trans reproduction, trans embodiment, trans materialities, gamete cryo-preservation

This article aims at tackling the issue of trans future through a critical discussion of trans reproductive injustice in France (Ross 2006). After decades of state-mandated sterilization, in 2016 France passed a bill that bans sterility as a requisite for legal gender recognition.[1] Approved under the pressure of an anticipated condemnation by the European Court of Human Rights, the law has been criticized by most trans organizations because it fails to make legal gender recognition an administrative procedure based on self-determination (see, e.g., Existrans 2017), thus leaving to a judge the power to decide whether the applicant successfully "presents and *is recognized*" in their gender (art. 56, law 2016-1547, November 18, 2016). This leaves the door open to any form of cisnormative prejudice and to the further exclusion of the most isolated and poor among trans people (Equal 2017). Although the law has been presented by some as an endpoint to trans reproductive oppression, this is far from being the case.[2]

TSQ: Transgender Studies Quarterly * Volume 6, Number 4 * November 2019 **579**
DOI 10.1215/23289252-7771737   © 2019 Duke University Press

Despite its self-portrayal as a nation of human rights and gender freedom, France is not a country where reproductive self-determination of trans people is guaranteed. The forces that affect trans reproductive self-determination are multifaceted. The cisnormativity[3] ingrained in health care and social services (Bauer et al. 2009); discrimination in employment, housing, and education; construction of trans identities as deviant and pathological; structural racism; immigration enforcement; criminalization of sex workers and their clients; as well as cisgenderist (Lennon and Misler 2014) and trans-misogynist (Serano 2007) violence all contribute to making the lives of trans and gender-diverse people, and especially trans and gender-diverse people of color, precarious. As a consequence, all these phenomena affect their ability to make free reproductive decisions, to have children if and when they wish, as well as to parent them (Ross 2006). Furthermore, the barriers to reproductive and sexual health services encountered by trans people, especially those who are racialized, live with HIV/AIDS, practice sex work, and are more marginalized, have a devastating impact on their reproductive lives.[4] In addition, trans parenthood is virtually invisible in political debates. This is even more so for trans people of color. As denounced by the collective Queer et Trans Révolutionnaires, trans people of color face enormous reproductive oppressions in a context impregnated by colonialism and institutional racism, and their reproductive desires are erased in dominant political discourses (QTR 2017).

Trans reproductive oppression in France is generated by a complex web of interacting factors and takes different shapes. In this article I want to focus on one of its many facets: the long-lived exclusion of trans people from access to publicly funded gamete cryo-preservation. Since the first decade of the twenty-first century, when trans women started to claim access to publicly funded gamete cryo-preservation in France, the institutions responsible for publicly funded gamete storage and administration (Novaes 1994), the Centres d'Étude et de Conservation des Œufs et du Sperme Humains (CECOSs), have persistently rejected trans people's requests. This policy has been endorsed by important medical and bio-ethical institutions. Only in the last year have a small number of CECOSs started to accept trans people's demands. Despite this, the right of all trans people to bank their gametes before undergoing medical treatments is far from being granted in the whole country.

In the first part of the article I will trace the genealogy of the exclusion of trans people from gamete cryo-preservation. To do so, I will tackle the history of the necropolitical governance of trans reproduction in France. In the second part of the article—through a close reading of a public controversy over trans gamete cryo-preservation that emerged in 2013—I will tackle the discourses that rationalize the exclusion of trans people from this technology of fertility preservation.

Despite an expanding scholarship in trans studies (see, e.g., Beaubatie 2017; Bourcier 2018; Espineira 2015a, 2015b; Espineira, Thomas, and Alessandrin 2013; Gabriell 2016; Reucher 2005; Thomas, Grüsig, Espineira 2015) and a growing interest in trans parenting and trans men's pregnancy (Fortier 2015; Hérault 2014; Thomas 2010), the issue of trans gamete preservation has received virtually no scholarly attention in France (with the exception of Hérault 2015). The aim of this article is to make a contribution to trans studies and trans/feminist scholarship on reproductive justice by addressing the discursive and material underpinnings of the cisnormative administration of gamete cryo-preservation in France. The decision to focus on this topic also comes from the fact that as a white, nonbinary, assigned-female-at-birth person and transfeminist activist I feel the responsibility to avoid reproducing the erasure of issues that concern trans women and trans women of color from the conversation about reproductive justice and transfeminism. As micha cárdenas (2016) contends, transmasculine people have been center stage in conversations about transgender pregnancy and family planning, while trans women's reproductive concerns (in particular gamete preservation) have been mostly ignored, and trans women of color have been completely excluded from conversations on reproductive rights and reduced to an image of death. Hence my decision to focus on gamete preservation and its material accessibility as an issue that—while of interest also for transmasculine people—has been raised as a concern for trans women and trans women of color (cárdenas 2016).

Reproductive Troubles in France

The control of reproduction has long been a central feature of the administration of trans lives and embodiments in France. When the demand for gender-affirming genital surgeries emerged in France in the 1950s, the medical community fiercely rejected it. The medico-legal argument against gender-affirming medical surgery relied on the idea that such procedures would constitute an "unacceptable" form of voluntary "castration" (L'Ordre des Médecins 1962). Genital surgery was thus refused to trans people in the name of the biopolitical imperative to optimize the reproductive potential of the nation by denying people control over their own bodies. Considering that, at the time, the determination of legal gender relied on genital status, trans people were unable to change their gender marker in the civil register. Even trans and gender-diverse people who managed to get operated abroad and filed an application at a district court to have their legal gender reclassified on the grounds of a "mistake" were generally rejected unless they could prove to be intersex. The impossibility for trans people who were not intersex to change legal gender contributed to their further exposure to marginalization, criminalization, and premature death. The governance of gender variance changed its mode of operation in the 1970s. While gender transitions were simply repressed in the previous decades, in the 1970s a medico-legal apparatus of control was put in place to sort out trans people who were deemed "worthy" of reintegrating into society in their lived gender from those whose lives were to be subject to institutionalized neglect, abandonment, and slow death. Similarly to what was happening in other countries at the time, in the 1970s a group of physicians created a "protocol for the management of transsexualism" that soon received institutional recognition. Following this protocol, which, despite some changes, is still in use in public hospitals in France, a team made up of medical "experts" was supposed to sort out "true transsexuals" from those who were categorized as "transvestites," "homosexuals," or "prostitutes" (Breton, Frohwirth, and Pottiez 1985). Only "true transsexuals" could have access to gender-affirming hormonal and surgical treatments and, as a consequence, to legal gender change. As is immediately apparent, racially charged, heterosexual, and classist notions of productive citizenship and respectability played a fundamental role in the selection of "true transsexuals." As a number of authors have highlighted, medical notions of deserving trans subjects were and are based on white and middle-class values (Snorton and Haritaworn 2013; Vipond 2015). The trans and gender-diverse subjects who did not fit the criteria for inclusion in the protocols and were destined to institutional abandonment and neglect were those who did not have class privilege and occupied the position of the "racialized other" (Snorton and Haritaworn 2013).[5] For instance, Brazilian trans women who practiced sex work were portrayed as the quintessential image of the "false transsexual" in medical literature and seminars. This racially and socially charged notion of transnormativity still haunts the medical management of gender transitions in public hospitals. Although practicing sex work or being HIV positive are no longer formal criteria of exclusion from treatment, the most marginalized and precarious trans people—among whom people of color and migrants are disproportionally represented—still face enormous barriers in accessing these services (Beaubatie 2017).

Under the new regime of (trans)gender governance that emerged in the 1970s, the biopolitical (the medicalization of gender transitions) and the necropolitical (the institutionalized neglect and marginalization of nonconforming trans people) were coextensive. But the necropolitical investment of the state in impeding trans continuation was also evident in the fact that trans people who were allowed to reintegrate into society as their real gender were allowed to do so only on the condition that they undergo sterilization. Indeed, in the jurisprudence of the Supreme Court, which in the following years institutionalized a procedure for legal gender change, having undergone genital surgery or proving irreversible sterility were prerequisites for having one's legal gender changed (Hérault 2014). A fundamental role in the naturalization of this form of state-mandated sterilization was played by current medical discourses on "transsexualism." The "pioneers" of the emerging field of trans medicine in France openly invoked sterilization as a requisite for legal gender change (Breton et al. 1985: 162). In addition, medical discourses on "transsexualism"—in line with the theories elaborated by Harry Benjamin on the other side of the Atlantic—coded the desire/need for genital surgery as the central feature of the "transsexual phenomenon." As a consequence, these discourses naturalized the idea that all "real transsexuals" would want, by definition, to undergo surgery, thus hiding the coercive and violent character of state-mandated sterilization in the frame of legal gender change.

Furthermore, the medical discourse on transsexualism also contributed to naturalize sterility as the inevitable "price" for medically transitioning. As Trystan T. Cotten (2014: 205) remarks, "The desire for surgery . . . was also narrowly conceived as the reconstruction of morphological sex, which excluded trans people who wanted to keep their genitals intact from treatment." In the last years medical practices have evolved, and genital surgery is no longer a requisite for accessing gender-affirming treatments. Nevertheless, in France gender transitions that do not involve sterilizing surgery are still appraised as "incomplete" by some health professionals. Indeed, some of them consider it "unethical" to surgically treat people who do not want to undergo "a complete transition" (e.g., practice top surgery on someone who does not want genital surgery).[6] Given these circumstances, it is not surprising that the desire to preserve fertility, expressed by a growing number of trans people who undergo medical transitions, has been regarded as problematic by many health professionals. In 2012, the French Society for the Study and Treatment of Transness (Societé Française d'Études et de Prise en Charge de la Transidentité, SoFECT), a federation of professionals working in trans health care services in public hospitals, demanded the advice of the National Consultative Committee of Ethics on the issue of fertility preservation. The text of the request filed by such a well-established professional organization is emblematic of the medical community's violent hostility toward trans people's reproductive and bodily self-determination: "Should physicians keep on accepting to create anatomical and parental chimeras? That is to say: is it acceptable that we let a person who has been turned into a man by hormones and surgery keep his uterus and ovaries? Is it acceptable to preserve the sperm of a person who has been transformed into a woman?" (Revol 2014).

Besides being symptomatic of the attitude of some health professionals, the complaint filed by SoFECT also demonstrates that a growing number of trans people are openly voicing the desire to preserve their fertility. Despite multiple forms of reproductive oppression, trans and gender-diverse people in France as elsewhere have always had children (Leprince and Taurisson 2008). Since the

1980s, some trans men, together with their cis women partners, have started to demand access to assisted reproductive technologies (ART) and in particular donor insemination. As shown by Laurence Hérault (2015), while some trans men with their cis women partners are formally "allowed" to access donor insemination, their actual possibility to do so is violently policed. In fact, a special protocol was created requiring that trans men who want to access ART must be in a couple relationship with a cis woman—who is the only one allowed to carry the baby—be legally recognized as men, and be sterile. Furthermore, prospective trans service users must undergo special counseling with a psychiatrist.

Gamete cryo-preservation—especially "sperm" banking, which, unlike "egg" banking, is a simple and non-necessarily medically assisted technique[7]— has a relatively long history, but it became openly accessible to trans people in some countries only around the turn of the century.[8] It is difficult to determine when trans people—and most notably trans women—living in France started to bank their gametes abroad (e.g., in Belgium and Spain), but this practice is well known (OUTrans 2017). Nevertheless, this form of gamete cryo-preservation must be paid with people's own money. Since the first decade of the twenty-first century in France, some trans women started to claim access to publicly funded gamete banking through the CECOSs (Leprince and Taurisson 2008: 23). In fact, one of the missions of these institutions is "preserving the fertility of those men, women and children who undergo a treatment . . . that might compromise their fertility in the future" (CECOS n.d.). Nevertheless, trans women's demands have been persistently rejected.

The Controversy over Gamete Cryo-preservation

In the face of the rejection encountered while trying to access publicly funded gamete cryo-preservation, in 2013 a group of trans women, backed by some associations (Arc en Ciel Toulouse, Inter-LGBT, HES-Socialistes LGBT+, ADHEOS, and Association Informations et Dialogues sur les Transidentités), filed a complaint to the Défenseur des Droits (DD), an independent authority created in 2011 to defend people against discrimination and grant equal access to rights. Indeed, based on the Public Health Code, "any person who undergoes a medical treatment that might affect their fertility or whose fertility risks being prematurely altered has the right to preserve their gametes in view of the possibility to access ART in the future or to see their fertility reestablished" (Code de la Santé Publique 2019: article L. 2141-11). Given that gender-affirming medical treatments can have "devastating effects on fertility" (De Roo et al. 2016), the complainants noted that the exclusion of trans women from the possibility to preserve their gametes is a form of discrimination.

Before expressing its opinion, the DD asked a number of medical and bio-ethical institutions as well as regulatory bodies for advice. The National Medical

Council, the National Academy of Medicine (NAM), and the Agency of Bio-medicine (AB)—which provide ethical and expert advice on different issues including organ tissue/cell transplantation and ART—all responded to the call for advice.[9] NAM and the AB (more precisely, its advisory committee) also published reports in which they extensively tackled the issue of gamete preservation for trans people more broadly (i.e., transmasculine and transfeminine people) (L'Académie Nationale de Médecine 2014; Agence de la Biomédecine 2014).[10] This debate offers an overview of the discourses that justify the exclusion of trans people from the technology of fertility preservation.

The first argument against trans gamete cryo-preservation advanced by the above-mentioned institutions is the fact that, in the current legal framework, those gametes would supposedly be "impossible" to use. As of today in France ART—the only frame within which the use of cryo-preserved gametes is allowed—is available only to heterosexual couples (Gross, Courduriès, and Federico 2014).[11] Unmindful of the endless possibilities of human reproduction, these institutions assume that trans people might "reasonably" use their own gametes only within a gay or lesbian relationship or through surrogacy: as a consequence, gamete cryo-preservation is deemed pointless.

The second argument against trans gamete cryo-preservation is that it would not be justified on medical grounds, as demanded by Article L 2141-11 of the Public Health Code, which regulates access to this technology. For instance, NAM argues that trans people who want to have children shouldn't receive a medical recommendation for genital surgeries but instead should be prescribed treatments that do not irreversibly affect fertility (i.e., low-dose hormonal treatments) (L'Académie Nationale de Médecine 2014). In this case, fertility could be reestablished on cessation of treatment, and thus gamete cryo-preservation would be elective rather than medically justified. The argument of NAM relies on a number of cisnormative assumptions. First, it reiterates the cisgenderist idea that trans people should choose between their fertility and the possibility to actualize their gender identity through desired/needed bodily modification, including genital surgery. Second, it erases the fact that interrupting hormonal treatments to reestablish fertility can be a destabilizing and painful process (cárdenas 2016): some trans people simply cannot afford—emotionally, socially, or otherwise—to get out of hormone treatment. Once again, the implicit assumption here is that for the "comfort" of society and in the name of cisnormative ideas about reproduction trans people should not enjoy the highest attainable quality of care free of charge.

Indeed, the extensive reports elaborated by NAM and the AB make clear that the problem with trans gamete cryo-preservation lies with the fact that trans biological reproduction is considered a problem per se. Trans people who use their own gametes to conceive a child are considered "trouble" for the "founda-tions" of human reproduction (Agence de la Biomédecine 2014: 13), as appraised within a cisnormative and heteronormative framework. NAM, whose position on gamete cryo-preservation seems to be more nuanced, offers a slightly different iteration of this idea. Indeed the institution estimates that while trans gamete cryo-preservation cannot be forbidden in principle, it shouldn't be acknowledged as fully acceptable either. In meeting a demand for gamete cryo-preservation, medical professionals should "discuss with the applicant their parental project, without omitting the incoherence that this might generate between their personal, parental, and reproductive identity. On the other hand, the consequences of this project for the health of the baby shouldn't be ignored" (L'Académie Nationale de Médecine 2014: 630). The considerations of NAM rely on a cis-centered and transnormative (Vipond 2015) paradigm of gender and parenthood. In this paradigm the only trans people who are "coherently" gendered are those who appear and act as similar as possible to cis people, even in relation to reproduction and parenting. This paradigm creates a demarcation between ways of being trans that "deserve" recognition and ways that don't. But it also creates a separation between "deserving" and "undeserving" modes of trans reproduction (and par-enting), in which those who bear the strongest resemblance with cis-heterosexual modes of reproduction (e.g., sterile trans men accessing donor insemination with their cis partners) are the only ones "worth" recognition and public support in the form of access to publicly funded ART. In this way transnormativity, that is, "the normalization of trans bodies and identities through the adoption of cisgender institutions" (Vipond 2015: 24), is imposed on trans people who want to be parents. This transnormative way of sorting out deserving and undeserving ways of being trans and reproducing is also racially charged. As a number of authors have pointed out, whiteness is a requisite of transnormativity (Snorton and Haritaworn 2013; Vipond 2015). "Deserving" modes of reproduction and par-enting are also racially charged. As the collective Queer and Trans Révolu-tionnaires (QTR 2017) contends, racialization and class are the main cleavages along which "deserving" and "undeserving" families—including trans and queer families—are sorted out. The discourse of NAM thus contributes to reinforcing the structures that tend to exclude trans people of color from the possibility to form a family.

Furthermore, NAM's argument about the supposed incoherence between trans biological parents' parental, reproductive, and personal identity operates through the assumption that body parts and capacities are inherently gendered. This assumption represents a form of "reality enforcement" (Bettcher 2014) that, if pushed to its extreme consequences, invalidates all trans people's identities. What is at stake in this kind of argumentation is thus the possibility of trans future itself.

A further element introduced by the above-mentioned recommendation of NAM is a preoccupation with the "health of the child," who would be put at risk by the supposedly inherent incoherence of trans biological reproduction (L'Académie Nationale de Médecine 2014). A preoccupation that is also shared by the AB, the "risk" envisaged here is made clear in a passage of NAM's report that describes psychiatric studies on the health of trans parents' children (625–26). The report focuses especially on the way these studies address children's gender identity and expression. What is immediately evident is that the most important issue at stake is whether the children of trans parents are more likely to be trans or gender nonconforming themselves. This preoccupation relies on the cisgenderist idea that being trans and gender nonconforming is inherently unhealthy and that transness should be prevented. This makes immediately clear that these discourses are a menace to trans futures.

Despite these recommendations, in 2015 the DD ruled that on the basis of current legislation trans women who undergo hormonal treatments have the right to preserve their gametes. Indeed, following the DD's notice, current legislation on ART cannot be used as an excuse to prevent trans people from banking their gametes because (1) the law might change one day and ART could be made available to nonheterosexual couples, and (2) even today, trans women might use their gametes in compliance with current legislation in the framework of a heterosexual couple (e.g., in partnership with a transmasculine person) or before/ without changing their legal gender. Furthermore, the DD has confirmed that hormonal treatments fall under the definition of "medical treatment that might affect fertility" as outlined in Article L 2141-11 of the Public Health Code (Défenseur des Droits 2015).

Although the DD recognized that excluding trans women from the possibility to preserve their gametes is discriminatory, it has also reinforced some of the arguments underpinning this policy. Most notably, far from affirming the principle that trans women—and trans people in general—have the right to preserve their fertility regardless of their treatment choices, it has reiterated the idea that sterilizing surgery should not be considered as a medical treatment falling under Article L 2141-11 of the Public Health Code (Défenseur des Droits 2015: 7). In this frame the reproductive rights of trans people are still acknowledged as conditional to their transitional pathways. Moreover, the verdict of the DD has not produced a radical change in the policies applied in the twenty-nine CECOSs operating in France at present. Even though the verdict was issued in 2015, it is only in the last year that a few CECOSs operating in Paris and its outskirts, as well as in Lille and Nancy, have started to openly accept trans people's demands or are considering doing so.[12] Nevertheless, given the current legal and social framework of ART in France, trans people who have stored their gametes have virtually no way to reclaim them to conceive a child. Gamete cryo-preservation is also becoming a matter of debate in medical circles: in the 2018 conference of SoFECT, a panel was dedicated to fertility.[13] Some health professionals are assuming a more permissive attitude toward trans gamete cryo-preservation (Condat et al. 2018). Nevertheless, more research on the development of trans parents' children is still routinely invoked in the literature, while the cisgenderist biases that affect existing studies are never questioned (8). As long as transness and gender nonconformity are uncritically categorized as potential "adverse effects" for the offspring of trans parents, trans futures will continue to be in question.

Conclusion

In France the necropolitical management of trans reproduction and embodiment has a long history, with roots in the medical construction of "transsexualism." One of the many outcomes of this history is the long-lived exclusion of trans people from publicly funded gamete cryo-preservation. Although the situation seems to be gradually changing, trans people who want to preserve their gametes still face great limitations because of the lack of recognition of their right to do so. To date, only people living nearby one of the few existing CECOSs that accept trans demands and those who can afford the possibility to travel and/or to pay out of their pocket to bank their gametes abroad have the possibility to freely choose their transitional pathway while preserving their right to become parents. The exclusion of trans persons from gamete cryo-preservation in France contributes to keeping bodily and reproductive self-determination a privilege that is out of reach for most poor and trans people of color who are exposed to multiple forms of precarity.

In a recent article, A. J. Lowik (2018) reads state-mandated sterilization for legal gender change through the prism of the history of eugenics, and especially negative eugenics, whose aim was restricting or prohibiting the reproduction of those who were considered "unfit." "Much like negative eugenics strategies directed at people of color, Indigenous people, those with a history of incarceration and people with disabilities (among others), trans people have had their reproduction restricted under the guise of doing what is in the best interest of children" (425). Although the end of state-mandated sterilization in France has been acknowledged by some as the end of trans reproductive oppression, I argue that the necropolitical administration of trans reproduction is perpetrated in the continuing misrecognition of trans and gender-diverse people's right to reproduce. As Laura Nixon (2013) remarked, the lack of policies supporting trans reproduction can be read as a form of "passive eugenics." Indeed, the analysis of the discourses that underpin the exclusion of trans people from gamete cryo-preservation shows that this policy is rooted in a quite explicit form of eugenics that aims at writing transness out of the future. Indeed the cisnormative governance of publicly funded gamete cryo-preservation tries to write a future in which necropolitical imperatives will continue to regulate trans embodiment in order to exclude poor trans people and trans people of color from the "privilege" of becoming parents, thus perpetrating racist and classist reproductive oppressions. Multiple forms of resistance such as gonad preservation, DIY gamete banking, and alternative modes of reproduction already exist and are writing resilient trans futures, as shown by cárdenas (2016). However, resistance can come at a social and affective cost: it is time to end institutional reproductive injustice and let trans futures and multiple embodiments and reproductive pathways thrive.

Olivia Fiorilli is a transfeminist activist and postdoc fellow in the Globhealth ERC project based at Cermes3 in Paris. They authored *La signorina dell'igiene: Genere e biopolitica nella costruzione dell'infermiera moderna* (*Miss Hygiene: Gender and Biopolitics in the Making of Modern Nursing*; 2015) and coauthored with Michela Baldo and Rachele Borghi *Il Re nudo: Per un archivio drag king in Italia* (*The Naked King: Toward a Drag King Archive in Italy*; 2014).

Acknowledgments

All translations from French to English are my own. This article was supported by funding from the Institut Francilien Recherche Innovation et Societé and the European Research Council. I am grateful to all the inspiring trans activists that I met in the course of my research. I am also grateful to the reviewers for their insightful and stimulating comments. I thank Vick Virtu and Michela Baldo for their feedback and help with proofreading. Finally, I want to thank Anne for inspiration.

Notes

1. In sixteen European and Central Asian states sterilization is a requisite for gender recognition (TGEU 2019).
2. Furthermore, the new law makes the situation of trans parents even more vulnerable: if a trans parent wants to list their name and legal gender on their child's birth certificate, the other parent (if present) must approve, thus exposing the trans parent to possible threat (ACHTÉ 2017).
3. By *cisnormativity* I mean the assumption that being cisgender is more normal, healthy, and desirable then being trans. Cisnormativity impregnates most social institutions, including health care (Bauer et al. 2009) in Western societies. As a consequence of cisnormativity, trans people are expected to act as similarly as possible to cis people in order to be recognized.
4. Some organizations such as Acceptess-T, Espace Santé Trans, OUTrans, and others provide grassroots, community-based sexual and reproductive health services.
5. On the intersections between transness and racialization processes in the French context, see Gabriell 2016 and Boeuf et al. 2008.

6.   Eighth Congress of the French Society for the Study and Treatment of Transness (SoFECT), Lyon, October 6–7, 2017, field notes.

7.   The cryo-preservation of ejaculated "sperm" is generally a simple and relatively low-cost procedure. "Sperm" can also be extracted surgically. "Oocyte" cryo-preservation is a more complicated procedure that requires hormonal stimulation and medically assisted extraction.

8.   Since 2001 the Standards of Care of the World Professional Association for Transgender Health (WPATH) recognize that fertility options should be discussed with clients (Meyer et al. 2001).

9.   The National Consultative Ethical Committee has not responded to the call.

10. The report of NAM was elaborated by a working group, which included the vice president of the CECOS federation as well as prominent members of SoFECT.

11. While this paper was in press, the French Parliament started to examine a bill that might allow lesbian couples and single women (but not transmasculine people) to access ART. The new bill might also legalize gamete preservation "on demand," i.e., without medical justification. Nevertheless gamete preservation "on demand" will not be publicly funded.

12. An analysis of the criteria that are mobilized to accept trans people's demands is beyond the scope of this article.

13. Ninth conference of SoFECT, Paris, October 11–13, 2018.

References

L'Académie Nationale de Médecine and Pierre Jouannet. 2014. "Autoconservation des gamètes de personnes transsexuelles et projet parental éventuel" ("Preservation of Transsexual People's Gametes and Possible Parental Project"). *Bulletin de l'Académie Nationale de Médecine* (*Bulletin of the National Academy of Medicine*) 198, no. 3: 613–31.

ACTHÉ. 2017. "Changement d'état civil, un décret catastrophique pour la filiation trans" ("Legal Gender Change: The New Decree Is Catastrophic for Trans Filiation"). Press release, April 3. www.acthe.fr/actualites/230--cp-changement-detat-civil-un-decret-catastrophique-pour-la-filiation-trans.html.

Agence de la Biomédecine. 2014. *Avis du conseil d'orientation: Autoconservaiton des gametes de personnes transsexualles souhaitant proceder à un traitement de reassignation sexuelle* (*Ruling of the Board: Gamete Preservation for Transsexual People Who Want to Undergo a Sex Reassignment Treatment*). www.agencebiomedecine.fr/IMG/pdf/avisco_autoconservationgametes_juin2014.pdf.

Bauer, Greta R., Rebecca Hammond, Robb Travers, Matthias Kaay, Karin M. Hohenadel, and Michelle Boyce. 2009. "'I Don't Think This Is Theoretical; This Is Our Lives': How Erasure Impacts Health Care for Transgender People." *Journal of the Association of Nurses in Aids Care* 20, no. 5: 348–61.

Beaubatie, Emmanuel. 2017. "Transfuge de sexe: Genre, santé et sexualité dans les parcours d'hommes et de femmes trans en France" ("Sex Defectors: Gender, Health, and Sexuality in the Pathways of Trans Men and Trans Women'"). PhD diss., L'École des Hautes Études en Science Sociales.

Bettcher, Talia M. 2014. "Trapped in the Wrong Theory: Re-thinking Trans Oppression and Resistance." *Signs: Journal of Women in Culture and Society* 39, no. 2: 43–65.

Boeuf, Carine, Morty Diamond, Jin Haritaworn, Vincent He-say, Jean Bobby Noble, and Stephen Whittle. 2008. "Masculinités queer, trans et post-trans: Les rejetons du féminisme (Propos recueillis par Sam Bourcier et Pascale Molinier)" ("Trans, Queer, and Posttrans Masculinities: The Offspring of Feminism"). *Cahier du genre*, no. 45: 85–124.

Bourcier, Sam. 2018. *Queer Zones: La trilogie.* (*Queer Zones: The Trilogy*). Paris: Éditions Amsterdam.

Breton, Jaques, Charles Frohwirth, and Serge Pottiez. 1985. *Le transsexualisme: Étude noso-graphique et médico-légale: Rapport de medicine légale* (*Transsexualism: Nosographic and Medico-legal Study: Medico-legal Report*). Paris: Masson.

cárdenas, micha. 2016. "Pregnancy: Reproductive Futures in Trans of Color Feminism." *TSQ* 3, nos. 1–2: 48–57.

CECOS (Centre d'Étude et de Conservation des Œufs et du Sperme Humains). n.d. "Qu'est-ce qu'un Cecos ?" ("What Is a Cecos?"). www.cecos.org/node/4204 (accessed July 16, 2019).

Code de la Santé Publique. 2019. "Code de la Santé Publique." Version consolidé au 10 Juillet 2019. www.legifrance.gouv.fr/affichCode.do?cidTexte=LEGITEXT000006072665&dateTexte=20190716 (accessed July 16, 2019).

Condat, Agnés, Nicolas Mendes, Véronique Drouineaud, Nouria Gründler, Chrystelle Lagrange, Colette Chiland, Jean-Philippe Wolf, François Ansermet, and David Cohen. 2018. "Bio-technologies That Empower Transgender Persons to Self-Actualize as Individuals, Partner, Spouses, and Parents Are Defining New Ways to Conceive a Child: Psychological Con-siderations and Ethical Issues." *Philosophy, Ethics, and Humanities in Medicine* 13, no. 1: 3–11.

Cotten, Trystan T. 2014. "Surgery." *TSQ* 1, nos. 1–2: 205–7.

Défenseur des Droits. 2015. *Avis du Défenseur des droits MSP-2015-009* (*Ruling of the Rights Defender MSP-2015-009*).

De Roo, Chloë, Kelly Tilleman, Guy T'Sjoen, and Petra De Sutter. 2016. "Fertility Options in Transgender People." *International Review of Psychiatry* 28, no. 1: 112–19.

Equal. 2017. "Être transgenre en France aujourd'hui" ("Being Transgender in France Nowadays"). Seminar, February 2, SciencePo, Paris.

Espineira, Karine. 2015a. *Médiacultures: La transidentité en television. Une recherché menée sur un corpus à l'INA (1946–2010)* (*Mediacultures: Trans Identity on Television. Study on a INA Corpus [1946–2010]*). Paris: L'Harmattan.

Espineira, Karine. 2015b. *Transidentités: Ordre et panique du genre* (*Trans Identities: Gender Order and Panic*). Paris: L'Harmattan.

Espineira, Karine, Maud-Yeuse Thomas, and Arnaud Alessandrin. 2013. *La Trancyclopedie: Tout savoir sur les transidentités* (*Transencyclopedia: Everything about Trans Identities*). Paris: L'Harmattan.

Existrans. 2017. "Communiqué de presse—Existrans no. 21, samedi 21 octobre 2017." Press release, October 21. existrans.org/?page_id=391.

Fortier, Corinne. 2015. "Transparentalité: Vécus sensibles de parents et d'enfants (France, Qué-bec)" ("Transparenthood: Delicate Experiences of Parents and Children [France, Que-bec]"). *Enfances familles générations* (*Childhoods, Families, Generations*), no. 23: 148–64.

Gabriell, João. 2016. "In Defense of a Radical Trans Perspective in the French Context." In *Decolonizing Sexualities: Transnational Perspectives Critical Interventions*, edited by Sandeep Bakshi, Suhraiya Jivraj, and Silvia Posocco, 60–70. Oxford: Counterpress.

Gross, Martine, Jérôme Courduriès, and Ainhoa De Federico. 2014. "Le recours à l'AMP dans les familles homoparentales: État des lieux. Résultats d'une enquête menée en 2012" ("Homoparental Families and ATR: State of the Art. Results of an Enquiry Conducted in 2012"). *Socio-logos*, no. 9. journals.openedition.org/socio-logos/2870.

Hérault, Laurence, ed. 2014. *La parenté transgenre* (*Trans Kinship*). Aix-en-Provence: Presses Universitaires de Provence.

Hérault, Laurence. 2015. "La gestion médicale de la parenté trans en France" ("Medical Man-agement of Trans Kinship in France"). *Enfances familles générations* (*Childhoods, Families, Generations*), no. 23. journals.openedition.org/efg/396.

Lennon, Erica, and Brian J. Misler. 2014. "Cisgenderism." *TSQ*, 1 nos. 1–2: 63–64.

Leprince, Laura, and Natacha Taurisson. 2008. *Rapport de la commission sur la transparentalité* (*Report of the Commission on Trans Parenthood*). Paris: Homosexualité et Socialisme.

Lowik, A. J. 2018. "Reproducing Eugenics, Reproducing while Trans: The State Sterilization of Trans People." *Journal of GLBT Family Studies* 15, no. 5: 425–45

Meyer, Walter, III. 2001. *The Harry Benjamin International Gender Dysphoria Association's Standards of Care for Gender Identity Disorders*. 6th ver. www.cpath.ca/wp-content/uploads /2009/12/WPATHsocv6.pdf.

Nixon, Laura. 2013. "The Right to (Trans) Parent: A Reproductive Justice Approach to Reproductive Rights, Fertility, and Family-Building Issues Facing Transgender People." *William and Mary Journal of Race, Gender, and Social Justice* 20, no. 1. scholarship.law.wm .edu/wmjowl/vol20/iss1/5/.

Novaes, Simone. 1994. *Les passeurs des gamètes* (*Gamete Smugglers*). Nancy: Presses Universitaires de Nancy.

L'Ordre des Médecins. 1962. "Des incidences morales et déontologiques de certains acts médicaux" ("Moral and Deontological Stakes of Certain Medical Acts"). *Bulletin de l'Ordre des Médecins (Bulletin of the Medical Council)* 13, no. 1.

OUTrans. 2017. "Hormones et parcours trans" ("Hormones and Trans Pathways"). outrans.org /ressources/hormones-et-parcours-trans/.

QTR (Queer et Trans Révolutionnaires). 2017. "Réflexions sur la parentalité non hétéro, non blanche et prolo: Bienvenue dans la 4e dimension" ("Notes on Nonheterosexual, Non-white, and Working Class Parenthood: Welcome to the Fourth Dimension"). qtresistance .wordpress.com/2017/03/01/reflexions-sur-la-parentalite-non-hetero-racisee-et-prolo -bienvenue-dans-la-4e-dimension-partie-1/.

Reucher, Tom. 2005. "Quand les trans deviennent experts: Le dévenir trans de l'expertise" ("When Trans People Become Experts: Expertise Becomes Trans"). *Moltitudes* 1, no. 20: 159–64.

Revol, Marc. 2014. "Chirurgie, médecine et societé, le transsexualisme" ("Surgery, Medicine, and Society: Transsexualism"). Fondation de l'Avenir, May 7. Vimeo video, 30:50. vimeo.com /95724122.

Ross, Loretta. 2006. "Understanding Reproductive Justice." Atlanta: Sister Song. d3n8a8pro7vhmx .cloudfront.net/rrfp/pages/33/attachments/original/1456425809/Understanding_RJ_Sister song.pdf?1456425809.

Serano, Julia. 2007. *Whipping Girl: A Transsexual Woman on Sexism and the Scapegoating of Femininity*. Berkeley, CA: Seal.

Snorton, C. Riley, and Jin Haritaworn. 2013. "Trans Necropolitics: A Transsnational Reflection on Violence, Death, and the Trans of Color Afterlife." In *The Transgender Studies Reader 2*, edited by Susan Stryker and Aren Z. Aizura, 66–76. London: Routledge.

Thomas, Maud-Yeuse. 2010. *La transparentalité aujourd'hui* (*Transparenting Nowadays*). Documentary, 50 min. www.observatoire-des-transidentites.com/2010/11/13/article-la-trans parentalite-aujourd-hui-60882458/.

Thomas, Maud-Yeuse, Noomi B. Grüsig, and Karine Espineira, eds. 2015. *Transféminismes*. Cahiers de la Transidentité, no. 5. Observatoire des Transidentités. Paris: L'Harmattan.

TGEU (Transgender Europe). 2019. "Trans Rights Europe and Central Asia Map and Index 2019." tgeu.org/trans-rights-europe-central-asia-map-index-2019/.

Vipond, Evan. 2015. "Resisting Transnormativity: Challenging the Medicalization and Regulation of Trans Bodies." *Theory in Action* 8, no. 2: 21–44.

From Duration to Self-Identification?

The Temporal Politics of the California Gender Recognition Act

MARIE DRAZ

Abstract This article examines the temporal politics of the 2017 California Gender Recognition Act (CGRA). The author first offers a brief history of the dominant temporal requirements for "gender recognition" in prior legislation around sex/gender markers on identity documents in the United States and United Kingdom, focusing on how this legislation places temporal boundaries around legitimate gender identity. Then, turning directly to the CGRA, the author asks to what extent the act's emphasis on self-identification revises or intervenes in these prior conceptualizations of time and identity by the state administration of sex/gender systems. The article closes with an exploration of the temporality of identity documentation itself, speculating about how this legislation might be placed more directly into conversation with the role of time in colonial and racial state building.
Keywords temporality, identity documents, gender recognition acts, state practices

In "'Time isn't after us': Some Tiresian Durations," Trish Salah (2017: 19) writes: "As trans and genderqueer people, how are we asterisked, deferred, or opaque, waiting to be translated? We often live alongside ourselves, long towards selves that are not yet: at the level of the pronoun, in conversation, introductions, there are anticipatory and pre-emptive movements, flash forwards and flashbacks; misnamings may bring forward a past in what might be a supple and smooth redoubling of selves, or a violent displacement." The experiences of time described by Salah here—waiting, longing, flashing forward, flashing back—emerge against a backdrop of a normative temporality in which gender identity is understood as a single discoverable thread moving from a knowable past to a knowable future. Departures from this expected temporal script produce complex experiences of both time and identity, witnessed in moments when one's assigned past gender is not easily linked with one's present gender, or when a desired future (a name, a pronoun, a gender marker) is not yet thinkable according to the terms of the present. As Salah notes, these looping and disjunctive experiences of time gesture toward the multiple temporalities of trans and genderqueer experience.

TSQ: Transgender Studies Quarterly ★ Volume 6, Number 4 ★ November 2019
DOI 10.1215/23289252-7771751 © 2019 Duke University Press

At the level of narrative, transgender studies has documented how it is precisely this temporal complexity that has regularly been flattened to legitimate identity according to linear, progressive temporal models in which past, present, and future are seamlessly linked together. This temporal management can be seen, among other places, in the range of dominant representational options for trans experience (born in the wrong body, born this way, trapped in the wrong body, etc.), wherein chrononormativity, or how the expected time line of a life comes to have a normative force, is the guiding logic (Amin 2014; Freeman 2010). These frameworks tie the legitimacy of an identity with its persistence across time. While these frameworks work for some, for others they prove limiting (Spade 2003). For example, Janet Mock (2014: 16) reflects on how, in her autobiographical writing, she has often given reductively linear narratives of her identity—such as "always knowing" that she was a woman—to avoid being seen as mistaken, confused, or lost. When she writes that she has instead turned in recent years to embrace a messier version of the past, a version in which she perhaps did not "always know," she recognizes that she risks losing the legitimation offered by the "born this way" model. Despite the overwhelming evidence that trans lives cannot be reduced to this temporal sequencing, the options for representation repeatedly circle back to these tropes.

Turning directly to the role of the future in trans narratives further clarifies how ideas about time are used to manage sex/gender systems. Regularly cast in the part of anxiety-inducing harbinger of non-cis futures, trans identity continues to be represented in popular media as perpetually new and strange, trapped in rhetoric of discovery and fetishizing curiosity that performatively justifies vigilant forms of temporal discipline.[1] Owing in part to a common syllogistic slide between *trans* and *future* (Halberstam 2005), trans experience is often mediated according to the rubric of its potential disruption to a knowable future. As a result, both experience and narratives are regularly slotted into normative temporal schemas so that the cracking open of a predictable future—present in the above hauntings and anticipatory temporalities of Salah's "flash forwards and flashbacks"—is kept at bay.

The prevalence of anxiety around the future in discourse on trans issues is perhaps nowhere more apparent than in the management of sex/gender systems by state institutions. The temporal norms used within practices of identity documentation must in turn be situated in their constitutive relation to racial and colonial histories. As I will explore in greater detail below, state institutions have often connected the legitimacy of an identity with its duration across time. This practice has been especially important in identity documentation, in which the focus is on making citizens cohere with stable identity markers as a way to manage large populations (Caplan and Torpey 2001). Numerous theorists of colonialism have demonstrated how linear and progressive models of temporality have repeatedly been used to justify racial and colonial projects. Consider, for example, the portrayal of the colonized as "backward" and therefore in need of saving (Fabian 1983), or the imposition of a Western European view of time through colonial practices (Mignolo 2011; Vallega 2014). Given that sex/gender systems have also been tools of racial and colonial projects (Lugones 2007; Miranda 2010), the linear, progressive narrative by which transgender identity is so often legitimated by state institutions should be read as an extension of this racial and colonial use of time (Draz 2017; Fisher, Phillips, and Katri 2017).

In what follows, however, I examine a piece of legislation that seems to offer another temporal option: the 2017 California Gender Recognition Act (CGRA). I argue that temporality is a generative framework with which to think about both the promise and the limits of the CGRA. By removing the temporal requirements commonly emphasized in discussions around changing sex/gender markers on identity documents, the CGRA seems to represent a more general shift to recognition grounded in self-identification rather than duration. As a result, the CGRA appears to open trans futures, and multiple temporalities of gender more broadly, rather than insist that a particular temporal model must legitimate all trans identity.

By first situating the CGRA as a challenge to the more common model of gender as temporal duration, I clarify the implicit temporal politics of the legislation and the reasons it appears as such an important departure from the status quo. In moving next to raise questions about the extent to which the CGRA does in fact successfully offer a different temporal politics of state documentation, I follow Kadji Amin's (2014) emphasis on the need to think trans temporality in terms of both individual experience as well as the structural and historical production of options. In other words, it is important to keep in mind both the felt experience (and resistant navigation) of this particular legislation as well as the forms of possibility it represents. I therefore close by asking how we can think about the temporal politics of the CGRA in connection to colonial, national projects of administrative state building.

Gender as Duration

Before turning directly to the CGRA, it is necessary to situate the legislation within a broader context. The demands of trans rights movements have increasingly been perceived as threats to state institutions that rely on sex/gender markers as one way to create a link between administrative systems and individuals. As Joanne Meyerowitz (2002) explains, when individuals began showing up in United States courts in the mid-twentieth century requesting to change the sex on their birth certificates, the courts had few precedents or definitions of sex to rely on in the decisions. Historically, one of the ways state institutions have managed these potential disruptions to documentation practices is by declaring that the initial assignment of sex could not be changed. In this way, sex markers have been made to live in a document despite any resemblance these markers might bear to one's lived experience of gender. To read this use of sex/gender markers temporally is to see how a particular version of the past is maintained through the work of the document.[2]

While the practice of refusing to change a past assignment despite a present identification remains alive and well in contemporary United States, the temporal tactics used by state institutions to administer gender have shifted significantly over the last several decades. Beginning in the late twentieth century and early twenty-first century, new measures were developed for maintaining temporal boundaries around sex/gender systems in the face of challenges to the fixed status of sex markers. In response to the work of trans advocates, sex/gender reclassifications were slowly granted on some identity documents as long as there were both individual and medical testimony about the legitimacy of the identity claim.

Importantly, this medical legitimation has often been granted through the logic of duration, such as in the requirement that one has "always known" (that one was assigned to the wrong gender) or has "lived as" a particular gender for a set period of time. In temporal terms, the past assignment is treated as an error that can be altered through the reissuing of another past. The *telos* is a legible gendered future aligned with past evidence that always already pointed in that direction. In Sandy Stone's (1991: 295) well-known phrase, trans people are then "programmed to disappear" through medical or state recognition. In other words, even when changes are granted to these policies, the underlying view of time and identity has often remained untouched. In this particular strand of compromises, the length of time an identity has existed is regularly positioned as key to whether that identity should be validated by the state.

In recent years, however, this use of duration has shifted to focus more explicitly on the permanence of an identity. In their article on changes to sex designations on New York birth certificates between 1965 and 2006, Paisley Currah and Lisa Jean Moore (2009) identify the increased focus on the permanence of the change to a gender marker as part of an intensification of a concern about the future. Rather than a primary preoccupation with fraud—which fixates on the need to maintain a record of the past through the document—the "permanence" compromise increasingly showing up in legislative discussions in the early twenty-first century allowed for the granting of a new origin, or a new past, as long as the future is positioned as knowable. In the example of the New York City birth certificate debates, the temporary compromise struck was that there would still be medical testimony about the social permanence of the change, even if there was no agreed-on medical form of such a guarantee. This was a departure, Currah and Moore argue, from a primary concern with the past. Likewise, albeit more dramatically rendered, the UK Gender Recognition Act of 2004 was a significant victory for trans advocates, allowing for changes to gender markers; however, the legislation also came with a requirement that applicants affirmed their intent to stay in the granted gender "until death." As Emily Grabham (2010) argues in her article "Governing Permanence," this requirement attempts to alleviate anxiety about the future by linking trans subjects to cohesive, stable state temporal narratives.

These legislative examples speak to the larger relationship between time and state practices. In *The Political Value of Time* (2018), Elizabeth Cohen examines how time acquires normative force in state institutions. From waiting periods and sentences to benefits eligibility and age restrictions, rules around time have become one of the ways that the state sets boundaries around the acquisition of rights and political status. For example, the very idea of "immutable" characteristics protected by law is deeply embedded in Western legal systems. It is the lack of change, or the duration of an identity across time, that is often used to justify the legitimacy of a marginalized identity, especially when it comes to claims of discrimination. For this reason, it is unsurprising that this framework has played such a central role in trans rights claims. (This is, of course, one of many reasons the "born this way" narrative is so compelling.) Crucially for my purposes here, Cohen also emphasizes that time is an especially effective tool of governance precisely because its normative force so often goes unnoticed. As witnessed in the standardization of the clock and calendar, this use of time extends to the very foundation of nation-states (Anderson 2006). Michael Shapiro (2000: 80) puts the connection between time and state practices as follows: "The primary understanding of the modern 'nation' segment of the 'nation-state' is that a nation embodies a coherent culture, united on the basis of shared descent or, at least, incorporating a 'people' with a historically stable coherence." Time becomes one of the ways a "coherent [national] culture" is shaped and managed. Daily rhythms and schedules, etiquette (tardiness, etc.), and acceptable waiting periods all create a shared vocabulary and set of expectations that are rooted in temporal norms.

Given the link between temporal norms and the nation-state, it is no accident that debates around sex/gender markers are often explicitly racially charged. For example, in the New York City birth certificate debates, the need to protect the nation against possible foreign threats was one of the reasons cited that documents with reliable (i.e., enduring across time and not easily changed) sex/gender markers were necessary. As Currah and Moore (2009) note, state officials expressed anxiety around "not knowing who you are" and the need to guarantee the permanence (the future) of an issued identity marker. In this debate as well as in the 2004 UK Gender Recognition Act, the anxiety surrounding the potential decoupling of duration and the legitimacy of an identity was inextricable from the racialized maintenance of administrative state systems, as officials described the need to maintain "federal identity requirements vital records post 9/11" (Currah and Moore 2009: 129) and performed the "broader flows of nationalistic rhetoric in which many recent sexual citizenship initiatives operate" (Grabham 2010: 120). Furthermore, with the passage of the 2005 Real ID act in the United States, there is now a federal mandate that all states must mark sex on driver's licenses and state ID cards or lose the validity of the license as a federal document (Davis 2017: 36). While the act was ostensibly passed in order to secure the nation-state and in the context of post 9/11 racialized discourse around foreign threats, sex/gender enforcement is positioned as necessary for that protection.

Managing the future repeatedly emerges as a primary concern in these debates around sex/gender classification. The identity document is supposed to connect a person's past with their present and future in a way that makes that person legible to state institutions. The use of linear and progressive temporal frameworks becomes one way to link trans and gender-nonconforming subjects with a national narrative, thereby reinforcing administrative power and state time lines. This context helps explain why the state administration of gender has so often relied on a connection between duration (seen in frameworks such as fraud and permanence) and the legitimacy of an identity. This context is also what makes the 2017 California Gender Recognition Act appear to be such a departure from business as usual at the level of time, gender, and the state.

Gender as Self-Identification

On October 15, 2017, the California Gender Recognition Act (SB 179) was signed into law. Lauded as a significant victory for trans, gender-nonconforming, and intersex people, the CGRA responds to research and advocacy work on the harmful effects of a binary system of state gender classification for those who do not fall easily within its boundaries, as well as the significant privileges accorded to those for whom such paperwork is barely noticeable, much less a source of harm (Grant et al. 2011; James et al. 2016; Spade 2015).[3] In addition to adding a third gender option (nonbinary) on state-issued identity documents, including birth certificates, the CGRA also removes the requirement that petitioners requesting a change of gender marker must present a physician-signed affidavit that they have undergone "clinically appropriate treatment for the purposes of transition." The legislation made California the first US state to issue comprehensive legislation providing a third gender option on all state identification documents (including birth certificates).[4] In what follows, I first read the legislation as representing a move to self-identification before focusing my analysis on two areas of the CGRA where temporality is at the fore: the discussions of fraud and provisional gender designations. By questioning these aspects of the legislation, I examine the extent to which it represents a transformation of temporal politics at the intersection of identity and state institutions.

The CGRA declares that gender is a "fundamentally personal" matter. For this reason, it can be understood as a significant move away from prior legislation that reinforces the connection between the duration of an identity and its legitimacy (i.e., either refusing to change the initial assignment or requiring affidavits concerning how long the identity has existed or is promised to exist).[5] Against this history, the CGRA places emphasis instead on the idea of gender as self-identification. Indeed, the idea of "self-attesting" to one's own gender has been an important cornerstone of activism by groups like the Sylvia Rivera Law Project (SRLP), which states the ability to self-identify as one of its central goals in its work on birth certificate gender markers in New York City and New York State. The CGRA therefore appears to remove the external institutional validation of gender (as evident in the lifting of the physician affidavit). While this is a striking change from prior legislation in California, its significance increases tenfold when placed within a larger history of legal and medical requirements, as briefly explored in the last section.

At present, there is a disorienting divergence in gender marker legislation between this recent move to self-identification, as represented by the CGRA, and the "permanence requirements," rooted in the model of gender as duration. On the one hand, in addition to the CGRA there are other examples of the lifting of "permanence" compromises: for example, the 2004 UK Gender Recognition Act has recently been debated along these lines, and the permanence affidavit has been successfully lifted from New York City birth certificate change requests as the result of hard-fought advocacy work from groups such as the SRLP. On the other hand, on the national level in the United States and across many states we also see a current reentrenchment of the sex-as-immutable origin story, an idea that relies on the legitimation of identities frozen in time (in this case, through an assignment given at birth that is supposed to stay the same throughout one's life).

Initially, self-identification appears to offer an alternative to the temporal rules set by state institutions around legitimate gender identity, affirming instead the multiple temporalities of gender that have been so regularly disallowed by the medical and legal understanding of gender transition. Rather than establishing specific criteria for the temporality of legitimate identity, the emphasis shifts instead to subjective interiority, an emphasis echoed in the insistence of the CGRA that gender is "fundamentally personal." (This reading of the CGRA is also apparent in the opposition to the bill, which disapprovingly named it the "pick your own gender" bill.) It is therefore tempting to think of the CGRA as opening trans futures in a way that at least potentially makes gender a more capacious category for everyone. Moreover, given that the linear, progressive model of gender identity has also been a tool of racial and colonial hierarchies, one could read the move to self-identification as furthering an anticolonial, antiracist politics as well. However, the temporal politics of this legislation is far from this straightforward. Temporality is a useful framework with which to simultaneously acknowledge the transformative aspects of legislation like the CGRA while also remaining critical about the extent to which it adequately represents a reworking of temporal politics at the level of state institutions.

Within the CGRA, there are several indications that the temporal politics of the legislation deserves closer attention. Recall that Currah, Moore, and Grabham all situate the permanence requirements as representing a shift from a primary concern with fraud (as a concern with the past) to a primary concern with controlling the future. While there are no explicit permanence requirements in the CGRA, it is significant that the language of fraud is used. The legislation states that the purpose of the request for a change of gender must be "to conform the person's legal gender to the person's gender identity and not for any fraudulent purpose." It is then noted that this potential for a fraudulent purpose "creates a crime." The charge of fraud has historically been "proven" with reference to the original gender assignment given at birth and preserved in a document. While those seeking to change a gender classification were once necessarily perceived as fraudulent, because such a change was not seen as possible and therefore was construed as necessarily attempting to conceal a past truth, here the possibility of fraud is negotiated through an emphasis on individual intent. Fraud continues to offer a way for state institutions to maintain a link to the idea that the document should preserve a truth about the person requesting a gender marker change. The difference is that that truth has shifted in the CGRA from an original, externally imposed assignment to a self-assessment. In this case, that mandated truth is that the document ("legal gender") should reflect a person's lived gender ("gender identity"), ostensibly in the present.

The significance of this language of fraud becomes even more apparent when turning to one of the few places where temporal language is explicitly used in the CGRA, which occurs in the discussion of intersex people. Here, it is emphasized that for intersex people it is especially important to be able to have a third option, or a nonbinary option, because a *provisional* gender designation" (emphasis added) is often necessary. For intersex people, then, such a provision may be mutable and temporary precisely because self-identification may not yet be clear. Through this language of provisionality, the third option of nonbinary becomes a category that is curiously marked by time. By contrast with a third, more provisional category, the two remaining categories of male and female are implicitly granted a more permanent status. Temporality appears to be one of the ways the third category is used to reconsolidate the normative status of the binary.

With the CGRA's use of fraud in mind, it is unclear what makes one gender marker more provisional than others. By testifying that one is changing one's marker for nonfraudulent reasons, one seems to claim that the document accurately reflects one's present, lived gender. When paired with the explicitly temporal language of a "provisional" third option in the section on intersex issues, the legislation indicates the belief that for most people this will not be a provisional designation. However, the temporal boundaries of this provisional status are vague. It remains unclear how often a person could change their gender classification, or even how quickly—after realizing that a gender marker no longer (to quote the legislation) "adequately conforms legal gender to gender identity"— one must request a change to avoid fraudulent purpose. In taking up these questions, it becomes clearer that there remains an expectation that the document, for most people, will continue to reflect an accurate relationship between person and gender marker. The language of provisionality in the case of intersex people therefore opens a line of questioning about the temporal limits of a framework of self-identification when dealing with identity documentation.

As suggested by the above questions, one way to see the limits of this focus on self-identification is to turn to the temporal function of the document itself. Despite the lifting of specific requirements for gender markers, the document still reflects a particular relation between time and identity that serves state institutions. In other words, the document continues to serve a promissory function that is supposed to project the present of the document holder into the future. The document continues to freeze a moment of identification in time. This line of questioning speaks directly to Grabham's examination of how the permanence requirement in the 2004 UK Gender Recognition Act forecloses postrecognition becoming, or what I am calling here the difficulty of thinking gender beyond duration. While there is one reading in which the CGRA affirms the present, lived experience of gender, the document (and its record) remains. Returning to the opening statement of the legislation that gender is a "fundamentally personal issue" is especially instructive in this regard. The emphasis on personal choice and preference—the three options (male, female, nonbinary) are described as "equally recognized" in the legislation—covers over the compulsory nature of this system of documentation. There is an important disconnect between the statements that gender is "personal" and that gender must be recognized as one of three options on a state-mandated identity document.[6] The questions left unanswered here (such as why gender markers are necessary at all on state identity documentation) indicate the limits of the move to self-identification offered by this legislation. In legislation like the CGRA that does loosen some of the more explicit forms of temporal gender management, the turn to self-identification must force—rather than distract from—the question of gender documentation more generally. I conclude now by gesturing to some of the questions that should be a part of this more direct reckoning with the temporality of identity documentation.

Documenting Time

In *Sleights of Reason*, Mary Beth Mader (2011: 3) argues that we should become more attuned to the "conceptual collaborations that function as switches or ruses important to the continuing centrality and pertinence [of a given social category such as sex]." The fictive category of sex, Mader writes, is a particularly "busy, gregarious one that operates with a loyal crowd of conceptual friends" (3). Trans studies scholars have thoroughly documented the slippery definitions of sex and gender at work in medical and legal institutions (e.g., Spade 2003; Latham 2017). In the state administration of sex/gender, there are any number of inconsistencies or, in Mader's terms, "sleights of reason" that can create problems for trans and gender-nonconforming people. These shifting "conceptual friends" allow sex/gender to maintain the multiple footholds of power necessary for state systems that seek to map and manage large groups of people. When one node is disproven (or a definition of sex is shown to be inconsistent in a way that cannot be ignored), another emerges to save the day.

The function of the identity document is key here. In Jane Caplan's (2001: 50) words, the identity document seeks to stabilize the "unruliness" at the heart of identity and identification so that state agencies can continue to collect data and track groups of people. Sex/gender systems have been key conduit points for this stabilization of the population, especially insofar as they have offered ways for the state to "stick" to those within its borders. As debates around changes to gender classification make clear (recall the anxiety on the part of New York state officials that "we won't know who you are"), this use of sex/gender markers is inseparable from nation-building practices. These practices, in turn, are steeped in the history of how binaristic notions of sex/gender have been tools of colonial, racial state building.

Approaching the CGRA through the question of "conceptual collaborations" asks us to pay attention to the switches or ruses through which sex/gender systems (and the racial systems with which they are intermeshed) continue in different forms. Here I have explored the idea that the shift to self-identification, especially accompanied by the third gender option, might be one of those ruses. By looking at the CGRA as an example of legislation that appears to offer an alternative to traditional temporal requirements for gender classification, I have argued that it is important to witness the significant changes wrought by this legislation while simultaneously remaining critical about the extent to which it adequately responds to the problems of identity documentation more broadly. Even without an explicit requirement of permanence, it is necessary to situate the identity document itself as a temporal mechanism that fixes a point between citizen and state. The temporality of recognition, when formalized in a document, continues to solidify a particular version of past, present, and future. To understand why this aspect of identity documentation is a problem, it is important to think about how the many "sleights of reason" constituting categories of sex and gender operate in the service of administrative systems that rely on these contact points between systems and individuals.

An alternative vision of documentation would question both the particular requirements for access to gender markers and the temporal function of identity documentation more broadly. To think the temporality of the document is not only to ask how the document itself persists across time but also how practices of documentation participate in precisely the kinds of temporal narratives of recognition foundational to administrative systems. For example, given the use of time to legitimate identity claims (on both an individual and state level), it is no accident that prior to the CGRA, a 2011 California law loosening the requirements for legal gender change was titled the "Vital Records Modernization Act" (VMRA). The language of modernization marks the legislation as participating in a particular narrative about time; to modernize is to update, to leave the past behind, to be ahead of the curve. Considering that the language of modernization relies on the idea that prior legislation was outdated, the 2011 act was portrayed as propelling California into the future, marking in particular its status as a progressive front-runner of trans and gender-nonconforming rights. The CGRA is therefore situated as fulfilling that modernizing promise. The legitimating force here is directed to state institutions; the movement into the future is used to justify the continuation of state practices (for example, maintaining record-keeping and classification schemes) that are bound up with the regulation of bodies and populations. To continue analyzing the temporal politics of the CGRA, then, should involve both looking at the specific requirements for identity markers and asking how nation-state building is still at work in the temporal function of identity documentation more broadly. Time becomes an analytic framework brought to bear not only on the legislation itself but also on the performative role of the legislation in crafting particular narratives about the past, present, and future of state practices.

To be clear, the testimony in support of this legislation powerfully explains the need for an alternative to the status quo. Again and again, people speak to the effects of having documents that do not appear to line up with their gender, and the discriminatory effects faced as a result. To state this need for continued reflection about this legislation is not intended to deny that the CGRA is the result of many years of hard work on the part of trans, intersex, and nonbinary activists working within serious constraints. It is to say again, however, that work of state recognition continues to require compromises and that the implicit agreements of these compromises should be closely examined for what Grabham (2010: 123) calls the "temporal effects" of rights projects. The move to self-identification and the addition of a third option for gender markers can therefore be simultaneously emancipatory and insidious, perhaps allowing for some degree of freedom on an individual level while potentially also distracting from the question of how temporal mechanisms of power remain at work in the documentation itself. The framework of time allows us to hold onto the dual function of temporality: both the individual experience of the document as well as the larger temporal narratives this kind of legislation participates in, narratives that are in turn tied to the legitimating performances of state administration and wrapped up with the racial and colonial use of time to establish legitimate identity, whether of nation-states or groups of people.

Trans futures have historically been managed through the state administration of sex/gender systems, which is not to minimize the myriad of ways that people creatively resist and thrive alongside, in response to, such management. Against this history, the CGRA is situated as progressive, as a sign of the future, and in particular as opening trans, nonbinary, and intersex futures. The language of self-identification, bolstered by rhetoric of personal preference and choice, promises a kind of flexibility that has not traditionally been offered by administrative systems. And yet the practice of state-issued gender documentation remains. It is necessary then, in raising questions about such legislation, to affirm efforts to think gender beyond duration while also continuing to think expansively about how and why sex/gender systems are made to endure in particular forms. What would it mean to think gender beyond duration, even or perhaps especially at the level of the identity document?

Marie Draz is assistant professor of philosophy at San Diego State University. Her scholarship has recently appeared in *PhiloSOPHIA: A Journal of Continental Feminism* (2017), the *Journal of Speculative Philosophy* (2017), and *Feminist Philosophy Quarterly* (2018).

Acknowledgments

The research for this article was supported by the University Grants Program at San Diego State University. I also thank *TSQ*'s editors and anonymous reviewers for their helpful feedback.

Notes

1. See Marvin (forthcoming) on the kind of curiosity that constricts trans experience. See Snorton 2017, especially chap. 5, for a discussion of the perpetual emphasis of newness in relation to the media coverage of Brandon Teena's murder. The point could also be extended to analyze the similar rhetoric at work in the coverage of Caitlyn Jenner and Christine Jorgensen across a period of more than fifty years.
2. Lars Mackenzie (2017) describes the effects of this preservation of the past through a sex marker assigned at birth as the "haunting" of documents, or the ways that the past is made to "linger" through administrative systems.
3. The critical response to SB 179 centered around two primary issues: identity fraud and Title IX. Conservative political groups also argue that the bill "endangers women and children" (Keller 2017). While responding to these critiques is not the focus of this essay, see McQueen 2016 for a response to the way the rhetoric of feminism (i.e., concern about women) and trans politics are so often pitted against each other in these legislation debates.
4. At the time of the signing of the CGRA, Washington, DC, and Oregon offered a nonbinary designation on driver's licenses and state-issued ID cards (without a required medical affidavit); however, the California legislation is arguably the first of its kind by also offering the nonbinary designation on birth certificates as well as a more comprehensive state-wide legal recognition of nonbinary gender. For an overview of current legislation around name and gender markers on state and federal IDs and records, see the National Center for Transgender Equality's online ID Documents Center.
5. I am indebted to Cassius Adair's (2019) unpublished manuscript "Is Transsexuality Chronic?" for its helpful framing of the problem of thinking the temporal boundaries of trans identity.
6. See Davis 2017 for an analysis of where and why sex/gender classification is needed, and how often such classification is included as part of a database or document without any clear need.

References

Adair, Cassius. 2019. "Is Transsexuality Chronic?" Unpublished manuscript.

Amin, Kadji. 2014. "Temporality." *TSQ* 1, nos. 1–2: 219–22.

Anderson, Benedict. 2006. *Imagined Communities: Reflections on the Origin and Spread of Nationalism.* New York: Verso.

Caplan, Jane. 2001. "'This or That Particular Person': Protocols of Identification in Nineteenth-Century Europe." In *Documenting Individual Identity: The Development of State Practices in the Modern World*, edited by Jane Caplan and John Torrey, 49–66. Princeton, NJ: Princeton University Press.

Caplan, Jane, and John Torpey, eds. 2001. *Documenting Individual Identity: The Development of State Practices in the Modern World.* Princeton, NJ: Princeton University Press.

Cohen, Elizabeth. 2018. *The Political Value of Time: Citizenship, Duration, and Democratic Justice.* Cambridge: Cambridge University Press.

Currah, Paisley, and Lisa Jean Moore. 2009. "'We Won't Know Who You Are': Contesting Sex Designations in New York City Birth Certificates." *Hypatia* 24, no. 3: 113–35.

Davis, Heath Fogg. 2017. *Beyond Trans: Does Gender Matter?* New York: New York University Press.

Draz, Marie. 2017. "Born This Way? Time and the Coloniality of Gender." *Journal of Speculative Philosophy* 31, no. 3: 372–84.

Fabian, Johannes. 1983. *Time and the Other: How Anthropology Makes Its Object*. New York: Columbia University Press.

Fisher, Simon D. Elin, Rasheedah Phillips, and Ido H. Katri. 2017. "Introduction: Trans Temporalities." *Somatechnics* 7, no. 1: 1–15.

Freeman, Elizabeth. 2010. *Time Binds: Queer Temporalities, Queer Histories*. Durham, NC: Duke University Press.

Grabham, Emily. 2010. "Governing Permanence: Trans Subjects, Time, and the Gender Recognition Act." *Social and Legal Studies* 19, no. 1: 107–26.

Grant, Jaime M., Lisa A. Mottet, Justin Tanis, Jack Harrison, Jody L. Herman, and Mara Keisling. 2011. *Injustice at Every Turn: A Report of the National Transgender Discrimination Survey*. Washington, DC: National Center for Transgender Equality and National Gay and Lesbian Task Force.

Halberstam, Jack. 2005. *In a Queer Time and Place: Transgender Bodies, Subcultural Lives*. New York: New York University Press.

James, Sandy E., Jody L. Herman, Susan Rankin, Mara Keisling, Lisa Mottet, and Ma'ayan Anafi. 2016. *The Report of the 2015 U.S. Transgender Survey*. Washington, DC: National Center for Transgender Equality.

Keller, Jonathan. 2017. "Three Serious Problems in California's Gender Identity Bill." *San Diego Union-Tribune*, July 12. www.sandiegouniontribune.com/opinion/commentary/sd-utbg -gender-identity-opposition-20170712-story.html.

Latham, J. R. 2017. "(Re)Making Sex: A Praxiography of the Gender Clinic." *Feminist Theory* 18, no. 2: 177–204.

Lugones, María. 2007. "Heterosexualism and the Colonial/Modern Gender System." *Hypatia* 22, no. 1: 186–209.

Mackenzie, Lars. 2017. "The Afterlife of Data Identity, Surveillance, and Capitalism in Trans Credit Reporting." *TSQ* 4, no. 1: 45–60.

Mader, Mary Beth. 2011. *Sleights of Reason: Norm, Bisexuality, Development*. Albany: SUNY Press.

Marvin, Amy. Forthcoming. "Transsexuality, the Curio, and the Transgender Tipping Point." In *Curiosity Studies: Toward a New Ecology of Knowledge*, edited by Perry Zurn and Arjun Shankar. Minneapolis: University of Minnesota Press.

McQueen, Paddy. 2016. "Feminist and Trans Perspectives on Identity and the UK Gender Recognition Act." *British Journal of Politics and International Relations* 18, no. 3: 671–87.

Meyerowitz, Joanne. 2004. *How Sex Changed: A History of Transsexuality in the United States*. Cambridge, MA: Harvard University Press.

Mignolo, Walter. 2011. *The Darker Side of Western Modernity: Global Futures, Decolonial Options*. Durham, NC: Duke University Press.

Miranda, Deborah. 2010. "Extermination of the Joyas: Gendercide in Spanish California." *GLQ* 16, nos. 1–2: 253–84.

Mock, Janet. 2014. *Redefining Realness: My Path to Womanhood, Identity, Love, and So Much More*. New York: Simon and Schuster.

National Center for Transgender Equality. n.d. "ID Documents Center." transequality.org /documents.

Salah, Trish. 2017. "'Time isn't after us': Some Tiresian Durations." *Somatechnics* 7, no. 1: 16–33.

Shapiro, Michael. 2000. "National Times and Other Times: Re-thinking Citizenship." *Cultural Studies* 14, no. 1: 79–98.

Snorton, C. Riley. 2017. *Black on Both Sides: A Racial History of Trans Identity*. Minneapolis: University of Minnesota Press.

Spade, Dean. 2003. "Resisting Medicine, Re/Modeling Gender." *Berkeley Women's Law Journal* 18, no. 5: 15–37.

Spade, Dean. 2015. *Normal Life: Administrative Violence, Critical Trans Politics, and the Limits of Law*. Durham, NC: Duke University Press.

Stone, Sandy. 1991. "The *Empire* Strikes Back: A Posttranssexual Manifesto." In *Body Guards: The Cultural Politics of Gender Ambiguity*, edited by Julia Epstein and Kristina Straub, 280–304. New York: Routledge.

Vallega, Alejandro. 2014. *Latin American Philosophy from Identity to Radical Exteriority*. Bloomington: Indiana University Press.

Imagining Otherwise

Transgender and Queer Youth of Color Who Contest
Standardized Futures in Secondary Schools

BESS COLLINS VAN ASSELT

Abstract This article explores the life history of Sam, a queer and transgender youth of color who contests standardized futures in secondary schools. Sam's school life is rife with expectations that seek to confine Sam and their way of being in the world. In response to their school life, Sam forwards new ways of thinking of the future that rely on remaining present, contesting identity politics and questioning the contours of humanity.
Keywords youth, transgender, Afropessimism, queer, education, standardization

Youth are consistently framed as out of control. The idea that their bodies are full of raging hormones, that they are susceptible to media, and that they are immature bolsters the need for proper direction and supervision from adults (Talburt and Lesko 2012). This is especially true in public secondary schools, where the national policy is to train teachers systematically so that they can offer differentiated education based on each student's level of development. These educational paths of success that are available to students are often racialized projects fueled by increasing standardization and neoliberal policies like the No Child Left Behind Act (NCLB) and Race to the Top (RTTT).

There is, as Zeus Leonardo (2007: 263) explains, "an absent marker of whiteness that defines the Standards Movement." As white supremacy is veiled by color-blind national policies like NCLB and RTTT, students of color are often blamed when they fail to meet the academic benchmarks as outlined by neoliberal school reforms. Policed by this "unspoken whiteness," students of color face the punishment of underachievement (e.g., not being able to graduate, being taught to the test) while educational policy makers "forget about the structural reasons for school failure" (263–64). At the same time, white students who continue to meet these academic requirements "receive a similar but beneficial message: that

TSQ: Transgender Studies Quarterly * Volume 6, Number 4 * November 2019
DOI 10.1215/23289252-7771765   © 2019 Duke University Press

their merit is entirely theirs" (264). Progress is thus embodied and perpetuated by the white student. The white student, emboldened by their success, also greatly benefits from the status of being fully human, which translates to the status of being fully a student—a subject that is "teachable" and considered a "knower" (608). Whereas students of color, as they have been relegated to the status of subhuman, are constructed as nonstudents and uneducable.

The soul-crushing outcome of these national policies means that learning or what Leigh Patel (2016: 397) describes as "departing from known automatic practices, venturing into experiences that aren't wholly predictable," and thereby transforming oneself and others, is not actually happening in schools. Instead, learning is replaced with ideas such as achievement that aim to stratify students into proper order. In this kind of schooling environment, transgender and queer youth of color are left with a curriculum that advances and ordains one type of mindset. This further perpetuates an inability to explore alternative worlds and futures or to actually learn. As Jonathan Grady, Rigoberto Marquez, and Peter McLaren (2012: 989) aptly explain, "Queer youth of color are not allowed to think. If they are not allowed to think, then essentially they are proscribed from exerting protagonist power in and on the world around them or even to exist as queer." Neoliberal school policies leave them with the question: "How do I survive on my own?" (989).

In my work with queer and transgender youth, I have found that, similar to Grady's sentiments, their ideas of the future stand in stark contrast to what schools offer them. The schools they attend often neglect the ways in which queer and transgender youth of color use their unique positioning and embodiments to generate new forms of knowledge and ways of being. In particular, Sam, a mixed-race (black and white), gender-fluid, pansexual, vegan witch, consistently questioned the nonsensical and teleological frameworks that schools attempted to place onto them. They argued throughout their interviews that the school favored white athletic bodies and programs like Advancement Via Individual Determination (AVID), which made them feel overwhelmingly inadequate. Instead of following the future hopes of school, Sam found a way to stay present and conceptualize time and space as endless. This allowed them moments of reprieve in an overcategorized world. As Sam played with creative ways of defining their body and desires, they also pushed against the confines of identity politics, white supremacy, and humanism and attempted to find some solace in leisure and the virtual. Finally, Sam momentarily identified one place in school where time and caring shifted so that they could revel in their weirdness and difference in a way that did not rely on the logics of standardized schooling and bleak futures.

Sam

Sam and I met at a queer and transgender youth storytelling and performance group that I mentored. The group did local public performances that raised awareness around issues faced by queer and transgender youth and, more specifically, queer and transgender youth of color. Topics such as being falsely accused of cheating, suicide, getting into trouble at school, and trying to figure out their place in the world were common. I asked Sam and several others if they would like to collaborate around creating their life history. I explained that the project was a way for them to tell their stories so that schools could ultimately change. Sam agreed, and for the next year we met and crafted an extensive life history that engaged the multimodal artifacts that make up Sam's life. Sam has read and commented on two versions of this particular piece of writing and has shared the pieces with their parents.

Struggling against Whiteness and Time

During our interviews, Sam attended a predominantly white (70 percent) secondary school that housed grades ten through twelve. The school ranks as a seven out of ten overall on greatschools.org but scored a meager one out of ten in their equity overview. The students and community suffered a loss of one of its black students to police violence in the spring of 2015. Years later, the school is still trying to open up dialogue and has been making local news for tweets by teachers who find the dialogue uncomfortable. Throughout the interviews, Sam relayed stories of bus rides with white supremacists, an overwhelming jock culture that was fostered by the school's attention to athletics, a burgeoning conservative force of students after the election of Donald Trump, and countless setbacks. Along with the antiblack sentiments at the school and in the wider community, Sam also explained a slow and painful process in which school went from fun to rote and meaningless. They explained, "School is not happiness anymore. It used to be, it used to be, like, yay, alright! Time to learn! But now I'm like, why are you making me learn these things in this way only? I don't like it. It's too restricting now." They elucidated further:

> School is meaningless. Meaningless. There's so many athletic white people, it's just, that's how it is and I hate it, like, ugh. Why is everyone athletic and white? They can do things for longer than I can do things. Like, even the people who are, like, "Ugh . . . I have to go up all these stairs . . . it sucks." I'm, like, "same. . . . " And then, there's the kids who take them three at a time, it's like, "Can you not?" Like, I'm clutching onto the railing for dear life, jeez. . . . We're all struggling right now, we're all trying to live and succeed and not drown in life. We're about to be seniors, we need to do all these things . . . all these things . . .

"School is meaningless" overtly repositions our commonsense understanding of schools. What is supposed to be a place of learning and growth is actually a place of anti-intellectualism for Sam. Sam learns about "things" and has to "do all these things" in a way that feels ultimately restrictive. Sam uses the story of the white athletic students to further prove their point. These white athletic people move in mass, upward and quickly in a way that feels preordained to Sam; it is "how it is." This motions to the sedimentation of segregation, standardization, and accountability as white athletic students cluster together, move in similar ways, and, presumably, arrive on time. The future is bright for them. The order of things reveals itself in the most mundane set of bodily articulations—moving up a staircase.

Sam's question, "Can you not?," opens up a set of possibilities. Instead of moving upward, Sam gestures toward the railing where "dear life" is located. Sam contends that holding on offers more promise to their survival than attempting to do as the white athletic kids. Still, they are compelled and forced, by being legally required to be at school and follow the schedule that they are given, to move in the same way and to abide by the architectural and structural demands of school. Thus, even though Sam moves up the staircase in their own way, at a pace that they try to keep, they still must shape their future time and place within the demands of the school.

This was further evidenced when Sam described their interaction with a school math teacher:

> She always made me feel like a delinquent or something, too, because I was late the first two days, first two or three days that I came to the class because I was just, I was talking with some storytelling friends at, like, the end of the hall and I was, like, "Oh, shoot! I got to get to class!" Like, I was just talking to them about theater stuff. And then the next time that I was on time, she was, like, "Oh, look who's here on time!" And, so, then I was, like, "Yeah, it's me." And then, the next couple of times I came in on time, and she still kept doing it. "Oh, look who's here on time . . . " like, every time I was here on time, because, like, the first two or three days I was late and, so, she just, kind of assumed I was going to be late all the time.

The math teacher marks Sam's body over and over again, reminding Sam that their chance for a revised narrative will never actually come to fruition—at least not in her math class. Sam's future is stalled by the past and lies in contrast to the white athletic population.

The Future in the Advancement Via Individual Determination Program
In the hope of closing the achievement gap, programs like Advancement Via Individual Determination (AVID) are ubiquitous in schools across the country.

Sam was placed in the program during middle school. The AVID program is a set of strategies and curriculum that starts as early as kindergarten for students in the academic middle (read: B or C students) and who are generally in a marginalized socioeconomic class. AVID claims that of the students they serve, 86 percent identify as a race or ethnicity historically underrepresented in higher education, 75 percent come from a low socioeconomic background, and 56 percent have parents with no college experience. They further state, "Regardless of their life circumstances, AVID students overcome obstacles and achieve success. They graduate and attend college at higher rates, but more importantly, they can think critically, collaborate, and set high expectations to confidently conquer the challenges that await them" (AVID n.d.). Painting a neoliberal picture of personal responsibility and drive, paired with a vision of a successful and critical academic, AVID promises a life that exceeds circumstances. The future they advertise is virtually disconnected from the unequal playing field that compromises achievement. How does AVID do it? They claim that it is through "engaging, rigorous, student-centered activities." Each year, AVID interviews students nominated by teachers; if admitted, students are given an extra class period in the day with an AVID instructor who teaches them how to take notes, dialogue, and organize a binder. Every student has their binder and notes checked each week so that teachers can see that they are following the AVID method. AVID was supposed to give Sam—a mixed-race student in a predominantly white suburban school—the tools to succeed in high school and make it to college. One method they commonly employed in Sam's AVID class was a Socratic seminar.

A process that "encourages dialogue" around a "rich" piece of text, Socratic seminars ask students to entertain open-ended and peer-driven questions. Students are asked to refer back to the text when making their claims and to work together to find a shared meaning (McCready 2014: 14). Framed as providing "critical skills for postsecondary success," the Socratic seminar is used widely in AVID curricula across the nation (14). Sam, once again, drew on the word *meaningless* to describe the Socratic experience. They explain:

> We all sit in a circle, you have to share three times and then you'll get full credit and then you have to watch somebody else and count how many times they share. It was, like, ugh . . . because then you're also spending time thinking, is she going to get all her sharing in? Like, I want to make sure that she gets all her sharing in because she's really quiet. She's being overshadowed. And everybody's just going around the circle. It's good in theory, but when you put rules on it, like, "you must share this amount of times," and "you cannot speak unless three people before you have spoken." It's like now I'm counting everything. *I don't want to sit here and count, I want to listen to other people.* I would typically sit there during the Socratic

seminar and just nod a whole bunch because that counted in one of the like grading categories. It's, like "appear to be listening," like, if you nod, that counts. So, I'd be, like [shakes head up and down] "Right . . . Right . . . " I'm just sitting like a bobble-head. It was meaningless.

In the beginning of their recounting, Sam's understanding of the Socratic process is made blatantly clear—they are doing the work for credit. There is no hope for a future shared meaning, as the dialogue aspect of the Socratic process is undermined by counting and "going around the circle," which completely inhibits Sam from listening. While Sam tries to get the right amount of sharing in while monitoring another student, Sam soon realizes that a huge part of the Socratic process is a performance. They figure out a way to get credit by simply sitting and nodding. Sam alters their way of being and becomes what the teacher and rubric expect—a listener who does not actually listen or "appears to be listening" and a sharer who shares exactly three times. Critical skills, the term as it is used here, does not actually imply criticality. Socratic seminars are not engaging students to criticize, judge, offer different readings, or create their own revised theory as the definition of *critical* might have us believe.[1] Instead the critical skill is bobble heading. The future is thus compliance. AVID directs students, predominantly students of color, to comply so that their dreams of higher education can come true. In one study on AVID attrition rates, which can be up to 50 percent depending on the district, a teacher is quoted as saying that AVID students "have to really want to be willing to surrender [themselves] to the system" and that those who do not are destined to be exited (McCready 2014: 19). Sam eventually joined the 50 percent and explained to me why they left:

> I quit it because it was stressing me out. Because the thing with AVID is you can do better, like, *always you can do better*. You can do better! Even if you do a pretty good job. Like, you're getting As. They're like "You can do better." I was like "How?" They're like, "Well, volunteer." It's like, "When? What are you, *what do you want from me?*" I say that a lot but, seriously like *what do you want from me?* I don't get it. So, I quit AVID because I was like crying before going to school on Sundays. I was like, "I can't do it. I'm doing my best and they keep telling me, '*You can do better.' Like, what am I supposed to be doing!?*" But it was a requirement that we had to do all those specific things. Plus, improve all the time. Always improve. So, my dad was, like, "You can quit. You're fine. You're allowed. Go for it. I'm not going to be mad. You've gotten the information you need, you know how to take the notes, you know how to look at the colleges by this point. That's what the whole plan was."

What Sam points to repeatedly is that AVID teachers could not explain why they wanted Sam to continually improve. There were "requirements" that Sam had to meet to stay in the program but no sufficient reasoning that allowed them to understand the endgame. Who were they getting better for, and what does getting better the AVID way look like? Sam's dad astutely points out that Sam gained what they needed to gain and that the experience of feeling so overwhelmed doesn't seem necessary or a part of the plan. While Sam was the one who quit, AVID simultaneously pushed them out. Sam could not embody the ambiguous version of success that AVID strived for, and Sam's continual questioning of AVID threatened AVID's future existence. AVID's system does not thrive on being questioned. In fact, those who question the system are framed as disruptors. It has been documented that teachers believe that students who cannot abide by the rules or who question the system need to leave so as not to upset other students who submit (McCready 2014: 150).

On a broader scale, Sam's critique and rejection of AVID fit in with a larger protest against neoliberal educational models and their commitment to diversity without disruption. Roderick Ferguson (2008: 162–63) describes this process as "cannibalizing difference," in which, when a college finds that diversity is profitable in specific ways, it engages its subjects in the "will to institutionality." This process requires that subjects speak to their profitability in markets of difference without upsetting the neoliberal norms. It is in the college's favor to anticipate future axes of difference so that they have the upper hand in shaping what subjectivities they will grant admission and what subjectivities they will overlook. This neoliberal movement to rein in difference and amplify it simultaneously is illustrative of the techniques the college uses to commodify dissent before it poses potential ruptural capacities. AVID assists colleges by starting the process as early as kindergarten. Sam fulfills the diversity demands of colleges, and if AVID was able to properly groom them, then the college would have benefitted from their arrival. AVID is the college's first line of defense in its quest to diversify without having to structurally transform. In short, AVID secures the future of college diversity. While Sam refused to be molded, they also had to give up the AVID name and the direct line to institutions of higher learning that AVID can promise to its students. Thus, the choice to disengage comes at a cost.

Finding a Means of Surviving against Identity Politics, White Supremacy, and Humanism

> Self-preservation warned some of us that we could not afford to settle for one easy definition, one narrow individuated self.
> —Audre Lorde, *Zami: A New Spelling of My Name*

The forces that are really hostile to black life . . . are so forceful and so powerful and they're always pushing against us, they always want to enforce forgetfulness. They always want to do something that forgets the African presence or reabsorbs it, reappropriates it in another way. The need to confront psychological violence, epistemic violence, intellectual violence is really powerful.
—Hortense Spillers, "'Whatcha Gonna Do?' Revisiting 'Mama's Baby, Papa's Maybe: An American Grammar Book'"

Sam's aforementioned protests and critiques of the futures provided throughout their secondary education experience speak to and with Audre Lorde and Hortense Spillers, whose quotes bear such gravity in the context of standardization in schools. As Lorde's and Sam's words remind us, the process of standardization is life threatening. And as Sam and Spillers contends, forces like AVID feed off a selection of racialized bodies who become representatives of a "working" neoliberal school system while covering up the violence done to those who do not benefit from AVID. How, in the midst of this, are queer and transgender youth of color supposed to create a different future?

For Sam, their investment in finding alternative ways of being was essential to their survival. More specifically, Sam uses terms like *weird* and *meat sack*, which gave them the ability to defy overdetermined identity categories and shape themselves in a way that pushed the confines of what makes up a human. Being able to express their embodiment in a nonlinear, nonhuman, and timeless way defied the logic of AVID's call to always improve and the mass of white athletic students moving upward. It allowed Sam to stay present. These ideas came out when I asked Sam to describe themself:

I'm a weirdo. Like, no matter where I am, I'm probably the minority. I figured that out a while ago. Like, no matter where I am, in some way, shape, or form, I'm a minority. Like, it's just how I am. I could be at a LGBT thing, I'm the only person of color. I could be at a witch thing and I could still be the only person of color, but I could be the only, like, vegan. Or I could be the only LGBT or something, like, I have so many different weird things that it's hard to be not the weird one. If I found someone just like me, I don't even know if I'd like them. My ex Caitlin, we had the sexuality weirdness and we had the mixed-race, we both have that in common, but I got my weird religion, all my hobbies that are strange, like I sit at home and watch YouTube forever. They, like, clean and watch movies like a normal human being. I'm not really, I'm just, weird. . . . I'm a blob flowing through space. It's me in my meat sack. That's what I call my body, it's my meat sack, basically.

At this moment, Sam understands their body as both more and less—they will always be otherwise and in excess of any given group's categorical assumptions (e.g., LGBT people are white; witches are white, eat meat, are straight and cis), and at the same time they are the only one or the "minority" in the group. As both more and less, their subjectivity exerts a certain form of pressure on each category. When Sam arrives with their "way, shape, or form," their presence suggests that categorization has its limitations. At the same time, Sam does not see much potential for change, as their history gestures to consistent reminders that they are the only one and that this may be an endless cycle.

Sam is joined by black feminists and afro-pessimists who, according to Treva Ellison et al. (2017), set the stage for Black and trans* theorizing. Black feminists have suggested that black women are always and already placed "out of the different symbolics of female gender" and that this "different social subject" has a wealth of "grammars" that could upend our commonsense notions of categories and lives (Spillers 2003: 228). This includes the category of human itself, as Calvin Warren (2017) argues. Drawing on Spillers, Warren argues that black bodies have been disqualified from "traditional gendered categories," and thus

> black existence becomes something other, a blend of sorts of categories that is unrecognizable as gender. We might call this symbiotic blend a form of transness, in which the blending troubles not just gender categories but also the categories of the human itself. . . . The problematic that black trans studies raises is that ontology itself is the fundamental issue—gender serves as the covering for a deeper onto-metaphysical challenge, the lack of the onto-phonological procedure. (269)

What Warren makes clear in this passage is that the call into being, the call that makes one human, is ultimately unavailable to black people, as their bodies are not given the same access to what makes someone human in the first place. Gender is but one of the many facets of humanity that are necessary for the call to be fulfilled. Eva Hayward (2017) explores this idea further, using the work of Frank Wilderson, who argues that white supremacy has created the ontological conditions that result in bodies being split between being human and black. She wonders, "Following Wilderson's critique of 'the human' as white beingness, might we ask: is beingness the problem, rather than the solution, for addressing antitrans violence[?]" (192). Hayward ends by suggesting that rejecting the protocols of humanness may actually be more life-saving than trying to play into the hands of an ontological state that has largely been refused to black people.

Thus, instead of trying to embody the perfect AVID student, move along with the white athletic population at their school, and thus play the game that makes Sam almost human, Sam finds solace in being weird and being a meat sack. The idea of weirdness that they conjure is linked to their rejecting the domestic calls for cleaning and watching contrived movies with a beginning, middle, and end. They would rather opt to be at home and watch YouTube, an endless stream of video, forever and thus reimagine home as a space of leisure, timelessness, and boundlessness. This positions them as not a "normal human being" but a "meat sack" or a "blob flowing through space." In many ways, their consumption of information at home, and the pleasure they get from consuming it endlessly, resists the tides of improving all the time or reaching a specified goal.

These desires are also akin to Denise Ferreira da Silva (2014), who suggests that our current conceptions of space and time bolster the ways in which the black body is categorized, commodified, and used in the pursuit of white progress, like what we have seen with AVID. In contrast, "Blackness's capacity to signify otherwise—beyond universality and its particular arrangement of Space and Time but also away from transcendentality (self-determination)—invites a consideration of knowing without modern categories" (84). Instead of engaging in space and time as we know it, as Ferreira da Silva suggests, we entertain the concept of a plenum or "a description of existence marked by virtuality: matter imaged as contingency and possibility" (92–93). The meat sack that Sam describes is something that is beyond self-determination, as it is a result of violence but still outside the catch of programs like AVID that rely on a specific type of legible and proper person of color to forward its cause. Moving beyond identity categories, pushing against white supremacy, and rendering a different way of being allows Sam the chance to rearticulate their present and potential future in ways that are uncatchable.

These ideas of the weird and uncatchable came up during one of our interviews when I asked Sam if they had any good memories of school. They responded that they had a favorite class, a creative writing course. When I asked them about what they would write about and do in class, they responded:

> Typically just a specific topic, but sometimes it would go off. We started every class period with ten minutes of journal writing and we'd talk about that for a while and then we do whatever he had planned. And so sometimes we'd end up talking about dreams for like an entire class period. And one time, we spent an entire class period just telling jokes because that was the problem, tell your best joke. And so everybody was like, "I got this!" We had a nonfiction prompt of the day, the fiction prompt of the day, and then you could also write about whatever. And sometimes people would share their whatever and we would talk about that. Sometimes people would share their fiction prompt and we'd be, like, "Wait, that doesn't make sense. Like, how did you do this?" Like, ask questions about the story they

wrote. The nonfiction ones would be like write a list of all your favorite food. People would share it and then ask, "Why?" and then we would all talk about the why. "Why is this your favorite?" "I like mac and cheese because I like cheese and macaroni." "Why?" "Because it tastes good." There's not as much of just because. I said, "I, actually am a weird one. I like brussels sprouts," and everyone was like, "Oh, okay. . . . " Then you listen to them and you care.

In this classroom space, time, a construct that marked Sam as always late, did not seem to matter. While there were classes when the teacher would instruct, other times the class would just "go off" or they would spend the entire time talking about their thoughts without any particular structure. Student thoughts were the central force in these lessons as they entertain the "why?" instead of "just because." This kind of discussion protocol goes against the frameworks of programs like AVID that seek to dissolve dissent in the name of critical thinking. The teacher does not know where the discussion will go and so has to relinquish the power of being able to foretell what students are thinking. Furthermore, the question of why is always situated as that which can be asked forever; it is timeless. As Sam delights in this classroom space, they confidently situate themselves as weird and reveal that they like brussels sprouts. This unexpected difference that arises from Sam's uncatchable claim creates connections and compels students to listen and care for one another. As students readily accept that difference will continually surface, a community of potential is formed against the grain of standardization, and imagining otherwise becomes possible.

Bess Collins Van Asselt is the associate director of the Center for the Integration of Teaching, Learning, and Scholarship at Lafayette College. Her work explores the life histories of queer and transgender youth and how queer and transgender youth embody and enact different forms of protest in secondary schools.

Note

1.   *Merriam-Webster*, s.v. "critical," www.merriam-webster.com/dictionary/critical (accessed May 6, 2018).

References

AVID. n.d. "What Is AVID Secondary?" www.avid.org/what-is-avid-secondary.ashx (accessed March 31, 2019).

Ellison, Treva, Kai M. Green, Matt Richardson, and C. Riley Snorton. 2017. "We Got Issues: Toward a Black Trans*/Studies." *TSQ* 4, no. 2: 162–69.

Ferguson, Roderick. 2008. "Administering Sexuality; or, The Will to Institutionality." *Radical History Review*, no. 100: 158–69.

Ferreira da Silva, Denise. 2014. "Toward a Black Feminist Poethics: The Question of Blackness toward the End of the World." *Black Scholar* 44, no. 2: 81–97.

Grady, Jonathan, Rigoberto Marquez, and Peter McLaren. 2012. "A Critique of Neoliberalism with Fierceness: Queer Youth of Color Creating Dialogues of Resistance." *Journal of Homosexuality* 59, no. 7: 982–1004.

Hayward, Eva. 2017. "Don't Exist." *TSQ* 4, no. 2: 191–94.

Leonardo, Zeis. 2007. "The War on Schools: NCLB, Nation Creation, and the Educational Construction of Whiteness." *Race, Ethnicity and Education* 10, no. 3: 261–78.

Leonardo, Zeis. 2013. "The Story of Schooling: Critical Race Theory and the Educational Racial Contract." *Discourse Studies in the Cultural Politics of Education* 34, no. 4: 599–610.

McCready, Bo. 2014. "Leaving the College Track? The Causes and Effects of High School Student Exit from Advancement Via Individual Determination (AVID)." PhD diss., University of Wisconsin–Madison.

Patel, Leigh. 2016. "Pedagogies of Resistance and Survivance: Learning as Marronage." *Equity and Excellence in Education* 49, no. 4: 397–401.

Spillers, Hortense. 2003. *Black, White, and in Color: Essays on American Literature and Culture.* Chicago: University of Chicago Press.

Talburt, Susan, and Nancy Lesko. 2012. "An Introduction to Seven Technologies of Youth Studies." In *Keywords in Youth Studies: Tracing Affects, Movements, Knowledges,* edited by Nancy Lesko and Susan Talburt, 1–10. New York: Routledge.

Warren, Calvin. 2017. "Calling into Being: Tranifestation, Black Trans, and the Problem of Ontology." *TSQ* 4, no. 2: 266–74.

Calling Self-Indulgence

Names, Pronouns, Poems

J DE LEON

Abstract Recent works by trans and nonbinary poets, including Oliver Baez Bendorf, Jos Charles, jayy dodd, Joshua Jennifer Espinoza, Paige Lewis, and Danez Smith, gesture to a new mode of trans-confessional poetry. Trans poets practice naming as a form of self-indulgence, and trans names and pronouns are a form of poetry—following Audre Lorde's articulation—read into the world to give it new shape. In trans naming practices and poetry, self-indulgences are also demands made of another, a new name or unexpected pronoun asking for an affirmative repetition, a performative reflection: mirror restaging. Gender, like self-indulgence, is never accomplished alone. It relies on an audience that either affirms and repeats—or refuses—one's request to be seen and understood in a way that breaks from expectation. I closely read two poems, by Oliver Baez Bendorf and Richard Siken, whose shared centering of names articulate a relational self-indulgence in their proposed call-and-response.
Keywords pronouns, naming, poetry, self-indulgence

Trans poets practice naming as a form of productive self-indulgence; and trans names and pronouns are forms of poetry, read into the world to give it new shape. Claiming "self-indulgence" in this context is far from an insult: self-indulgence is a virtue when the alternative for minoritized subjects is following a prescribed self-annihilation. I invoke *self-indulgence*, instead of refusing its sting and finding another term, to emphasize the social and political stakes of self-indulgence for those selves who are regularly and brutally shut out of the social. Self-indulgence, in this context, is a necessity as we live toward unknown futures, carving new words and ways forward for and with our selves. Laying claim to self-indulgence, from a demeaned position in the social, is an insistence on the value of one's being in the world despite arguments to the contrary. This is paradoxically a matter of life and death for those whose desire for a livable life is precisely the thing that's called self-indulgence. In trans and nonbinary poets' rewording of the self in language, self-indulgence is an ethics of reciprocal flourishing, through which we can care for one another and/as our selves: as Joshua Jennifer Espinoza

TSQ: Transgender Studies Quarterly ★ Volume 6, Number 4 ★ November 2019
DOI 10.1215/23289252-7771779   © 2019 Duke University Press

(2017c) puts it, in "gushing bloody dreams of escape, / of listening to one's self and caring for other selves." To reconfigure one's self in language—name and/or pronoun—is to indulge in an idea of another way of being in the world, to imagine a way into or out of something binding, and to hold open space for a different sense of movement for one's self instead; that is, the possibility of change.

The recurring focus on naming in the work of many contemporary trans and nonbinary poets helps articulate the power and precarity of this particular self-indulgence. I begin with these examples to suggest a logic that extends from the formalized work of trans and nonbinary poets, to argue that trans and nonbinary names and pronouns are themselves poetry—following Audre Lorde's (1984: 37) argument that "poetry is the way we help give name to the nameless so it can be thought." Writing and reading names into and as poems allows trans and nonbinary poets to further play with the potentiality of language as a tool of trans futurity. Paige Lewis (2016) calls naming "the only power we're left with," in their poem "Turn Me Over, I'm Done on This Side." Jos Charles (2018: 1) gestures to this potentiality in the opening poem of *feeld*, in which she works to reshape and resound a language that can accommodate "tran" subjectivities:

> inn 1 virsion off thynges /
> alarum is mye nayme

In Danez Smith's (2014) poem "Alternate Names for Black Boys," they set out a numbered list that includes upward of a dozen names. The names they list flicker between stark: "8. gone"; "10. going, going, gone"—and luminous: "13. fireworks at dawn"; "14. brilliant, shadow hued coral" (17). Laying claim to alternate names requires a shared self-regard that Smith recognizes and asserts near the end of their list, invoking an "us" in their dreams of alternatives for black boys:

> 15. (I thought to leave this blank
>   but who am I to name us nothing?)

Smith marks, with the poem's only parenthetical, the crucial difference in holding a space for someone else to fill for themselves versus an unmarked blank that invokes nothingness or non-naming. This parenthetical is a form of openness, inviting another option, while refusing violent namelessness.

Smith's (2017: 3) theology centers the name: "we say our own names when we pray." In their "summer, somewhere," naming is also a crucial form of self-creation. The shape of an imagined black afterlife slowly emerges in their couplets, starting with the necessity for proper forms of address. In their logic, a new name is congruent with aliveness:

> please, don't call
> us dead, call us alive someplace better. (3)
>
> we send him off to wander for a day
> or ever, let him pick his new name. (4)

While this long work specifically addresses racist violence and police brutality, following the murders of black men and boys from Emmett Till to Trayvon Martin, the opportunity to choose one's name as a mark of paradise resonates with Smith's "Alternate Names for Black Boys" and the self-indulgent, queer audacity of naming oneself—the "us/we" of the work insistently aligning Smith's queer and nonbinary voice in relation to experiences of systemic racism and articulating the shared urgency of self-determination and self-indulgence for brutalized communities: "don't call us dead." Here, too, one's name is not taken for granted, but offered as an opportunity to situate oneself in a new context, an imagined future in which aliveness is possible. The chosen names Smith lists include "*RainKing*," "*I do, I do*," and simply "*alive*" (4).

Rendering these "alternate names" in verse aestheticizes the name itself as an art form for trans and nonbinary poets, whose names and pronouns are overdetermined and anxiously read even without any explicit invocation in their work. In bringing these challenges to language into verse, these poets invoke and claim the mythic power of naming. In Lewis's poem "Last Night I Dreamed I Made Myself" (2017), they further elaborate the pleasurable self-indulgent power of naming in relation to their own dream of self-making:

> —and I think
> about how hard it is for me to believe
>
> in the first Adam because if Adam
> had the power to name everything,
> everything would be named Adam.

Lewis's too-consuming proliferation of Adams, the desire to rename all things to hear one's own name echoed back, is an inversion of Rumpelstiltskinian mythologies of naming in which one's name must be protected as a precious secret and self-disclosures are a risk.

In contrast, Joshua Jennifer Espinoza (2018a) articulates an adverse option, the betrayal or the name given back bad—"I am afraid of being seen. / I am afraid of being named."—reflecting the ease with which these words can change shape in other mouths that refuse to self-indulge with us. Concern with names and the power of naming is aligned with the heightened dangers of self-expression for trans and gender-nonconforming people of color, which shapes the readiness for violence present in Espinoza's work as an anticipation of hostility. Rather than asking for an affirmation she does not expect, she instead anticipates hostility, and emphasizes the limitations others' words have put on her own claim to life:

> The time has come for me to be alive
> and for you to stop speaking. Please stop speaking. Please, oh
> please stop speaking. (Espinoza 2016: 12)

Espinoza's ambivalence toward the possibility of a present/presence, let alone any imagined futurity, complicates any reading of the self-indulgence of trans names and poetry as straightforward or simply pleasurable. She wavers between an insistence on aliveness, and a hopelessness she alternately claims and refutes: "i have so much hope for the future / or no i don't"—later amended with "full of hope despite everything" (Espinoza 2015: 11).

Espinoza's work returns often to the ambivalence of naming, and her own name sets the stage for the work of the work: her writing is signed with a doubled name (Joshua/Jennifer) that elides cis or binary identification, challenging even an unknowing reader to reconsider the gendered voice of the poem. Names thread through her work as well, even as her concern is oriented more toward the stranger than the beloved or trusted, suspicious of what she might hear: "I have five hundred / names and all of them are bad" (Espinoza 2017a: 80). The double-edged sword of a name is a paradox that recurs in Espinoza's work, as she acknowledges the opportunity to name oneself as both utility and trap:

> *What will I call myself now? . . .*
> It helps to have a name even though
> a name is a room you can never leave. (Espinoza 2017b)

She juxtaposes the limitations and necessities of naming in a Foucauldian turn of thought, followed with her own persistence in naming, in several poems. In "Things Haunt" (2018b), the name she turns to is gestural and vague: "Something else like that. / That should be my name." Elsewhere, she is not naming herself, but her body, emphasizing the constitutive violence of subjectivity even as she lays claim to "hope despite everything":

> the same violence swallows itself and produces bodies
> and names for bodies

> i name my body girl of my dreams
> i name my body proximity
> i name my body full of hope despite everything
> i name my body dead girl who hasn't died yet (Espinoza 2015: 11)

Espinoza's concern with the stakes of naming in relation to trans bodies opens into the complex relationality of self-indulgence that I am interested in arguing for as a necessarily shared undertaking. In "To the Queer Woman Who Asked Me If I Have a Dick," she uses the title to very specifically frame the address of the poem. Here, she calls on the inadequacy of given language, rather than a bodily exactness, as a site for potentiality:

> Everything I adore about women cannot be spoken
>
> because the words have not yet been invented.
> I imagine another life, a possibility of healing, of knowing, of
>   listening.
>
> It could appear the day we stop relying upon the materials of this
>   one. (Espinoza 2018c)

This brief poem articulates the shared stakes of self-indulgence, which both puts Espinoza under a kind of scrutiny that carries a risk of violence, and also relies on others—the "we" she invokes—to move toward something like futurity, a shared imagination of other ways to be in the world that might begin in language, in these words that "have not yet been invented" but may yet appear. Relying on "the materials of this one"—the words and bodies inadequate for trans flourishing— and refusing to self-indulge, Espinoza (2018c) is a means of "sustaining a narrower, uglier world," rather than imagining, together, "another life, a possibility of healing, of knowing, of listening." The listening, in particular, is a mark of the peculiar relationality of self-indulgence, requiring a particular kind of listening for felicity.

While the poem is addressed to an eponymous "queer woman," Espinoza gives herself the opportunity to revisit this encounter for an audience of readers who may be more receptive. She is able to articulate a response to the titular question through poetry in a way that she may or may not have been able to accomplish in the moment of confrontation or in the accumulation of such moments. She takes this strategy into other poems, such as "Pardon My Gender" (Espinoza 2017c), whose tone refuses any kind of apology, taking instead a scalding read on the regularly occurring, rudely shocked and appalled responses to trans embodiment and language.

> Pardon my gender—
> I didn't mean to make you
> question the nature of our reality
> or the walls that surround us.

This sarcasm builds into a concise articulation of the self-indulgence I read for in these works, as she links her gender with the possibility of "listening to one's self and caring for other selves":

> please don't worry
> about the fact that this situation is beating us senseless
> with its violent meaningless gestures and its gorgeous
> high ceilings and its gushing bloody dreams of escape,
> of listening to one's self and caring for other selves. (Espinoza 2017c)

In her poetry, Espinoza offers the opportunity to accomplish the questioning of reality the language of her gender evokes, not just for herself, but for others who might also want that possibility. She describes the potential violent infelicities of given names and the trappings of gender that precede one's self-awareness and the ways these "gorgeous" structures are intended to preclude other possibilities for forming one's self. Her break with these "meaningless gestures" of given name and pronoun is the start of a proposed shift in self-articulation that allows for her dreams of shared escape.

Transition often begins in language, the rest following in the wake of words. Our names and pronouns are spoken into the world to give it a new shape, one that can better accommodate our selves. A new name or pronoun can be a way toward what Espinoza (2018c) imagines for herself: "another life, a possibility of healing, of knowing, of listening." But the process of being gendered in language is ongoing, with continued reaffirmation or refusal from friends and strangers. The self-indulgence articulated in trans poetry, pronouns, and names makes clear that self-indulgence can't be a solo accomplishment.

Turning back to Audre Lorde: reading trans names and pronouns in/as poetry, builds on Lorde's (1984) argument for the uses of poetry in "Poetry Is Not a Luxury." She argues for "poetry as a revelatory distillation of experience, not . . . sterile word play": "Poetry is not a luxury. It is a vital necessity of our existence. It forms the quality of the light within which we predicate our hopes and dreams toward survival and change, first made into language, then into idea, then into more tangible action. Poetry is the way we help give name to the nameless so it can be thought" (37). The urgent work of poetry in relation to trans self-identification—not only reliant on one's own sense of self but also requiring interlocutors—is in its ability to mark out a map toward "more tangible action" and begin to name the ways we might move ahead, with "dreams of escape" shaped around listening to and caring for one's self and others. The recurring concern with naming in contemporary trans and genderqueer poetry helps articulate the importance of this self-indulgence. To name ourselves is poetry.

Lorde argues that often what is considered to be a "luxury," in excess of bare survival, is a crucial part of our ability to persist and dream despite a context that would rather we did not. She argues that "poetry is not a luxury" but rather exactly what gives us "the strength and courage to see, to feel, to speak, and to dare" (39). My argument for the urgent, necessary self-indulgence of trans self-identification builds on Lorde's insistence on poetry, while also proposing that we value the luxury of poetry differently—as she does in other essays, with the uses of the erotic, and the uses of anger. Poetry, like self-indulgence, is a luxury that we need. To justify the need for poetry as other than luxurious undermines its importance, as it works in defiant excess of the narrow, ascetic standards to which we are supposed to aspire. Or, if poetry is not a luxury, then it nonetheless helps us articulate and luxuriate in what sustains us, beyond the respectable limits of self-restraint and self-control. In jayy dodd's "ars poetica" (2017: 27), they can be read as elaborating on and expanding Lorde's argument for poetry:

or

every poem is masturbation. the gesture of naming
in so many words, crafting metered stroke, in lyric & verse & still,
every poem,   even in its most spectacular excitement,
        must know how to finish itself   off.

Masturbatory is an easy synonym for *self-indulgent,* a way to dismiss a work as unimportant. dodd broadens this demeaning implication to encompass the entirety of poetry, rather than defending against such an undermining accusation toward particular works. Lorde, arguing variously for the uses of pleasure and anger, builds a case for the kinds of self-expression—made, crucially, by certain kinds of ill-regarded selves—that are disregarded as masturbatory or self-indulgent and therefore easily dismissed. dodd shifts the terms of Lorde's reclamation if all of poetry, "even in its most spectacular excitement," falls under this rubric of pleasure. In their "ars poetica," dodd describes poetry as "the gesture of naming / *in so many words*" and wholly masturbatory, without marking either of these as negative statements. dodd does not refute or refuse accusations of masturbatory work, instead leveling the field with this grand assertion.

The poets I cite here can be read as examples of contemporary trans and nonbinary poets' uses of naming as "tangible action" toward trans futurities, following Lorde's (1984: 37) articulation of the urgent and necessary work of poetry as the work of rewriting one's world to better accommodate one's self. Trans and nonbinary poets practice and play with naming in their writing, complicating linear narratives of transition by articulating their relation to naming as a form of self-making. The proliferation of names in the work of many contemporary trans and genderqueer poets could be termed a new school of confessional poetry, in which poets whose bodies may confess in myriad ways reframe their experience through language and take on a different kind of refusal of stealth or passing in language. dodd (2017: 27) ties this exposing, confessional logic to the particular "grammar" of poetry, the masturbatory pleasures of language bound up in the self-exposure of expression.

> every poem costs some mass, some
> measure—requires a body to expose itself. a grammar
> called recompense.

If our names, bodies, voices, pronouns, and pasts all confess us in various ways, then the names invoked in these examples of trans-confessional poetry take up confession and expand the potentiality in these experiences, complicating the linearity of trans narratives of self-naming and also laying claim to the pleasures of language and experimentation. These self-indulgences are also demands made of another, a new name or unexpected pronoun asking for an affirmative repetition, a performative reflection—mirror restaging. Gender is never accomplished alone. It relies on an audience that either affirms and repeats—or refuses—one's desire to be seen and understood in a way that breaks from normative expectation.

I turn to pronouns as an example here in addition to names, specifically the nonbinary *they/their*, because they are also a kind of poetry, in Lorde's rendering of the form—a naming that we may use to move toward a shared future. This is not to say that binary pronouns don't also function as a crucial tool for trans futurities, but that nonbinary pronouns emphasize both the particular self-indulgence and the reliance on others inherent in any pronoun choice. Choosing different pronouns allows us to collaboratively work to reshape language with others and to better articulate a world for our selves—a reshaping with language that calls on the proliferation of names in the trans-confessional poems I cite here, and the forms of address they invite and anticipate. Using nonbinary pronouns is an opportunity to reflect on the necessarily collaborative formation of gender, and the reliance on others that is already present in all our interactions but is heightened by the break with normative grammar. This break underlines the ways in which gender works through language on bodies. *They/their* holds open the possibility for reconsidering the quotidian work of grammar as gender in all pronouns—a logic on which we rely and yet often goes unremarked. Considering the possibilities available in language that challenges our understandings of what it means to be a gendered "self" requires another understanding of self-indulgence, as it prompts us to reconsider what that self might look and sound and feel like. To fully articulate this change, one must consider that the rewording insists on an audience receptive to hearing and recognizing that change. These transitional sentences, in which *they* is practiced and repeated, sounding change word by word, also make clear the always-present dynamic in which one's self is shaped by others' language all the time, and only in the attempted intervention is this made strange. Projects of cultivating a collaborative self-indulgence remain urgent in contemporary contexts as we learn to self-indulge more than one self, rather than brutalizing difference. Toying with language in this way offers opportunities to make and give the space in which such ideas can be undertaken, forming a shared reworking of gender via language.

In my own relation to this pronoun, I hear it as a form of address with a productive ambivalence that allows me to listen for and practice a form of futurity that is otherwise elusive. With this request in the form of self-revelation, I offer others the opportunity to trip over and interrupt expectation in language, with and for me, and performatively refuse the limits of a binary. By asking to be addressed via the singular *they*, I ask those in the position to conjure me in the third person to indulge in my self, perhaps at the expense of their own sense of the solidity of both gender and language. This is a form of self-indulgence that others may offer me in language, and my desire to resignify the grammar of gender is also self-indulgent: both make room for a different reading of our selves. This self-indulgence requires a shared commitment to a certain rendering of futurity that hinges on a remaking of language; I must continually express my self as out of alignment with gendered expectation in language, in order to invite others to let me hear what that sounds like. The third-person pronoun necessitates collaboration, the other's voice. I am never "they" without affirmative reflection from interlocutors willing to go out on a limb of language, with and for me. I offer the opportunity to care for me in this form of address, in excess of all other forms of care already present in the person of whom I make this request. This is a kind of care of the self that is oriented toward a shift in the way we each imagine inhabiting the world, the mutability of language offering an opportunity to reconsider both the role of language in our self-makings and the ways we each contribute to one another's selves with such everyday speech acts.

In this reading of self-indulgence as a productive and collaborative form of queer sustenance, I am considering the work of affirming names and pronouns specifically as it might function in relation to those who do care to collaborate with and indulge us. Self-indulgence is not just in choosing a name or pronoun but in hearing it repeated back and relying on interlocutors to self-indulge with us. Hearing the poetry of names and pronouns allows us to luxuriate in these pleasures—the taste of such a bon mot as a new name after grinding through so many utterances of one that wasn't working. The shared queer pleasure of hearing and saying names and pronouns can also form the framework for an ethics of self-indulgence as a form of mutual self-making that centers a more expansive understanding of how we may exist in the world with and for one another.

Here, I turn to two works by two queer poets—one trans, one cis—to amplify this argument, with an imagined diptych of collaborative self-indulgence via the poetry of trans names and pronouns. In Oliver Baez Bendorf's "Split It Open Just to Count the Pieces" (2015), he lays claim to dozens of names in exuberant succession, while Richard Siken's "Saying Your Names" (2004) matches Bendorf's exultation and offers back these names, an affirmative reflection. Siken's "Saying Your Names" can be read as a model of self-indulging another's self, and the distinct pleasure interlocutors offer in affirming one's identity. His practice with a lover's many names is a tripping litany that builds as he enumerates all the kinds of names his lover may lay claim to and have affirmed:

> Chemical names, bird names, names of fire
> and flight and snow, baby names, paint names,
> delicate names like bones in the body,
> Rumplestiltskin names that are always changing,
> names that no one's ever able to figure out.
> Names of spells and names of hexes, names
> cursed quietly under the breath, or called out
> loudly to fill the yard, calling you inside again,
> calling you home. (33)

These names carry on for pages, sentences overflowing lines in a rush of options; more densely packed on the page than most poems in Siken's award-winning debut *Crush*, this poem is presented as a solid column of text rather than the lacy cascade of lines that build negative space into the page with a painterly eye throughout the rest of the text. "Saying Your Names," in contrast, clips along at speed, rhythmic in its repetition, pursuing the page's tracks in steady, narrow returns. The momentum of Siken's work presents a kind of reverberating affirmation of these many names, shifting from one to the next, often multiple names within the same line, hundreds accumulating. Siken, breathless halfway through the poem, builds and leaps into a culminating "O" in this excerpt, but then

continues on, shifting from one set of repetitions to another without pause—
"your name like" shifting into a leaner pattern, "to mark, to hold, to keep":

>   Your name like
>   a song I sing to myself, your name like a box
>   where I keep my love, your name like a nest
>   in the tree of love, your name like a boat in the
>   sea of love—O now we're in the sea of love!
>   Your name like detergent in the washing machine.
>   Your name like two X's like punched-in eyes,
>   like a drunk cartoon passed out in the gutter,
>   your name with two X's to mark the spots,
>   to hold the place, to keep the treasure from
>   becoming ever lost. (34)

Reading Siken's text alongside Bendorf's "Split It Open Just to Count the Pieces"
(2015) presents an idealized duet of call-and-response: Bendorf deliberating the
many possible names he might hold, Siken saying yes to each. Bendorf's "me" is
answered and affirmed, again and again, by Siken's "you," the litany of names
returned in kind. Read together with Bendorf's work, Siken's many names reflect
an exuberance, the joy of Bendorf's naming reflected back.

Bendorf's poem—reproduced here in its entirety—is barely a fifth of the
hundred-plus lines of Siken's "Saying Your Names," but it conveys a similar
prolific delight in possibility and the pleasures of language in self-determination:

>   Call me tumblefish, rip-roar, pocket of light,
>   haberdash and milkman, velveteen and silverbreath,
>   your bitch, your little brother, Ponderosa pine,
>   almanac and crabshack and dandelion weed. Call me
>   babyface, kidege—little bird or little plane—thorn of rose
>   and loaded gun, a pile of walnut shells. Egg whites
>   and sandpaper, crown of Gabriel, hand-rolled sea,
>   call me cobblestone and half-pint, your Spanish
>   red-brick empire. Call me panic and Orion, Pinocchio
>   and buttercream. Saltlick, shooting star, August peach
>   and hurricane. Call me giddyup and Tarzan, riot boy
>   and monk, flavor-trip and soldier and departure.
>   Call me Eiffel Tower, arrondissement, le garçon,
>   call me the cigarette tossed near the leak
>   of gasoline. Call me and tell me that Paris is on fire at last,

> that the queens of Harlem can have their operations
> and their washing machines. Call me seamless,
>   call me sir. Call me tomorrow's inevitable sunrise. (4)

Bendorf's imperatives retain a gleefulness, rather than an imperious tone. These commands are given familiarly: for example, the aside "kidege—little bird or little plane—" offers access to potentially obscure vocabulary. The language here is delicious and textured, the soft and sweet "buttercream" and "August peach" complementing the salt and crunch of "saltlick" and "walnut shells." The internal rhymes and alliteration—"almanac" and "crabshack," "panic" and "Pinocchio"—maintain a playfulness; while the shifts between possessive diminuitives—"your bitch, your little brother"—and powerful dangers—the thorns, the "loaded gun" and the lit cigarette—articulate a kinetic and animated dynamic between the "me" and "you," contributing to the poem's momentum.

This was first published before Bendorf changed his name and pronouns and so can also be read in retrospect with a certain playfulness in advance of decision—at least as far as bylines are concerned. "Call me": trying on a range of options and identities, tasting potential names rather than implying any one inevitability. The seamlessness invoked in the penultimate line speaks to this proliferation, all these names existing in a smooth continuum, rather than presenting a binary of name or identity: none of these need be renounced. Originally published online in 2011, this is also included in Bendorf's first volume of poetry, *The Spectral Wilderness* (2015). Bendorf's own name is not yet explicitly articulated in this poem, but it may be hinted at—the *olive* in Oliver emerging in "saltlick," "flavor-trip"—or may be simply the feeling of "tomorrow's inevitable sunrise" when he hears it repeated back (4). Even this inevitability is not singular, each day offering the potential for a tomorrow, the name itself, the demand—"call me" —offering a bridge toward that imagined near future.

Siken's (2004: 33) names, "called out / loudly to fill the yard . . . calling you home," skip into a doubled naming, a beckoning rather than an identification. *Home* is another name for the lover among these many, as well as a request for return. To be addressed as one asks is also an address to which one may turn, creating a home in the affirmative recognition Siken offers in his long list. Siken's play with *call* matches Bendorf's (2015: 4) "call me and tell me," as a slip from imperative to invitation:

> Call me and tell me that Paris is on fire at last,
>   that the queens of Harlem can have their operations
>   and their washing machines.

With this turn from his own many potential names to an outreach for conversation, Bendorf instead requests news of a shared plenitude, the reciprocal self-indulgence of being bolstered not simply by his own self-making but also in the hearing of someone else's. To hear this news is on par with his own demands for new and different names, linking his own new names to a wider context. The washing machines are echoed between Bendorf and Siken, too; the latter, just after the "sea of love" couplets, tripping from self-deprecating to quotidian domesticity, "your name like detergent in the washing machine" (Siken 2005: 34). The washing machines in these poems call on Venus Xtravaganza's sharp analysis—using a "washer and dryer set" as example—of the logic of reciprocity in heteronormative relationships in *Paris Is Burning* (Livingston 1990), which she positions as analogous to her own and something she can comfortably imagine inhabiting: "married, a woman, in the suburbs," but still reliant on others in order to achieve her desires. In her logic, such reliance is "regular" and unremarkable. "A regular woman is married to her husband and she wants him to buy her a washer and dryer set. In order for her to buy that, I'm sure she'd have to go to bed with him anyway to give him what he wants, for her to get what she wants. So in the long run, it all ends up the same way."

Bendorf invokes *Paris Is Burning* explicitly, builds his desire for more and new names in relation to and in step with the larger stakes of trans self-identification; a new name also gestures toward a potential futurity in which "Paris is on fire at last," signaling the arrival of the washing machine, the surgery, the way out of whatever closing-in spaces that mark the present. Xtravaganza's dreamy rendering of her imagined future in *Paris Is Burning* aligns the domesticity of the washing machine with gender-affirming surgery, linking them as both aspirational and quotidian, a desire that helps create a sense of home. She is attentive to race and class, building from twinned aspirations of wealth and whiteness to further specify the security of domesticity, within which litany her own "sex change" is embedded: "I would like to be a spoiled rich white girl. . . . I want a car, I want to be with the man I love, I want a nice home away from New York . . . somewhere far where no one knows me. I want my sex change. I want to get married in church, in white. I want to be a complete woman and I want to be a professional model, behind cameras in a high-fashion world. I want this. This is what I want. And I'm gonna go for it." She's already made herself a name, a daughter of the House of Xtravaganza; her belonging is also marked through this name and by those who help her hear a potential future in it. Her name offers her access to the certainty with which she articulates the inevitability of her success. In this context, the imagined world Bendorf writes toward—"their operations / and their washing machines"—echoes Xtravaganza's, and is one in which the name, the surgery, and the washing machine are all within the realm of possibility, and the name serves to speak the possibility of these other dreams into existence "at last" (4).

A name can be a place to start, something to play with out loud before risking other moves toward exacting one's self. Of course, the breathless self-indulgences of Siken's "Saying Your Names" are not always the outcome of trans self-disclosures. And despite his exuberance, the potential for irruptive violence is never forgotten in Siken's work, which he reflects in the quick shift from "the sea of love" to "punched-in eyes, / like a drunk cartoon passed out in the gutter" to signal the always-proximate bodily risk of queer and trans self-indulgence. Language is a test for potential violence, as the invocation of Venus Xtravaganza in Bendorf's work reminds us: another option for what we can expect when giving another person the opportunity to reconsider our selves.

While the "you" Siken addresses is not explicitly named or identified as trans, Siken's marveling repetition of these many names, read in concert with Bendorf's ebullient demands, evoke an idealized iteration of collaborative self-indulgence and a model for ecstatic affirmation of trans names and pronouns. These two works are a call-and-response, reveling in the potentialities in a name, in many names, "names that are always changing," rather than landing on any single one (Siken 2004: 33). The opportunity to play with potential naming options is one that Bendorf and Siken both suggest in their profusion of names, never landing on or suggesting the necessity for a definitive or single choice, instead presenting excess as a pleasure that's available in such collaborative self-indulgences as asking for and hearing a new name or names, opening into unarticulated possibilities. These exchanges propel an enactment of Lorde's understanding of poetry as "the way we help give name to the nameless so it can be thought"; the "we" here speaking to the pleasure and necessity of shared projects of self-indulgence in queer and trans self- and world-making practices (37).

J de Leon holds a PhD in performance studies from New York University, where they are also an MFA candidate in creative writing.

Acknowledgments
Oliver Baez Bendorf's "Split It Open Just to Count the Pieces" appears by permission of Kent State University Press.

References
Bendorf, Oliver Baez. 2015. *The Spectral Wilderness*. Kent, OH: Kent State University Press.

Charles, Jos, 2018. *feeld*. Minneapolis: Milkweed Editions.

dodd, jayy. 2017. *Mannish Tongues*. England: Platypus.

Espinoza, Joshua Jennifer. 2015. "I Dream of Horses Eating Cops." *Nepantla*, no. 2: 11.

Espinoza, Joshua Jennifer. 2016. *There Should Be Flowers*. Fairfax, VA: Civil Coping Mechanisms.

Espinoza, Joshua Jennifer. 2017a. "The Heat Death of the Universe." *West Branch*, no. 84: 80.

Espinoza, Joshua Jennifer. 2017b. "Makeup Ritual." *Them*, November 19. www.them.us/story
/pardon-my-gender.

Espinoza, Joshua Jennifer. 2017c. "Pardon My Gender." *Them*, November 19. www.them.us/story
/pardon-my-gender.

Espinoza, Joshua Jennifer. 2018a. "Every Day Was Ordinary." *Granta*, no. 144. granta.com/every
-day-was-ordinary/.

Espinoza, Joshua Jennifer. 2018b. "Things Haunt." *Academy of American Poets*, December 11. poets
.org/poem/things-haunt.

Espinoza, Joshua Jennifer. 2018c. "To the Queer Woman Who Asked Me If I Have a Dick."
Buzzfeed, July 24. www.buzzfeednews.com/article/jjenniferespinoza/poetry-to-the-queer
-woman-who-asked-me-if-i-have-a-dick.

Lewis, Paige. 2016. "Turn Me Over, I'm Done on This Side." *Journal* 40, no. 3. thejournalmag.org
/archives/11648.

Lewis, Paige. 2017. "Last Night I Dreamed I Made Myself." *TriQuarterly*, no. 152. www.triquarterly
.org/issues/issue-152/last-night-i-dreamed-i-made-myself.

Livingston, Jenny, dir. *Paris Is Burning*. 1990. Los Angeles, CA: Miramax.

Lorde, Audre. 1984. *Sister Outsider*. New York: Ten Speed.

Siken, Richard. 2004. *Crush*. New Haven, CT: Yale University Press.

Smith, Danez. 2014. *[insert] boy*. Portland, OR: YesYes.

Smith, Danez. 2017. *Don't Call Us Dead*. Minneapolis: Graywolf.

Future Fatigue

Trans Intimacies and Trans Presents (or How to Survive the Interregnum)

HIL MALATINO

Abstract This essay explores the ways that teleological narratives of transition come coupled with corresponding affective narratives that frame life "pre" transition as characterized by a reductively bleak emotional surround and cathect life "post" transition to a bright-sided promise of social ease, domestic comfort, and existential peace. Building on Lauren Berlant's theorization of cruel optimism and the work of Tobias Raun and Laura Horak on video narratives of hormonal and surgical transition, I position the figuration of futurity in these narratives as generative of a form of intense antici-patory anxiety in the present, one that may actually impede the flourishing of trans subjects, particularly those who encounter difficulty accessing technologies of transition. These teleological affective narratives generate an inhabitation of the present as a dwelling in lag — a form of being out of temporal sync, left behind, with the life one desires deferred (perhaps perennially). As an ame-liorative to the effects of such cruelly optimistic futural narratives, I theorize a trans for trans (t4t) praxis of love, drawing on the fantastic and dystopic imaginaries at work in the fiction of Kai Cheng Thom and Torrey Peters to account for the creative and caring acts of trans intimacy that render life in the interregnum — in the moments during transition, which may very well not have a definite end — not only livable but also, sometimes, joyous.

Keywords trans temporalities, trans embodiments, cruel optimism, negative affect, t4t, medical transition

Lag: Rethinking the Affective Temporalities of Transition

What makes a future bleak? Is it a question of one's orientation to futurity? Is a future bleak because of the anticipation, anxiety, and fear that imbues one's relationship to it? Is it a failure of ability to envision oneself happy in one's projections of the future? Or a failure to envision oneself in any kind of future at all?

Sometimes, perhaps, what makes a future bleak is also that which makes it promising. This is the key insight of Lauren Berlant's (2011) theorization of cruel optimism, her name for the affective complex that occurs when that which you profoundly desire is also that which inhibits your flourishing, when that which you imagine to one day deliver happiness, security, comfort, or joy actually wears you down and out through your attachment to it.

This essay interprets certain visions of the future that circulate in hegemonic narratives of medicalized transition as generative of a form of cruel optimism that stems from the affective promises they offer. These narratives emanate from diverse sites. Sometimes, they are framed and marketed by medical specialists addressing trans folk as a surgical niche market. Other times, they are produced within DIY spaces of trans cultural production that document medical transition. In this essay, I focus specifically on the futural narratives at work in the genre of trans vlogs concerned with documenting the impacts of transition produced by folks residing in the United States. These vlogs fulfill a crucial function for trans folks and communities, making specialized medical information accessible across disparate healthscapes, offering interactive forums for communication about experiences with hormones and surgery, and documenting the corporeal and affective changes that accompany medicalized forms of transition. They are a critical stopgap in the notoriously uneven terrain of trans health care access in the United States, one shaped by a long legacy of rigorous and problematic gatekeeping, a historic and ongoing dearth of insurance coverage, high out-of-pocket fees, and a metro-centricity that makes it quite difficult for trans subjects in rural areas and small towns and cities to access transition-related care (as well as trans-competent medical care, broadly construed). The folks composing, editing, and posting these vlogs are engaged in forms of care labor for, and on behalf of, trans communities, documenting their own experiences to educate and potentially mitigate feelings of isolation and anomie. They perform, with a much wider reach, the work of trans community newsletters and magazines like *Chrysalis*, *AEGIS News*, the *Erickson Educational Foundation Newsletter*, and *Transgender Tapestry* that circulated throughout the 1970s, 1980s, and 1990s, informing scattered and disparate trans subjects and communities of developments in transition-related health care and giving advice on how to navigate a too-often byzantine and difficult process.

However, the crucial care labor of these vloggers is frequently shaped by an affective orientation to futurity that I interpret as a trans-specific, biomedicalized variant of the much-criticized "It gets better" genre of inspirational, affirmative messaging. The It Gets Better Project was initiated by gay journalist Dan Savage and his partner Terry Miller in 2010 as a social media campaign to address high instances of depression and suicidality among LGBTQ youth, a public response to the highly publicized suicides of teenagers like Billy Lucas and Tyler Clementi who were bullied for being—or suspected of being—gay. The project seeks to offer hope to LGBTQ adolescents and teens with the repeated assurance that "it"—

one's life and life chances, the degree of discrimination one encounters—improves significantly as one ages. This project was roundly critiqued by many prominent North American queer academics and activists almost immediately for failing to grapple with questions of intersectionality. Jasbir Puar (2010) penned a paradigmatic editorial in the *Guardian* that succinctly outlines the prevailing grounds for such critique, highlighting how "many . . . have been struck with how these deaths have been made to serve the purpose of highlighting an exceptional class of aspirational gay citizens at the expense of others. Part of the outrage and upset generated by these deaths is precisely afforded through a fundamental belief that things *are* indeed, better, especially for a particular class of white gay men."

Unlike the initial, official iterations of the It Gets Better campaign, these vlogs are geared specifically toward trans folks who are contemplating or in the midst of transition, offering palliative reassurances that once one moves through the process of medical gatekeeping and accesses the forms of medical transition that make up the normative ensemble of interventions, life improves on most all registers: economically, romantically, in terms of body image and self-esteem, social belonging, mental health, and so forth. Like the It Gets Better Project they seek to offer reassurances and support in the face of high rates of depression and suicidality. The promise implicit in these narratives is that, as one takes steps to bring their embodiment in line with their gender identity, a radical metamorphosis takes place that makes the rhythms and patterns of everyday life easier, more bearable, and less traumatic. Insofar as vloggers proffer this affective narrative, they echo and enhance the promissory narrative of transition articulated by trans-specialized medical professionals, whose practices and reputations rely on such repetitions and amplifications, especially in the form of patient testimonials. Trans vloggers working in this genre are positioned proximally to the medical industry, radically lacking institutional power and authority but able to harness their communal social credit to attest to the promise of (and, sometimes, to critique) trans medical practice.

Tobias Raun (2015: 702), in an examination of trans male vloggers on the "digital *Wunderkammer*" of YouTube, understands this genre as offering a "database for the display of everyday trans life" (703). What strikes him, however, is how redundant this database is, establishing and reifying specific generic conventions in performances of trans masculine self-making. Raun provides an account of the specific tropes that shape the genre, including titling and cataloging vlogs by the number of months one has been on testosterone and assiduously detailing the transformations wrought by testosterone injections, a process through which testosterone becomes the "structuring principle" (704) of the genre. Raun highlights the ways in which "the drug and the camera are mutually constitutive, instantiating and confirming maleness, thereby allowing the vlogger and the viewer to witness the process (documenting effects) while also being a site for staging what and how to witness (performative effects)" (705–6). More than a visual record of transition, these videos also have a pedagogical or coaching function, directing the viewer's attention, establishing zones of corporeal significance (facial hair, the postsurgical chest), and showing us how to gaze, what to notice. This visual coaching does, indeed, do more than document the effects of transition—it also teaches us what constitutes the transition process. Raun concludes that "while trans male vlogs manifest potentials—and possible futures—they also create norms for how trans men look, feel, and talk about their transition, and how they vlog about it" (707), operating as both "commencement and commandment" (707). These vlogs are part of a cultural ensemble that installs narratives of transnormativity, teaching viewers what transition is supposed to look like, what they might one day look like, operating as a visual litmus test against which one might measure their "progress" and gauge what the process and the "post" of transition might be. Inevitably, this entails self-objectification and anxiety, as it invites a practice of corporeal comparison (will my chest hair grow in like his? Will my top surgery scars heal that well?) that, while undergirded by the hope of inhabiting something closer to one's corporeal ideal, hinges on an uncertain and projected future that may very well not turn out to be what one wishes. The affective surround produced by this kind of media is one of anticipation, in all its tense complexity, with all the desire, hope, fear, and dread that anticipation entails.

Jordan F. Miller (2018: 822) comments on the transnormative assumptions that circulate in the trans vlogosphere, writing that many vlogs reflect the "mainstream media portrayal of trans people" insofar as they focus on "documenting the changing body during the early stages of hormone replacement therapy (HRT) or after various gender-affirming surgeries" (822) and frame medical intervention "as a life-or-death step to achieving happiness" (821). In doing so, they fail to reflect the diversity of trans subjects and communities. Miller writes that "the privileging of such a limiting narrative has, among other negative outcomes, created damaging expectations for trans people who identify outside of a male/female binary or do not desire medical intervention" (8), as well as those subjects who encounter substantial difficulty accessing the forms of medical transition they do desire, given that such access is intensively stratified. This surfeit of transnormative narratives makes it difficult, Miller argues, to locate trans vlogs that offer alternative and critical accounts of trans experience, particularly those that foreground questions of race and racism in relation to trans identity and the politics of transition, refuse to overemphasize physical transformation, or depict nonbinary and/or nonmedically transitioning trans experiences. Though the trans vlog archive is vast, the most popular and readily accessible vlogs tend to reiterate, rather than destabilize, transnormative tropologies, producing a misleading sense of coherence that can result in viewers assuming, as Miller did early in his research, that trans YouTube is almost exclusively informed by the perspectives of class-privileged, white, straight, and binary trans subjects (5).

By highlighting this, I don't mean to dismiss the crucial world-building work done by even the most ostensibly transnormative vlogs. In a fundamentally transphobic institutional, political, and cultural environment, providing digital community and transition-related support is both radical and necessary. I call attention to the limits of these narratives only because I believe that other, additional forms of support, solidarity, and intimacy are needed to grapple with the all-too-common experience of lag—a form of being out of temporal sync, left behind—and the negative affects associated with it. This is especially so because the shape of most trans lives doesn't mimic the progressive teleological contours of such narratives, and the ascendancy of these narratives has been far from frictionless, with a well-articulated trans critique of transnormative teleologies of medical transition dating back at least to the work of Sandy Stone in her foundational essay "The *Empire* Strikes Back" (1991) and continuing through the present, with important contributions from Dean Spade (2003), Julian Carter (2013), Julian Gill-Peterson (2017), C. Riley Snorton (2017), and others. Rather, transnormativity and trans exceptionalism are aspirational fantasies that very, very few trans subjects are able to live out phenomenologically. Because the embodied reality of living in and through forms of transphobic violence is so often articulated with the indignities, harms, and aggressions that characterize poverty, disability, and debility; the inhabitation of perceptually queer forms of embodiment; and the differential and compounded violence that attends processes of racialization as nonwhite, the number of trans subjects who live in any kind of comfortable proximity to transnormativity is slim indeed. If there is a phenomenon that cross-cuts much of trans experience—in this moment, in those zones of dispossession, extraction, expropriation, and brutal reterritorialization that some of us call North America—it is the experience of "near life," what Eric Stanley (2011: 15) refers to as "that which emerges in the place of the question of humanity," a term that indexes the experience of living with one's humanity withheld, insistently interrogated, rarely ever assumed.

Laura Horak (2014: 580) builds on Raun's scholarship, unpacking the temporality of these narratives structured around hormonal transition, which she refers to as "hormone time." She writes that "hormone time is linear and teleological, directed toward the end of living full time in the desired gender. It borrows a Christian temporal structure—time begins with moment of rupture and points in a particular direction. . . . While hormone time is not as grandiose, it also points toward a utopian future, in which the subject experiences harmony between the felt and perceived body" (580). Hormone time is both teleological and utopian. The future is always better than the present, a site of promise, deliverance; transition is framed as a period of trial and potential duress that is rewarded with the experience of harmony, good feeling, corporeal comfort, and ease when navigating everyday social interactions. For this reason, Horak links hormone time to "straight time," writing that "it appropriates the 'straight' temporality of progress for radical ends—proving that trans self-determination is not only possible but viable and even joyful. Unlike 'straight' time, the goal is not children or the future of the nation but expansive trans subjects and communities" (581). Hormone time is quite distinct from reproductive futurism—a politics molded by a heterocisnormative investment in providing a better future for the child (Edelman 2004)—but nevertheless appropriates a teleological utopian temporality to provide hope to trans subjects and communities. The futural horizon, the promised telos, is, as Horak (2014: 580) writes, the moment of "harmony between the felt and perceived body."

The trouble is that this horizon sometimes seems to be infinitely receding. When is one "post" transition? Who experiences such unity between feeling and perception, given how radically thrown—nonsovereign, out of one's control—modes of intersubjective corporeal perception are? Is there ever an experience of subjectivity-in-sociality that isn't, to some (significant) extent, shaped by dissonance and misrecognition, particularly if, as Berlant (2011: 26) reminds us, "recognition is the misrecognition you can bear"? Is there ever a moment when we are—transparently, in all our complexity, intuitively and deeply—known by those others we share space with? Where those others understand our bodyminds in precisely the ways in which we desire them to? Even if such moments are possible, or at least feel possible, that doesn't erase the prior years of consistent dissonance, misgendering, and misrecognition, nor does it easily transform the anxiety and fear that one cultivates as a product of living through such (routine, quotidian, incessant) moments.

What hormone time does—and what related futural narratives of medicalized transition do, such as those that prioritize top or bottom surgery (or both) as the sine qua non of a "completed" transition—is position biomedical intervention as necessary and fundamental to securing the future one desires, to achieving the promised moment of harmony between the felt and the perceived body. I want to push against this promissory narrative for a few different reasons. First, it encourages trans subjects to cathect hope for a more livable life to a for-profit medical industry that, too often, lacks empathy and sensitivity and treats trans subjects as a niche market rife for economic exploitation. This means that doctors become saviors, capable of enabling or disabling the possibility of a better future for trans subjects. It also means that the politics of access to forms of medical transition—which are simultaneously geographical, economic, racialized, and gendered, not to mention contingent on questions of employment, insurance, citizenship, and carceral status—aren't significantly engaged, and those that experience compromised access are encouraged to understand this as tantamount to a foreclosed future. If one is unable to access, or has compromised access to, the large ensemble of transition-related technologies, they are placed in a position of lag, their desired future deferred, perhaps perennially. Lag shapes the experience of saving up for transition, putting away a little bit of money each paycheck for specialist appointments not covered, or only partially covered, by insurance (if one has it). Economic considerations aside, the experience of lag structures transition at least as much as transition-related technologies themselves, manifesting in the days, months, and years before one takes steps toward transition and shaping the experience of waiting for each new appointment, each treatment, each follow-up visit. The tropic conventions of hormone time that shape the narratives of transition critiqued by Horak and Raun tend to downplay the affects that correspond to the temporal experience of lag. Lag often comes coupled with an experience of repeated, persistent, and dogged misrecognition and allied forms of transphobic hostility operative at both macro and micro levels. This misrecognition wears away at the resilience of trans subjects and makes the daily arts of living more difficult—in other words, it produces fatigue. I think, largely, we invest in the promises of hormone time because we hope, sincerely, that one day this fatigue will lessen, subside, surcease.

Hormone time and related futural narratives are undergirded by the promise of a time (not yet, but someday) when the relation between one's gendered sense of self and the way that self is perceived socially are aligned. Within this alluring future vision, recognition is conferred explicitly through social interaction, which is understood in a bifurcated manner—either folks get it right or get it wrong, and what they get right or wrong is explicitly linked back to questions of medical access, binary understandings of gender, and the gender-ideal aesthetic "success" of trans subjects. My concern with this understanding of the conferral of gendered recognition is that the granting of legibility lies solely with the perceiver, rather than with the subject being perceived. If we take seriously the fact that access to technologies of transition is shaped by multiple, intersecting vectors of privilege (not to mention differing degrees of interest in and desire for medical transition), and that, both because of and despite this, many trans subjects experience "passing" only in discontinuous, situationally dependent ways, a teleological account of transition that ends with an experience of "harmony between the felt and perceived body" is radically inadequate; it doesn't begin to dignify the complexities of trans experiences of gendered (mis)recognition and the complicated interplay, linkages, and feedback loops that inform the relationship between the "felt" and "perceived" body.

The desire for this experience of harmony between the felt and perceived body is common to trans and cis folks alike—it undergirds all efforts to acquire and inhabit a body unlike the one inhabited at any present moment. I don't mean to suggest that an investment in the promise of experiencing such harmony is the province of trans folks exclusively, though the stakes of such hopes are often much higher for us. The experience, however durable or fleeting, of being recognized in gendered ways that resonate with how we understand ourselves is a form of legibility that isn't only pleasurable but quite crucial to survival, and this is true for both our own perception of our bodies and the ways in which others perceive them. What I am trying to think, however, is how trans subjects might (and do) cultivate forms of self-regard and intracommunal recognition that bolster our ability to see ourselves—and love ourselves, and each other—even as crucial forms of intersubjective gendered recognition are withheld, even as we don't pass as cis, even as we're deprived of the forms of social mooring that gendered legibility and recognition provides, even as we inhabit lag time.

I am accompanied by the work of Gayle Salamon (2010) as I think through the interrelation of trans recognition and livability. She draws on Maurice Merleau-Ponty's phenomenological account of perception and embodiment to develop the idea that perception is fundamentally relational, and that, on account of this, the reality of the perceived body is always situationally coproduced. Therefore, the "reality" of the body always lies "'further on' than any objective perception" (62)—which means that the conferral of gendered recognition never lies solely with an external perceiver. She goes on to clarify what this means for trans and gender-variant bodies:

> What one might read from the contours of the body is something less than the truth of that body's sex, which cannot be located in an external observation of the body, but exists instead in the relation between the material and the ideal, between the perceiver and the perceived, between the material particularity of any body and the network of forces and contexts that shape the material and the meaning of that body. (62)

The task, for Salamon and for me, is how to develop relational ways of witnessing and perceiving trans and gender-variant bodies regardless of their relation to, positioning within, or investment in medicalized teleologies of transition.

Further, I want to suggest that, despite the proliferation of temporally linear, progressive, transnormative narratives, it would be deeply misleading to understand them as offering nuanced experiential accounts of transition or trans experience. They move quickly to affirm an affective experience of embodiment characterized by comfort, joy, recognition, and pleasure, and they tarry with negative affect only insofar as they work to reassure subjects who might be dwelling in an existential space saturated with such affect that it will one day improve, especially if they heed the hegemonic pedagogy of transition offered. I think these narratives, while seeking to provide hope—to trans folk beginning to consider medical transition but also, perhaps, to cis audiences grappling with the affective politics of the transition of a loved one—also (albeit unintentionally) shut down possibilities for empathic identification across and exploration of the more difficult affective experiences of trans becoming—becomings that are often shaped by a dwelling in lag time, and that are no stranger to ensembles of negative affect that manifest in both routine and unpredictable ways.

I prefer to use the language of becoming rather than being because it offers a way of understanding trans experience that exists to the side of (though not incompatible with) hegemonic understandings of transition. Borrowing the term from Gilles Deleuze and Félix Guattari's account in *A Thousand Plateaus* (1987), and drawing on its history of deployment within trans studies scholarship (see Crawford 2008; Sullivan 2006), I understand becoming as the unfolding of difference in time, as an experience of ontological shifts that don't necessarily cohere as shifts in identity at the level of representation. Rather, becoming undermines the fixed, stable terms that give shape and sense to the taxonomies of identity offered up within a given milieu; as philosopher and Deleuze scholar Todd May glosses (2003: 150), "to become is to be part of a process by which the stable identities—the majorities—are dissolved in creative acts in which more fluid 'identities' are created, but only as the by-products of the process itself." Placing emphasis on becoming enables me to think through some of the aspects of transition that fall to the wayside when the focus is solely on questions of representation, identity, and social legibility. This is not to suggest that political and scholarly emphasis on representation and recognition isn't important, only to call attention to the fact that these terms don't do justice to the affective textures of trans experience. Identity is a (very important) part-object in a broader ensemble of relations, and it shouldn't be taken as coidentical or coterminous with transness—or, rather, trans-ing.

Susan Stryker, Paisley Currah, and Lisa Jean Moore propose the concept of trans-ing in the introduction to a 2008 special issue of *WSQ* titled "Trans-" and concerned with the concept of transition, broadly conceived. They write that

> rather than seeing genders as classes or categories that by definition contain only one kind of thing (which raises unavoidable questions about the masked rules and normativities that constitute qualifications for categorical membership), we

understand genders as potentially porous and permeable spatial territories (arguably numbering more than two), each capable of supporting rich and rapidly proliferating ecologies of embodied difference. (12)

The understanding of gender fleshed out here shifts our attention away from questions of identity constitution ("classes or categories that by definition contain only one kind of thing") and towards questions of becoming. If gender isn't an identity, but rather a territory that supports "rapidly proliferating ecologies of embodied difference," then "trans" names not a specific entity, but a process; it is not a noun, but an adjective. Trans-ing, then, "is a practice that takes place within, as well as across or between, gendered spaces . . . a practice that assembles gender into contingent structures of association with other attributes of bodily being, and that allows for their reassembly" (13).

Thinking of transition as a practice of "trans-ing" allows one to focus on how gender is a practice of assembly and reassembly, a process without a delimited outcome. I find this shift in perspective helpful when trying to think slantwise in relation to the emphasis on surgical and hormonal outcomes and normative gendered legibility that forcefully structures transnormative teleologies of transition. To think transition otherwise, especially to think through the aporias produced by such hegemonic accounts of transition, an emphasis on assemblage, process, and practice is key.

Another way to put this: I want to focus on transition as a journey, rather than a destination, and a particularly unpredictable journey at that—one with shifting itineraries, detours, roadblocks, and breakdowns; comprising various speeds and slownesses; with no given return "home," and no guarantee that home might not be profoundly changed if and when one does return. I want to focus on trans lives in interregnum, in the crucial and transformative moments between past and future, between the regime of what was and the promise of what might be. I don't understand the interregnum as the midpoint of a linear temporal narrative, however. It is a kind of nowness that shuttles transversally between different imaginaries of pasts and futures and remains malleable and differentially molded by these imaginaries. Typically understood as a moment between state regimes, or the moments between state failure and the installation of a new system of power, the meaning of the interregnum shifts if we refuse to place emphasis on what was and what might be, and instead focus on the pause, the interim, as a moment of foment, generation, complexity, and fervor, rife with unexpected partnerships, chance events, and connections fortuitous and less so—a space of looseness and possibility, not yet overcoded and fixed in meaning, signification, or representative economy. What possibilities open up when we cease to run toward promissory futures from pasts that we're (sometimes, literally) dying to leave behind?

What I'm proposing is a trans-specific reconsideration of queer theorizations of temporal drag: the refusal to embrace narratives of queer modernity and the attendant march toward ever-increasing progress on account of a stubborn attachment to an often-traumatic past, what Heather Love (2007: 9) has called a "history of queer damage [that] retains its capacity to do harm in the present." Like Love, I'm calling for a necessary grappling with the negativity that doesn't ever seem to stay planted firmly in the past, and the affects allied to the forms of social marginality and abjection that suffuse trans experience regardless of how passable-as-cis one may be in the wake of transition.

This isn't the same as an embrace of a queer temporality of developmental lag that solidifies through being positioned askew in relation to heteronormative reproductive time. This queer embrace of arrested development, articulated by Jack Halberstam in *In a Queer Time and Place* (2005) and trenchantly critiqued by Julian Carter (2013: 142), is the kind that refuses to grow up in order to embrace, instead, a form of not-quite-adulthood that "opens the space for same-sex bonding and polymorphous perversity," but also shuts down "the space for becoming-trans." The inhabitation of the interregnum entails not the refusal to grow up but instead an approach to temporality that understands it as multiply enfolded, rather than merely delayed or deferred. This is how Carter envisions what he calls "transitional time" (142), writing that the folding of such time may produce a sense of lag, but it also might "heighten a body's sensitivity, invaginating it so that it touches itself in several different moments at once" (142), and that these temporal "pleats may propel the body forward . . . toward an embodied future, even as that future is summoned into being in and through a body that does not yet exist, and while the body that does exist in the present is the medium for the future body's becoming-form" (142). Such an enfolded temporality is inevitably affectively complex, with traumas residual and fresh existing alongside— rather, knotted together with—moments of joy, hope, and recognition. As Gwen Benaway (2018) writes, in a beautiful essay on surgical transition and the long process of coming home to one's body, "the events that surround our becoming leave an imprint on us." The memories of these events are carried with us and come to help constitute our divergent and overlapping experiences of embodiment. Meditating on the complexities of the relations between trans embodiment, selfhood, and temporality, and figuring her self and her body as a "we" in negotiation, Benaway (2018) offers the following account: "Together, we imagined a possibility instead of an ending. This is the real story of bodies. Movement, joy, and release into new configurations. Our bodies do not need to be perfect or exactly as they were when we were born. We are not ruled by the shape we arrive in. We adapt, heal, and expand. Our bodies are not an ending, but a beginning. This is a truth I am willing to die for." While transnormative futural narratives envision the time of posttransition as characterized by the structure of feeling associated with domesticity—comfort, ease, happiness, safety—and are underwritten by the promise of finally feeling at home in one's skin, this affective narrative of what the body as home feels like belies the complex temporalities of transition. Benaway points out the ways that such a coming home involves moving through trauma, grappling with the enormous existential difficulties and forms of violence, both structural and interpersonal, that attend processes of trans becoming. She argues that these experiences leave an imprint, that the traces of these events are, following Carter, always temporally enfolded within, part and parcel of, the experience of embodiment.

Some of the difficulties that attend affective experiences of transition have to do with the forms of disconnection, withdrawal, and dissociation that often accompany it. As trans scholar Atalia Israeli-Nevo (2017: 38) writes, in a meditation on her own (slow, circuitous) transition process,

> as trans subjects in this transphobic world, we are encouraged and forced into a position of not being present. We are dissociated from our bodies, our loved ones, and our general environment. This dissociation throws us into a far future in which we are safe after we have passed and found a bodily and social home. However, this future is imagined and unreachable, resulting in us being out of time.

When Israeli-Nevo articulates being "forced into a position of not being present," she's referring to the ensemble of strategies that trans subjects cultivate in response to consistent misrecognition, phobic response, and shunning. One of these responses is social withdrawal: if one's appearance in a situation or social world is contingent on misrecognition and encounters with macro- and microaggressions, they may do their best to limit or altogether avoid—to the best of their ability—such situations. Another, related response is that of skepticism and mistrust. This entails a carefully considered curation of where and how one appears, among whom, in what kinds of built spaces. This means that any form of public or semipublic encounter is subject to premeditation and scrutiny with reference to the maintenance of one's physical and emotional well-being (though often one has very limited agency over whether to inhabit certain spaces and must appear in and engage ones they'd rather avoid). If "being present" means occupying space with a degree of un-self-consciousness, lack of anxiety, and without projections about what forms of violence might occur, then "being present" is a form of privilege that the majority of trans subjects lack. The word Israeli-Nevo gives to this complex experience is *dissociation*—detaching physically, psychologically, and emotionally from spaces, institutions, situations, relationships, and our own bodies, even as we must continue to inhabit them. In the midst of this dissociation, we are offered narratives about finding home and safety, but this is contingent on a process of medical transition that may be out of reach, differentially deferred, or not even desired; it is on this narrative that we are encouraged to pin our hopes and dreams. Even for those of us who are able to access medical technologies of transition, the experience of dissociation, once endured, remains pleated into the present moment, a memory imprinted, informing our relationship to our own bodies and the multiple milieus they move with and within.

#t4t: Trans Intimacies and Trans Presents (or How to Survive the Interregnum)

The form of futural imaginary I've been critiquing has trouble holding the complexities that attend the enfolded time of transition. It isn't adequate to the task of dignifying the ways in which past trauma emerges suddenly in a present moment, the ways that negative affect that we might be tempted to associate with a closeted past or the turbulence of transition persists and endures, resonating across life spans and irrefutably transforming the subjects so impacted. I have found, in the speculative dystopic trans fictions of Kai Cheng Thom (2018) and Torrey Peters (2017), disruptive reworkings of temporalities of transition that offer a more capacious frame through which to incorporate the ongoing lived effects of negative affect. The dystopic visions they offer resist the tendency to link joyful affect to futural hope, even as they vividly depict the scrappy inventiveness, creativity, and intimacy cultivated by trans folks to survive in radically imperfect, irreparably broken worlds.

Kai Cheng Thom's *Fierce Femmes and Notorious Liars* (2018) takes place in a fantastic fictional near future that very much mirrors the North American present. The narrator—who is never named—leaves home in her late teens, running from a city called Gloom where she has lived with her parents, both Chinese migrants, and a beloved younger sister named Charity, toward the City of Smoke and Lights, a place where "the streets are crooked, and the light is heavy, and the air is stained ash grey from the glamorous cigarette lips of hungry ghosts swimming through the fog"; a place where "anything can happen if you dream it," where "you can be anything you want" (20). She has moved to the City of Smoke and Lights to transition, to "become nobody" in order to "become someone else" (21). She finds the Street of Miracles, a vice district populated by trans femmes and queers and cops and johns, and is quickly taken in by a circle of trans women and placed under the protective wing of Kimaya, a trans elder whose smile is "ancient and battered and mysterious, punctuated by several cracked teeth . . . from getting hit in the face by her boyfriend ten years ago . . . from a police baton during a protest" (40). Kimaya's smile, which the narrator calls "bright and beautiful" (40), is a living testimonial to the forms of trans resilience in the face of trauma that the narrator is about to be initiated into. Over the course of the "confabulous memoir," she will fight (and kill) cops and johns to defend herself and her trans sisterhood, fall in love, navigate exploitative specialists in trans medicine, negotiate the difficulties of political solidarity through debates about the most effective modes of trans insurgency, struggle to find and afford a place to live, and cultivate strategies for ensuring her physical and emotional safety in situations of explicit transmisogynistic targeting.

Peter's novella, *Infect Your Friends and Loved Ones* (2017), takes place in a dystopic near future in which an unnamed narrator negotiates the fallout wrought by a global "contagion" that comes about when her on-again, off-again girlfriend, Lexi, invents a new form of bacteria that prevents human bodies from responding to endogenous hormonal production, ushering in an era wherein everyone—cis and trans folks alike—must rely on exogenous hormones to manifest gendered embodiment in the ways they desire. Over the course of the novel, we shuttle back and forth in time, with the orienting event that structures before and after being "contagion." This contagion is both personal—the narrator is one of the first people infected, in a deliberate move by Lexi that would cease the narrator's biological responsiveness to androgens. She is also a Patient Zero figure, initiating global contagion. It tweaks the temporal function of hormone injection and ingestion in mainstream trans narratives, which, as Horak and Raun note, so often functions as a temporally structuring principle. In the novella, this moment is not individuated, not a tale of personal gender transformation, but an event of world-shifting magnitude; Peters even refers to trans folks in the novel as "antediluvian trans," situating contagion on par with the cataclysmic great biblical Flood. Because of the polysemy of the word *antediluvian*—which can also mean old-fashioned, behind the times—Peters also implicitly raises questions about how we might understand trans subjectivities in a near future in which everyone partakes of exogenous hormonal body modification. It's worth noting that this near future is very much like the present, insofar as cis and trans folks alike routinely utilize exogenous hormones for all sorts of reasons.

Both books are animated by the questions that Alexis Lothian (2016: 448) poses about the work of speculative dystopia, which she articulates as such: "A dystopian impulse leads us to ask: what do speculative narrative futures look and feel like without either a redemptive kernel of hope or an implicit acceptance of the way things are? And what pleasures . . . and politics grow from this kind of speculation"? In other words, how can we think futurity without acquiescing to the narrative lures of optimism, salvation, rebirth, and redemption? The genre of trans speculative dystopia, of which Peters and Thom are but two examples, offers us rich resources for envisioning such futures. They are part of a broader set of literatures theorized by Adrienne Maree Brown, Walidah Imarisha, and Sheree Renee Thomas (2015: 10) as "visionary fiction," a term they use to distinguish speculative fiction that "has relevance towards building new, freer worlds from mainstream science fiction, which most often reinforces dominant narratives of power."

The fact that Thom calls *Fierce Femmes* a "confabulous memoir" highlights the limitations of traditional (linear, redemptive) narrative strategies of trans memoir. Unpacking the portmanteau *confabulous* means, first, grasping that it is shaped by confabulation, an unintentional memory error that takes the form of fabricated or distorted retellings of experience; second, that it takes part in a process of fabulation, a postmodern narrative form emerging out of resistance to the conventions of both realism and romanticism, one that we most readily associate with magical realism in its combination of the mundane and the fantastic; and third, that such forms of revised and invented narratives are fabulous. A "confabulous memoir" offers us a way of getting at both the mundane and extraordinary valences of trans experiences and can be enacted only by leaving behind the dominant temporal and affective tropes of trans memoir. As Thom (2017) comments in an interview with *Teen Vogue*, the book is

> a struggle to break out of the memoir genre that trans women have been relegated to for a really long time, this idea that we are only important or readable as objects to study, as objects to be used as titillation for a cisgender audience. [This narrative of] us explaining our life story of being born in the wrong body and being oppressed and overcoming it and then assimilating into a happy cis-passing straight life. That is not the reality of the vast majority of trans women I know.

The book begins with a critique of this narrative, opening with the narrator watching a wealthy white trans woman—a thinly veiled proxy for Caitlyn Jenner—who has just gotten "The Surgery" (Thom 2018: 2) receive an "Upstanding Good Samaritan Pillar of the Community Award for, like, being brave or whatever" (2).

> What really works me up is the *way* that this whole story is being told: Everyone look at this poor little trans girl desperate for a ~~fairy godmother~~doctor to give her boobs and a vagina and a pretty face and wear nice dresses! Save the trans girls! Save the whales! Put them in a zoo!
>
> It's actually a very old archetype that trans girl stories get put into: this sort of tragic, plucky-little-orphan character who is just supposed to suffer through everything and wait, and if you're good and brave and patient (and white and rich) enough, then you get the big reward . . . which is that you get to be just like

everybody else who is white and rich and boring. And then you marry the prince or the football player and live boringly ever after. We're like Cinderella, waiting to go to the ball. Like the Little Mermaid, getting her tail surgically altered and her voice removed, so that she can walk around on land. Those are the stories we get, these days.

Or, you know, the ones where we're dead. (2–3)

The character slippage Thom's narrator highlights—between fairy godmother and doctor—highlights the messianic temporal structure that tends to characterize transition, shifting the register to a princess narrative, which (like narratives of being saved by religion) charts a move from wretchedness and despair to effulgence and fulfillment. Thom's narrator also raises the question of deservedness: Who is a good trans person? Who is an ideal candidate for transition? The long history of medical gatekeeping around transition is the obvious target of commentary here, with the "~~fairy godmother~~doctor" the arbiter of whether one might become what they so desire. The proper affective disposition in relation to this phenomenon is one of deference and hope—one is exhorted to fulfill the role of the "tragic, plucky-little-orphan character" or the rare and endangered species in need of rescue ("Save the trans girls! Save the whales! Put them in a zoo!"). The orphan, the endangered species: both are figures of severely curtailed agency, victims of their environment almost entirely dependent on the good will, grace, and assistance of others. Importantly, in the case of the endangered species, these others are often precisely those who did the harm in the first place. These metaphors suggest that trans girls are radically unable to save themselves, though desperately in need of saving. What Thom's narrator insinuates here is that trans girls are consistently framed as both radically vulnerable and incapable of saving themselves—a disempowering, deleterious, and limiting trope if ever there was one. Further, she suggests that the possibility of rescue is not just predicated on the successful performance of deference, desire, and gratitude but also explicitly tied to racial and economic privilege (being "good and brave and patient (and white and rich) enough"). One is worth saving only if they already bear certain markers of existential value, only if they are already, in Foucauldian terms, counted as part of the population conceptualized as worthy of life, rather than cathected to the slow process of neglect that so profoundly shapes his articulation of biopolitics as "the power to 'make' live and 'let' die" (Foucault 2003: 239). Thom's narrator highlights the radically bifurcated mainstream narratives of trans femme existence; they vacillate between princess narratives and accounts of brutal homicide, and the difference between the two hinges on questions of racial and economic status. Temporally speaking, this is a vacillation between the brightest of futures and no future, between hope and the radical negation of hope. Both of these temporalities yoke (and reduce) the complexities of trans experience to a future, either promised or foreclosed. Both temporalities place trans *presents*, and trans presences (the forms in which we manifest here, now, whatever those may be) under erasure.

What Thom's (2018) novel does, instead, is radically refuse a futural narrative of redemption by grounding the story in the complicated intimacies of a group of trans femmes living and loving alongside one another, supporting each other, arguing with each other, forming an "all-trans girl vigilante gang" (178) with each other, making love, breaking up, and reconciling. We shuttle to the past from time to time, through memory narratives offered by several different characters, but the bulk of the book takes place in a now wherein the narrator is learning, gradually, hard lessons about self-care and the importance of trans communality in a broader necropolitical context wherein violence is routinized, normalized, and rarely contested unless by trans subjects themselves. At the conclusion of the book, the narrator even explicitly refuses attachment to a fairy tale ending: the arrival of her prince. She meets and falls for a trans guy named Josh, a graduate student from a wealthy family who is kind, generous, and committed to building a future with the narrator; he invites her to move into his (extraordinarily fancy) condo, bankrolled by his family, and encourages her to go to college and take writing classes. While discussing this turn of events with her elder protectress Kimaya, she pauses to envision their future together:

> And now I'm going to move in with him, and he keeps on saying I should think about auditing classes at the University and probably I could get a scholarship and what a great writer I could be with my "gift for storytelling." And then I'll get published and become a super-famous Transgender Writer and we'll get married and be a Transgender Power Couple and have Transgender Children and raise them on a cloud of Transgender Happiness™.
> And the thing is, I *want* that. I want it so, so bad. (178–79)

But she also senses that Josh is pushing her toward this fairy tale ending, toward the fulfillment of their promise as a Trans Power Couple; she resents this projection while also being lured by it. She then turns to Kimaya and asks, "What do you think the difference is between hunger and love?" (179). Kimaya responds, after some deliberation: "Hunger is a story you get stuck in. Love's the story that takes you somewhere new" (180). Thom gives vivid shape here to both the absolutely understandable lure of transnormative futural narratives—framing them as informed by a deep yearning for something better—and the danger of such futural attachments, manifest in the ways they produce a certain stuckness. This stuckness is precisely what Berlant notes as integral to cruel optimism, insofar as it produces difficulty improvising in the context of an ever-shifting present because of fidelity to a particular cluster of futural promises about what constitutes the good life. A practice of love is proposed, in the place of such hunger, as that which might transform the conditions of the present; Berlant (2011: 262) calls this "solidarity," which, she writes, "comes from the scavenging for survival that absorbs increasingly more people's lives." The most profound love that we witness in Thom's work is that between the trans women who dwell, scavenging for survival, in the Street of Miracles; and it is the practice of love cultivated there that enables each of them to not get stuck in a story, to go "somewhere new." Thom's narrator rejects the scripted futures on offer, choosing instead the sustaining unpredictability of a praxis of love. Thom's work helps us explore the affective structures of trans presents, which are always more nuanced, more variegated, than the Janus-faced structure of conventional narratives of trans futurity would have us believe.

I turn now to the dystopian trans alter-world on offer in the work of Torrey Peters as it deals directly with questions of negative affect, grappling with the way the everyday is shot through with traumas residual and fresh, which make themselves more or less available within the present, depending on conjuncture, chance, affinity, and trigger. Crucially, however, these traumas are positioned not as wounds to be healed, finally sutured in some future-perfect. Rather, the narrative—like Thom's—is resolutely irresolute, refusing to wrap up loose ends, refusing the lure of the palliative gestures of happily ever after, yet offering glimmers of possibility for living otherwise, in and through trauma, and maybe perhaps beyond it. These glimmers are routed through trans-for-trans (t4t) love, affection, and intimacy, presented as simultaneously radically difficult and radically transformative.

The central love story—if one can call it that—in Peter's novella *Infect Your Friends and Loved Ones* occurs between trans folk, between the narrator and Lexi, another trans woman. This fact alone merits pause. Peters, through this narratological decision, renders a world that actively decenters cis subjectivities, perceptions, and erotic economies of meaning, recognition, and validation. Emphasis is placed on t4t circuits of recognition, attraction, solidarity, and support, and a central animating question emerges: how can trans folk learn to love each other? In exploring the dynamics of t4t intimacy, Peters intentionally performs a radical revision of the meaning of the acronym.

T4t began its life as a category within the personals section of Craigslist (a regionally tailored online version of classified advertisements), one of the handful of options that enabled folks to search through online personals by gender identification. I consider the intimacy elaborated in Peters's work a détourned take-up of the t4t acronym. Détournement—a tactic developed by Guy Debord

(2000) (and affiliated with radical French Lettrists) in the 1950s and later taken up by the Situationist International—is most easily understood as the appropriation and repurposing (rerouting, hijacking, derailing) of an existing media artifact in a manner that troubles, subverts, or resists the intended messaging of the original artifact. Understanding the détournement t4t undergoes in Peter's work begins with admitting the obvious transphobic logic that undergirds the initial iteration of t4t: it sequesters trans folks from Ms and Ws (as in M4M, W4W), partaking of the kind of trans-exclusionary (not to mention cisnormative and homo-normative) logic that misconstrues trans as a sexualized gender category unto itself. As Susan Stryker (2008: 148) clarifies in her critical rereading of the importance of trans exclusion for the emergence of homonormative political/communal forms,

> As a sexual orientation category, trans appears as a desire, akin to kink and fetish desire, for cross-dressing or (more extremely) genital modification. The "T" in this version of the LGBT community becomes a group of people who are attracted to one another on the basis of enjoying certain sexual practices—in the same way that gay men are attracted to gay men, and lesbians are attracted to lesbians, on the basis of a shared desire for particular sexual practices.

When the digital architectonics of Craigslist partake of this logic, misinterpreting trans identity as kink—and drawing on a long history of such problematic interpretations, ranging from John Money and Margaret Lamacz's (1984) writing on gynemimetophiles to the work of J. Michael Bailey (2003) and beyond—they also deploy "T" as an insulating function, intending to prevent trans-identified individuals from cropping up in the rest of the personals. As Stryker (2008: 148) clarifies, "Trans thus conceived of does not trouble the basis of the other categories [M, W, hetero, homo]—indeed, it becomes a containment mechanism for 'gender trouble' of various sorts that works in tandem with assimilative gender-normative tendencies within the sexual identities." It also derealizes the authenticity of trans gender identifications, partaking of the double bind Talia Mae Bettcher so eloquently parses in "Evil Deceivers and Make-Believers" (2007), in which trans folk can only be perceived within cisnormative framings as "fooling" cis folks—particularly in intimate/sexual contexts—or "pretending" to be the gender that one is; it is implicit in the structuring logic of Craigslist personals that trans folks are sequestered precisely to guard against cis experiences of ostensible deception.

However, the designers of Craigslist personals also unintentionally produced a kind of proto-trans-separatist space with the invention of t4t, and it is this by-product, this form of alternative usage, that is taken up by contemporary manifestations of the acronym, both as a hashtag and a descriptor of intimacies extant and desired. T4t is a form of contingent, strategic separatism that Chela Sandoval (2000: 57) usefully glosses as a mode of oppositional consciousness that is initiated "to protect and nurture the differences that define its practitioners through their complete separation from the dominant social order." It is in the tradition of other forms of politicized and eroticized separatism, echoing Marlon Riggs's assertion in *Tongues Untied* (dir. Marlon Riggs, 1989) that "black men loving black men is *the* revolutionary act," and resonating with the formulation of lesbian separatism as a praxis engaged by "woman-loving women" (Radicalesbians 1970) to invent modes of life beyond the stranglehold of interlocking (male, heterosexual, white) supremacies. T4t emerges from a recognition that trans subjects, too, might benefit from a severing of ties to cissexist modes of interpellating trans bodies (as failures, fakes, inorganic, inauthentic), and, moreover, that such strategic separatism might be one of the most direct routes toward cultivating self-love, self-regard, and self-care, especially because it confronts and disrupts the assimilationist logics that structure the limiting forms of individuated futural aspiration already discussed. The hope is that, in community with one another, insulated—however temporarily—from cissexist modes of perception, some significant healing might be possible.

Peters's (2017) work fleshes out this détourned reinvention of t4t for the purposes of trans intimacy. She is quite explicit about her reconceptualization of it: the acronym appears on the cover of *Infect Your Friends and Loved Ones*, is spoken as a secret code of care and solidarity at crucial points in the novella, and appears as a stick-and-poke tattoo on Lexi, one of the central characters (the former/maybe future lover and complex frenemy of the narrator). Lexi and the narrator also met through the t4t personals, where the narrator answered Lexi's ad, despite being in a sexless relationship with her current girlfriend (whom she started dating prior to transition) and already involved in clandestine Skype and phone-sex hookups with random men. She wants to meet Lexi, though not necessarily for sex: "Why do I want to meet Lexi? The answer is things I can't say. That I can barely think" (25). The narrator's desire to reach out to another trans woman is opaque, oblique, ineffable—not predetermined, scripted, or prefigured, but an opening to possibilities not yet articulable or even quite imaginable. For me, this admission of uncertainty raises several significant questions: What does it mean that the narrator—and perhaps, by extension, many other trans folk—lack scripts, expectations, and assumptions for t4t intimacy? What possibilities inhere in the space of such unscriptedness? What might t4t intimacy enable in a world less overcoded by forms of genital-centricity that naturalize linkages between morphology and intimacy?

Peters builds such a world in *Infect Your Friends and Loved Ones* and does this by, first, making everyone trans. Lexi and her trans girl gang concoct a contagious bacteriological infection (derived from agricultural research on pigs) that "causes a body's antibodies to bind to gonadotropin (GnRH)"—as the narrator explains, "the hormone that signals the production of all sex hormones in mammals" (28). This means that the antibodies then attack GnRH, resulting in "a complete cessation of the production of all sex hormones" (28). What this contagion effectively ushers in is a near-global reliance on exogenous hormones—an intensification of what Paul Preciado (2013: 23) has called the "pharmacoporno-graphic era" and a quite literal reimagining of Halberstam's (1994: 226) early-career assertion that "we are all transsexuals. There are no transsexuals." While we certainly live in a world that is (albeit discontinuously) biomedicalized and in bodies, whether cis or trans, that are deeply imbricated with and reliant on all sorts of exogenous hormones—whether we're on birth control, supplementing ostensibly "low T," on hormone replacement therapy to mitigate menopause, or taking hormones to transition—Peters removes the question of agency, establishing a new biological baseline that asks everyone to choose, and thus to deal with questions of access, scarcity, and gatekeeping the way trans folk have had to for the last several decades.

In the postcontagion world that Peters (2017) constructs, where the body modified by exogenous hormones has become a general ontology, where one's intentional relation to practices of biomolecular modification must be grappled with and there is no recourse to a purportedly "natural" form of biological dimorphism, the phrase "antediluvian trans" (52) comes to mark a difference of identity and agential relation to transition that might otherwise be lost in a world of "auntie-boys" and "T-slabs" (the names Peters gives to folks accessing exogenous estrogen and testosterone postcontagion). The register of trans identity thus shifts, as does the meaning of trans solidarity. What differentiates "antediluvian trans" folk from others has to do primarily with shared desires and affective orientations, rather than access to technologies of transition. In Peters's world, hormones are scarce, subject to a black-market economy, and liable to be tainted with harmful chemicals. Transition-related surgeries have ceased to be available; in a world increasingly given over to scarcity and subsistence, the market for such technologies has dried up. Nevertheless, the networks that trans women had formed before contagion persist, shaped by a t4t praxis of love.

Explicating the meaning of this praxis, Zoey—a member of a trans femme separatist farmhouse on the plains—says, "It's a promise. You just promise to love trans girls above all else. The idea—although maybe not the practice—is that a girl could be your worst enemy, the girl you wouldn't piss on to put out a fire, but if she's trans, you're gonna offer her your bed, you're gonna share your last hormone shot" (54). The narrator responds that this sounds like "some kind of trans girl utopia," to which Zoey laughs and clarifies: "Do you think the words trans women and utopia ever go together in the same sentence? Even when we're not starved for hormones, we're still bitches. Crabs in a barrel. Fucking utopia, my ass" (54). And finally, closing the scene, Zoey drives the point home: "We aim high, trying to love each other and then we take what we can get. We settle for looking out for each other. And even if we don't all love each other, we mostly all respect one another" (54).

T4t, in Peters's work, is many things: an ideal, a promise, an identifier, a way of flagging an ethic of being. It is antiutopian, guiding a praxis of solidarity in the interregnum; it is about small acts guided by a commitment to trans love, small acts that make life more livable in and through difficult circumstances. It has no truck with cruel optimism, with the attachment to a toxic present because of a promised future that wears you down and out. It is cynical, skeptical; t4t is set up to fail, about aiming high and taking what one can get. It embraces ethical imperfection and complexity. It dwells in difficulty without the expectation that such difficulties will cease by and through a t4t praxis of love. It is about being with and bearing with; about witnessing one another, being mirrors for one another that avoid some of the not-so-funhouse effects of cisnormative percep-tive habits that frame trans folk as too much, not enough, failed, or not yet realized. Nevertheless, it doesn't rely on a frictionless and easeful understanding of trans relationality; it hinges on the admittance that trans people often have a very, very difficult time with one another. Appearing together in public might increase the likelihood of being clocked; dwelling in intimate spaces with one another might render one's home places more difficult, rather than less, as trans-related trauma is shared and thus, perhaps, affectively amplified rather than dimin-ished (a phenomenon that is not bad, per se, just complex and—sometimes—tiring). Then there are those other dynamics Zoey obliquely references with the phrase "crabs in a barrel"—the forms of envy, annoyance, jealousy, and judgment borne out of survival struggles and economies of scarcity, an emotional ensemble shorthanded by Zoey in one word: *bitches*, a word that is simultaneously an indicator of relational difficulty and a badge of honor, a sign of tenacity, bull-headedness, ambition, and brassiness. Not to mention competing and sometimes incompatible personalities, politics, expectations, and assumptions.

To recall Eve Sedgwick's (1990: 22) very first axiom: (trans) people are different from one another. T4t is inevitably a difficult practice of love across difference in the name of coalition and survival, and it thus can't presuppose or predicate such love on identitarian or subjective sameness. Too often, "trans folk/people/communities" gets deployed as an abstract and overcoded monolith, coming to signify for diversely stratified communities. When used monolithically, *trans* coheres in ways that minimize colonial and racial differences and operates as implicitly white and settler, presuming a form of trans belonging sutured through the experience of "trans" as a single-axis form of minoritization. A t4t praxis of love enables and elicits more finely grained attention to differences between and among trans folk, with all the dissonance and difficulty engaging such differences entails. In this movement toward one another, this contingent separatism, space is made to signify and be understood differently, in greater complexity, in excess of reductive cis- and transnormative interpellations of trans subjects. Ultimately, what a t4t praxis of love does is offer a blueprint for surviving lag time, for getting by in the interregnum, which may end up being the only time we have.

Hil Malatino is an assistant professor in the Department of Women's, Gender, and Sexuality Studies and a research associate in the Rock Ethics Institute at Pennsylvania State University. Their research and teaching draws on trans and intersex studies, critical sexuality studies, transnational feminisms, disability studies, and medical ethics to theorize how experiences of violence, trauma, and resilience play out in intersex, trans, and gender-nonconforming lives. Their first book, *Queer Embodiment: Monstrosity, Medical Violence, and Intersex Experience* (2019), examines the relationship between intersex embodiment, biomedical technologies, and the forms of subjectivity both enabled and constrained by the medicalization of gender nonconformance.

References

Bailey, J. Michael. 2003. *The Man Who Would Be Queen*. Washington, DC: Joseph Henry.

Benaway, Gwen. 2018. "A Body like a Home." *Hazlitt*, May 30. hazlitt.net/longreads/body-home.

Berlant, Lauren. 2011. *Cruel Optimism*. Durham, NC: Duke University Press.

Bettcher, Talia Mae. 2007. "Evil-Deceivers and Make-Believers: On Transphobic Violence and the Politics of Illusion." *Hypatia* 22, no. 3: 43–65.

Carter, Julian. 2013. "Embracing Transition, or Dancing in the Folds of Time." In *The Transgender Studies Reader 2*, edited by Susan Stryker and Arin Z. Aizura, 130–43. New York: Routledge.

Crawford, Lucas Cassidy. 2008. "Transgender without Organs? Mobilizing a Geo-Affective Theory of Gender Modification." *WSQ* 36, nos. 3–4: 127–43.

Debord, Guy. 2000. *Society of the Spectacle*. Detroit: Black and Red.

Deleuze, Gilles, and Félix Guattari. 1987. *A Thousand Plateaus*. Minneapolis: University of Minnesota Press.

Edelman, Lee. 2004. *No Future*. Durham, NC: Duke University Press.

Foucault, Michel. 2003. *Society Must Be Defended: Lectures at the Collège de France, 1975–76*. New York: Picador.

Gill-Peterson, Julian. 2017. "Implanting Plasticity into Sex and Trans/Gender." *Angelaki* 22, no. 2: 47–60.

Halberstam, Jack. 1994. "F2M: The Making of Female Masculinity." In *The Lesbian Postmodern*, edited by Laura Doan, 210–28. New York: Columbia University Press.

Halberstam, Jack. 2005. *In a Queer Time and Place*. New York: New York University Press.

Horak, Laura. 2014. "Trans on YouTube: Intimacy, Visibility, Temporality." *TSQ* 1, no. 4: 572–85.

Imarisha, Walidah. 2015. Foreword to *Octavia's Brood: Science Fiction Stories from Social Justice Movements*, edited by Walidah Imarisha, Adrienne M. Brown, and Sheree R. Thomas, 10–11. Oakland, CA: AK.

Israeli-Nevo, Atalia. 2017. "Taking (My) Time: Temporality in Transition, Queer Delays, and Being (in the) Present." *Somatechnics* 7, no. 1: 34–49.

Lothian, Alexis. 2016. "A Speculative History of No Future: Feminist Negativity and the Queer Dystopian Impulses of Katharine Burdekin's *Swastika Night*." *Poetics Today* 37, no. 3: 443–72.

Love, Heather. 2007. *Feeling Backward*. Cambridge, MA: Harvard University Press.

May, Todd. 2003. "When Is a Deleuzian Becoming?" *Continental Philosophy Review* 36, no. 2: 139–53.

Miller, Jordan F. 2018. "YouTube as a Site of Counternarratives to Transnormativity." *Journal of Homosexuality* 66, no. 6: 815–37.

Money, John, and Margaret Lamacz. 1984. "Gynemimesis and Gynemimetophilia: Individual and Cross-cultural Manifestations of a Gender-Coping Strategy Hitherto Unnamed." *Comparative Psychiatry* 25, no. 4: 392–403.

Peters, Torrey. 2017. *Infect Your Friends and Loved Ones*. Self-published.

Preciado, Paul. 2013. *Testo-Junkie*. New York: Feminist Press.

Puar, Jasbir. 2010. "In the Wake of It Gets Better." *Guardian*, November 16. www.theguardian.com /commentisfree/cifamerica/2010/nov/16/wake-it-gets-better-campaign.

Radicalesbians. 1970. "The Woman-Identified Woman." Documents from the Women's Liberation Movement, Special Collections Library, Duke University, Durham, NC.

Raun, Tobias. 2015. "Archiving the Wonders of Testosterone via YouTube." *TSQ* 2, no. 4: 701–09.

Salamon, Gayle. 2010. *Assuming a Body*. New York: Columbia University Press.

Sandoval, Chela. 2000. *Methodology of the Oppressed*. Minneapolis: University of Minnesota Press.

Sedgwick, Eve. 1990. *Epistemology of the Closet*. Berkeley: University of California Press.

Snorton, C. Riley. 2017. *Black on Both Sides*. Minneapolis: University of Minnesota Press.

Spade, Dean. 2003. "Resisting Medicine, Remodeling Gender." *Berkeley Women's Law Journal* 15: 15–37.

Stanley, Eric. 2011. "Near Life, Queer Death: Overkill and Ontological Capture." *Social Text*, no. 107: 1–19.

Stone, Sandy. 1991. "The *Empire* Strikes Back: A Posttranssexual Manifesto." In *Body Guards: The Cultural Politics of Gender Ambiguity*, edited by Julia Epstein and Kristina Straub, 280–304. New York: Routledge.

Stryker, Susan. 2008. "Transgender History, Homonormativity, and Disciplinarity." *Radical History Review*, no. 100: 145–57.

Stryker, Susan, Paisley Currah, and Lisa Jean Moore. 2008. "Introduction: Trans, Tran-, or Transgender?" *WSQ* 36, no. 3: 11–22.

Sullivan, Nikki. 2006. "Transmogrification: (Un)Becoming Other(s)." In *The Transgender Studies Reader*, edited by Susan Stryker and Stephen Whittle, 552–64. New York: Routledge.

Thom, Kai Cheng. 2017. "Author Kai Cheng Thom on Writing a New Kind of Transgender Memoir." Interview by Britni de la Cretaz. *Teen Vogue*, April 5. www.teenvogue.com /story/author-kai-cheng-thom-on-writing-a-new-kind-of-transgender-memoir.

Thom, Kai Cheng. 2018. *Fierce Femmes and Notorious Liars: A Dangerous Trans Girl's Confabulous Memoir*. Montreal: Metonymy.

The Transfeminine Futurity in Knowing Where to Look

Vivek Shraya on Selfies

NICOLE ERIN MORSE

Abstract In this interview, trans artist Vivek Shraya discusses the gendered politics of self-representation, the misogynistic stigma that attaches to her selfies, and the power of controlling the gaze and knowing "where to look."
Keywords Vivek Shraya, selfie, futurity, stigma

V ivek Shraya is an interdisciplinary artist and an assistant professor of creative writing at the University of Calgary. Her award-winning books include the children's book *God Loves Hair* (2014), the novel *She of the Mountains* (2014), and the poetry collection *even this page is white* (2016). Her latest books, *I'm Afraid of Men* and *Death Threat*, were released in 2018 and 2019. She writes and performs original music, including the coming-out song "Girl, It's Your Time" from her album with Queer Songbook Orchestra *Part-Time Woman* (2017). In her portrait project *Trisha* (2016) she restages photographs of her mother from the 1970s, playing both her mother and the role of "Trisha," the daughter her mother thought she would never have. As she stands in for her mother, with costumes, props, and poses that both resemble and transform elements of the original images, Shraya reimagines her family's history as she produces a future that once seemed impossible. On social media, Shraya's reflexive work continues in her selfies (figs. 1–2), which attract intense interest but also elicit strong feelings of discomfort. While Anne Burns (2015) has shown that the disciplining of selfies operates as a stand-in for the disciplining of the young, cisgender women who are most closely associated with selfie culture, Shraya speaks to the specifically racialized and transmisogynistic anxieties that arise in response to her selfie practice.

Figure 1. Vivek Shraya, Selfie #1.

As Shraya says in this interview, "a good selfie is one where you know where to look." In her selfies, I contend that this idea of "knowing where to look" is both a practical question of her pose and a metaphorical issue of where to direct one's attention—how to aim toward brown transfeminine futurity.

For example, in a selfie originally captioned "something wicked this way comes" (Shraya 2018b), Shraya's look at first appears to be barred by the sunglasses she wears, although her pose allows us to read the likely direction of her look toward the lens. However, within the depths of the reflective glasses, we can catch a glimpse of the screen of the smartphone with which she captured the image. The line of her arm, illuminated by sunlight, leads toward the shadowed screen that we know duplicates the image we see. Although obscured by shadow within the image, the vision of futurity that "this way comes" simultaneously emerges in vibrant color in this relay between the selfie, Shraya, her camera, and the spectator. Like Kara Keeling's (2008: 137) "black femme function," which points to a future "elsewhere," Shraya's selfies point to the potentiality of brown transfeminine futurity, something that is distant and difficult to see but simultaneously vibrantly imminent, as long as she—and we—know where to look.

Nicole Morse: Just to start: why do you take selfies?

Vivek Shraya: Let's see, where do I start? For me, I use selfies as a political tool to disrupt people's Instagram feeds, or Facebook feeds, or Twitter feeds. Because unless your feed is very curated, even if it's not very white, it can be very cis. So here you go. I'm going to give you a trans selfie in your day. I think selfies have been a way for me to reclaim the gaze or return the gaze back to me. It's one of the only times that I can essentially own the gaze, and certainly it has been pivotal in my coming out as trans. I got an iPhone in 2011, and I came out as trans in 2016; I really think that there's a deep connection between being able to photograph and document myself while seeing gestures of who I want to see, and I think the more that I took selfies the more I started to see a truer sense of who I was. Selfies, in a lot of ways, have revealed my truth to me.

NM: What are the differences between selfies, or any photography even, and other forms of self-representational art? Because some of your other work is also very self-reflective, or self-representational.

VS: I often make jokes like, "Why do I even bother making art? I could just post selfies all the time," because if you look at what my most popular posts are, they tend to be my selfies. Increasingly, I've been using selfies as a way to get people to check out my art, because posting about the art directly isn't always successful. I'll post a random selfie, but I'll write, "Have you checked out my new single?" I have had to be strategic about how to deploy selfies because first and foremost I really want to be known as an artist. It does feel challenging when your audience online seems to engage more with your selfies than your art. I guess the obvious answer would be that selfies tend to be confined to the face. A lot of my work is based on my own experience, whether that's writing songs, or poems, or whatever, but I'm not really ever explicitly writing about my face. I mean, I might be writing about race, and that sort of thing, but there's something about selfies that is a lot more physical.

NM: One of the things I like the most about selfies is the way that they allow us to see the faces of people that we care about—or even people that we're getting to know—so regularly in ways that wouldn't be possible outside this technology. And that makes me want to know more about your experiences looking at other people's selfies.

VS: I'm laughing because some of my friends have had me give them, like, informal selfie tutorials just because I'm so passionate about selfies. I'm definitely

Figure 2. Vivek Shraya, Selfie #2.

inspired by other people's selfies. We talk about selfie game, right, and this idea of upping your selfie game, and there are certain celebrities whose selfies I really admire and am inspired by. But at the same time, people post selfies that are blurry, or out-of-focus selfies, or selfies that aren't (in my perspective) particularly flattering. I always find that a little bit troubling, because I feel like selfies are this really accessible form of self-love, and when I see a blurry selfie, I'm like, "Girl, why don't you love yourself enough to just take another one?"

I think one of the reasons people are really uncomfortable with selfies is that looking at yourself in the mirror, and appreciating your face, is a really challenging thing to do, especially for a lot of people of color, especially for feminine people. Seeing someone engaging in that practice can feel uncomfortable because we don't always know how to engage in that practice; and I mean, truthfully, I have found it uncomfortable in the past myself.

NM: What is your selfie aesthetic? What makes good selfie game?

VS: It's really about knowing where to face the light. Like, don't backlight yourself. Don't backlight yourself, right? Find a nice window, get that natural light. Some people really like taking selfies from way above, especially feminine people or older people feel like it makes you look younger or thinner. There's all sorts of feelings about taking selfies from above. But I think it's about finding a balance. You don't want a selfie where your face looks like an alien unless that's what you're going for. So for me, it's like holding the camera just slightly above your face, maybe, or directly, like the same height as your face. And, I've acknowledged with my friends that I have a bit of arm privilege. It's funny teaching friends who have shorter arms to take selfies, because it is, I think, a lot more challenging.

A good selfie is one where you know where to look. A lot of people don't know where the camera is, but don't be afraid to look back at that camera. I think another part of it is owning the gaze, you know? So many of us, especially feminine people, have been taught not to look at ourselves, because it's vanity, and not to appreciate ourselves, because it's vanity. That's certainly what I grew up with, and it just feels really good to look back at yourself.

NM: For a lot of people writing about selfies, there seems to be this kind of discomfort about the fact that people refer to group photos as selfies. I know you've taken a lot of selfies with other people. Is there a tension there for you?

VS: It's interesting to think about how people define a selfie. If I were to get my boyfriend to take a photo of me, to me, that's not a selfie. Like, if someone else is handling the camera for you it's not a selfie. But it's interesting, because I like the expansion of selfie too. Sometimes I'll take a picture of something else and then caption it #selfie, like . . . I don't know, I'm trying to think of something goofy. Let's say french fries. That's quite clearly not me, and not my face. But something I have some sort of aspirational desire for, or that I think I share some sort of aesthetic with. I like that the definition of *selfie* gets continually expanded. For me, a selfie is less about the number of people, or subjects in the photo, and more about who's in control of the camera.

NM: This brings up questions around the gendering of selfies. It seems that whether people are comfortable taking selfies in public, and being seen taking a selfie, is very gendered. I'm assuming that you're comfortable being seen taking a selfie, but so often the negativity around selfies is concentrated on the fact that there's this moment of self-performance.

VS: It's funny, I just had a photo shoot in Toronto, and the photographer was telling me this long story about how he and his girlfriend "caught" me taking a selfie. And I felt like I had to perform embarrassment, which felt irritating; like, "oh haha, you caught me." As if I was doing something bad or wrong, you know? I've been very vocal about selfie shaming. A selfie, for me, sometimes, is the only time in the world that I feel beautiful. There's a whole Wikipedia page about selfies, and selfie deaths, and the ways that selfies are tied to low self-esteem and the lack of ability to build friendships. So much of that feels so gendered to me in a world where my aesthetic as a transfeminine/nonbinary trans person isn't desirable. One of the things I've noticed the most in transitioning is just the lack of desirability. People will comment on your selfies and say "fierce," or like, "queen" or whatever, and that's really nice, but I seldom feel like someone wants to throw me on the bed and fuck me, you know? I really miss that feeling, and sometimes a selfie is the only time that I can assert my sexiness. Even though it's not the same as someone else showing desire for me, it feels like the closest thing—to show desire for myself. Selfies are just a really crucial way for me to show love back to myself.

NM: In the story you just told, it was a photographer, or someone who's going to be taking a picture of you, who was shaming you for taking a selfie. To me, that says something about portraiture, and who controls the camera.

VS: Totally. We're doing this shoot, and he's like, "I gotta tell you this story!" And I thought it was going to be really funny or something, the way it was presented. And then he was like, "Me and my girlfriend were in my car, and we saw you, and you know, you were doing this thing, and then later we went home, and we saw the photo on Instagram, and we were like, 'Oh my god, we saw . . .'" I don't know how much of it was mocking, but the whole thing felt a little goofy. Like, what is the story here? "We saw you take a selfie."

I will own that I am very defensive about selfies because they are seen as narcissistic. The whole thing is kind of vulnerable, too. I was up for a cover of a magazine in Toronto, and I'll never forget how the editor of the magazine said that the creative director pulled up my Instagram, just to get a sense of my aesthetic, and said, "Well, she really loves herself." I was like, "So is that a criticism?" For me as a feminine person, I'm supposed to perform some sort of humility or passivity, and God forbid you look at a feminine person's Instagram and there's lots of pictures of her. And the funny thing is I don't love myself, you know? I think that loving yourself is not a destination; I think it's something that's a work in progress. There are moments that I like myself more than others, and taking selfies helps me get there, but it doesn't mean that every time I post a selfie, like, I personally feel fierce, or whatever. Sometimes I'm actually having a really bad day and feeling terrible. I've experienced some sort of antitrans harassment or violence, or I'm just feeling undesirable as a trans person. Posting a selfie says, "Well, on the inside, I don't feel great. But on the outside . . ." It's less about projecting it to someone else, and it's more about projecting it to myself. I think a lot of people think it's about just acquiring likes. And don't get me wrong, that's really nice. But a lot of it is also for me to remember my face. To be like, "No matter how ugly you feel, and how ugly the world is telling you that you are, look at this photo, and appreciate this moment, and appreciate your beauty."

NM: If they're saying that "she really loves herself" they must be talking specifically about your selfies. But you also share photos from photo shoots and projects. When you share images of yourself, what's the difference between sharing portraits that are taken by other people, and selfies?

VS: Honestly, I have found that sometimes a selfie will do better than professional photographs. It's really interesting and it's really complicated. I don't really know the magic of what's behind the likes but I've certainly observed that disparity and thought, "Wow, this is a professional photo shoot, with lighting, and you know, my dinky selfie I took in my bedroom is connecting with people more." I find that interesting and puzzling at the same time.

NM: Do you have a hunch about why selfies speak to people so much?

VS: There's something about controlling the gaze that creates or produces a stronger visual. I've been really fortunate to be photographed quite a bit, but it's still nerve wracking, right? Sometimes I've selected the photographer because it's my project, but half the time it's somebody I don't really know. There are some photographers who I feel like really get me, and I get a photo back, and I'm like, "I see myself." But there's this weird thing that happens sometimes when I get photos back from photographers, where I'm like, "This doesn't look like how I felt at that shoot," or "This doesn't look like how I thought I looked at the shoot." I think this is such a human experience, where you think you look great and then someone takes a photo of you, and you're like, "Oh my God, I look like shit." But then you go in the washroom, and you take a photo of yourself and you're like, "No actually, I look as good as I thought." There's something about controlling the gaze that allows you to create a photo that's more representative than when someone else does it, even if they're a professional. That might be one of the reasons why it translates more, or it connects more online, or why it gets more likes, because that's what people are seeing.

*   *   *

As Shraya details in this interview, selfies provoke strong reactions that are closely linked to anxieties about femininity, about who controls the camera, and, finally, about the power of the look back into the lens—knowing "where to look." Selfies are often imagined to create a solipsistic, timeless loop between self and self-image, but it seems to me that Shraya's assertion that selfie creators should "know where to look" introduces a future-oriented temporality into the encounter with the image of the self. Rather than a narcissistic circuit confined to the present, the question of where to look—where to direct one's attention—recalls Sara Ahmed's (2006: 72) work on how queer subjects navigate the tension between society's "straightening devices" and our own aslant orientations. Within a world that marks queer, brown transfemininity as not only undesirable but abject, Shraya's act of directing her look toward herself is not merely a practice of self-love in the present. Instead, the directionality of the look, and the iterative act of repeatedly staging the look toward the self, points toward alternative futures. As Shraya notes, her selfies may interrupt social media feeds that are otherwise exclusively cisgender and white; yet her selfies also punctuate the feeds of people for whom these glimpses of brown transfeminine potentiality may be a welcome relief from the "irregular, but inexorable, rhythm" of online news of racist and transphobic violence (cárdenas 2017: 161). In this way, Shraya's selfies interpolate the viewer into her look toward a brown, transfeminine futurity.

Nicole Erin Morse is an assistant professor in the School of Communication and Multimedia Studies at Florida Atlantic University. Their work has been published in *Jump Cut, Feminist Media Studies, Porn Studies, M/C Journal*, and *[in]Transition*.

Acknowledgments
Thanks to Vita Eya Cleveland for transcribing the interview, which I edited lightly for clarity.

References

Ahmed, Sara. 2006. *Queer Phenomenology: Orientations, Objects, Others.* Durham, NC: Duke University Press.

Burns, Anne. 2015. "Self(ie)-Discipline: Social Regulation as Enacted through the Discussion of Photographic Practice." *International Journal of Communication* 9: 1716–33. ijoc.org /index.php/ijoc/article/view/3138.

cárdenas, micha. 2017. "Dark Shimmers: The Rhythm of Necropolitical Affect in Digital Media." In *Trap Door: Trans Cultural Production and the Politics of Visibility*, edited by Tourmaline, Eric A. Stanley, and Johanna Burton, 161–81. Cambridge, MA: MIT Press.

Keeling, Kara. 2008. *The Witch's Flight: The Cinematic, the Black Femme, and the Image of Common Sense.* Durham, NC: Duke University Press.

Shraya, Vivek. 2014a. *God Loves Hair.* Vancouver, BC: Arsenal Pulp.

Shraya, Vivek. 2014b. *She of the Mountains.* Vancouver, BC: Arsenal Pulp.

Shraya, Vivek. 2016. *even this page is white.* Vancouver, BC: Arsenal Pulp.

Shraya, Vivek. 2018a. *I'm Afraid of Men.* Toronto: Penguin Random House Canada.

Shraya, Vivek (@vivekshraya). 2018b. "Something wicked this way comes." Instagram photo, August 13. www.instagram.com/p/BmcZyM4g1Hl.

Shraya, Vivek, and Ness Lee. 2019. *Death Threat.* Vancouver, BC: Arsenal Pulp.

Shraya, Vivek, and Queer Songbook Orchestra. 2017. *Part-Time Woman.* Digital Album.

"I Sexually Identify as an Attack Helicopter"

HARPER SHALLOE

Abstract This article jumps off and theorizes out from the viral meme "I Sexually Identify as an Attack Helicopter" to think trans as a cut across diagrams of control and counterinsurgency. Terming the set of digital and discursive technologies for capturing the threat of trans potentiality the "biopolitics of identification," it traces spectral appearances of trans as a contrivance for violence through lived and imagined scenes of surveillance and security.
Keywords meme, media, big data, gender identity

In 2014, an avid participant in the online multiplayer game *Team Fortress 2* posted a copypasta to his pastebin. Known by its polemical opening words, "I sexually Identify as an Attack Helicopter," the meme describes its author's identification as a Boeing AH-64 Apache and plan to be surgically weaponized to resemble one:

> I sexually Identify as an Attack Helicopter. Ever since I was a boy I dreamed of soaring over the oilfields dropping hot sticky loads on disgusting foreigners. People say to me that a person being a helicopter is Impossible and I'm fucking retarded but I don't care, I'm beautiful. I'm having a plastic surgeon install rotary blades, 30mm cannons and AMG-114 Hellfire missiles on my body. From now on I want you guys to call me "Apache" and respect my right to kill from above and kill needlessly. If you can't accept me you're a heliphobe and need to check your vehicle privilege. Thank you for being so understanding.

Written to be copied and pasted to the in-game chat "during arguments on gender identity politics," according to the esteemed scholarly source knowyourmeme .com, the copypasta quickly migrated and mutated, appearing across a number of sites and in various derivative forms, including the eminently self-reflexive

TSQ: Transgender Studies Quarterly ∗ Volume 6, Number 4 ∗ November 2019
DOI 10.1215/23289252-7771824 © 2019 Duke University Press

Figure 1. "All Gender Restroom." knowyourmeme.com/photos/1182873-i
-sexually-identify-as-an-attack-helicopter (accessed June 30, 2019).

"I sexually identify as a meme."[1] But lest this seem to trumpet a game of media studies show-and-tell, a genre in which I might ultimately argue that the repugnant object I began with is, on closer reading, radical and resistive, let me briefly suggest the reason for this (I hope) rousingly titled review. "I Sexually Identify as an Attack Helicopter" brings into view transness as a crucial node in networks of control and counterinsurgency; it opens onto what I call the "biopolitics of identification," a set of digital and discursive capture technologies adjudicating who edges toward livable life, who tarries near death, and who lingers precariously in between. At the same time as it posits, through its mocking announcement of helicopter gender, that identification is mere declaration, a kind of fanciful claim forming one side of the unbridgeable divide between what one identifies as and what one is, it inadvertently gestures toward just the opposite, signaling identification's capacity to extend the good life to some, while denying others access to vital resources. With this meme in mind, I hope to stage an encounter between some dominant media-theoretical diagrams of power and the spectral "toolness" of transness, the persistent conjuring of trans as a contrivance for violence executed both by and against the US nation-state.

My hypothesis is twofold: we have to think corporate tracking, state surveillance, and counterinsurgency together, and we have to take transness as one of their tethers, to trace what big data and ubiquitous sensing are doing to our models of power. In other words, those of us working at the intersections of digital media and surveillance studies must attend to how transness transverses the variegated fields of control that we describe. This also requires that we conceive of transness beyond transgender subjects, noticing how the threatening potentiality of trans is affixed to bodies that would not describe themselves as such, and often without describing them as such. And this not because transness offers a conceptual stand-in for dangerous disruption or the threat of difference, but because technologies deployed across loci of liberalism and increasingly unexceptional spaces of exception, between bounded nations and mobile conflict zones, are concerned with capturing a kind of trans technicity, securitizing transgender subjects and phantasmatic trans terrorists alike.[2]

This biopolitical work, which I take to include the necropolitical as well, is linked to the wider cultural imaginary of trans instrumentality, the conceit that people will claim transgender identity to reap its apparently abundant benefits, whether expensive medical care that will drain the meager resources of the US military, access to women's restrooms to traumatize young girls, or the convivial camaraderie of participating in a plot to convince confused children, who might otherwise have turned out normal, that they are trans. "I Sexually Identify as an Attack Helicopter" extends this hypothesis: here trans identification demands a self-realization that is at once a realization of imperialist ambition, an authorization of the sovereign right to kill. While I focus on invocations-cum-incantations of trans technicity in discourses and practices of digital surveillance, which the meme invites through its appeal to lethal military oversight, these observations should be situated within a broader inquiry into the strange fantasy of what I am tempted to call—and only half-jokingly—trans tool-being.

We are witnessing, and feeling and weathering, a moment at which identification is both a sign of gender's unavailability to visual verification and the impetus of ever more pervasive surveillance, both a performative act of resistance to prescription and a function of state biometrics, corporate data analytics, and military intelligence, surveillance, and reconnaissance tactics that compute always already raced and gendered data to manage the movement of bodies through digital and physical space. That identification and sensing traverse trans self- and world-making practices and surveillance and security protocols attunes us, if only preliminarily, to the tangle of transness, domination, and digitality that I want to unravel here.

Media theory is centrally concerned with mapping the digital machinations of domination, uncovering how emergent technologies and the epistemologies they inaugurate (re)shape the nexus of knowledge-power, and particular attention has been paid of late to the spread of data-driven predictive analytics in applications as apparently disparate as targeted advertising and prison sentencing.[3] In light of this algorithmic ascendency, John Cheney-Lippold (2017: 35) has theorized "soft biopolitics" as an update to Gilles Deleuze's schematization of societies of control. Describing the cybernetic system of gender classification used by corporate marketing firms, Cheney-Lippold argues that this and other operations of algorithmic identification inaugurate a form of power more proximate and personal and yet more distant and diffuse, an assemblage of technologies that "regulate life without our direct participation or realization" (35). But

Cheney-Lippold opens his first chapter with former National Security Agency director Michael Hayden's resounding claim that "we kill people based on metadata," describing the process by which the aggregated surveillance data of suspected insurgents in Yemen, Pakistan, and Somalia is measured against vectorized "terrorist" behavior patterns in a biometrics of risk calculation, an identification of a body's terrorist potential, and the forestalling of that potential's actualization through preemptive drone strikes (39). Cheney-Lippold comes close to thinking gender and terrorist identity together but ultimately cannot but make them interchangeable, fungible "measurable type[s]" that do not enter the same analytic frame except as abstractions, failing to integrate the lethal identification practices of the Global War on Terror into his theorization of the biopolitical difference that the digital makes (143).

Writing against the tendency to overemphasize the slickness and imperceptibility of power in the information age, Tung-Hui Hu (2016) argues that both territorial sovereignty and the sovereign right to kill mutate with control. Drawing on Caren Kaplan's (2006) claim that subjects of warfare and marketing alike are produced through the precision targeting of geographic information systems, Hu (2016: 139, 115) theorizes the "sovereignty of data" as a hybrid form of biopolitical regulation and necropolitical violence, which "may manifest itself primarily through targeted advertisements, and through the bloodless forms of control and governmentality typically described by new media scholars, but occasionally appears as a targeted killing."

To these and other accounts of how the digital is redrawing global lines of force, I propose to add "I Sexually Identify as an Attack Helicopter," that is, to think transness as a pivot between control and counterinsurgency, to ask how surveillance and security technologies work to capture the threat of trans technicity. Though the meme positively (if derisively) aligns trans technicity with US militarism, or trans identification with the elimination of those who threaten the nation, it also conjures the opposite: the trans terrorist who embodies that threat, and who is the target of, rather than a tool in, the Global War on Terror. Following this ambulant figure through discourses and practices of digital capture, I suggest, reveals the cut of transness across cartographies of power.

Control is often theorized as a biopolitical turn to affect, to the management not of subjects but of pre- and subindividual capacities, which is perhaps part of the reason why it is so easily or so frequently cordoned off from models of less modular and minute force relations. That is, if control is concerned with the adjustment of an infinity of somatic intensities, then the brute killing of suspected insurgents in extrajudicial drone strikes would seem a far cry from it. And setting aside debates raging over transgender military service, transness too might seem to dwell at some remove from the digitality of counterinsurgency. But I am suggesting, again, that practices of predicting and preempting threatening bodily potentials transverse control and counterinsurgency. This is not to abstract transness as capacity par excellence but to suggest that the array of identification technologies that gather affect as information to monitor and manage bodily movement, to determine, say, whether a body can cross a border, or whether it is threateningly different from what it is expected to be, form part of a conceptual and material network of national security, affective control, and trans technicity.

Nascent and uneven freedoms for trans identification are inextricable from contrivances of capture, and by this I want to signal not only the surfeit of stoppages keeping trans people, and trans people of color in particular, from moving up the ladder of life chances, but also the processes by which identification is incorporated into a digital logic of personalization operationalized by agents of corporate and state surveillance.[4] For example, the ability to specify one's gender identity on Facebook, and the increasing presence of options beyond "male" and "female" in drop-down menus demanding gender disclosure, enable the more precise production of the "data double," a kind of digital gestalt at once less than and in excess of the in-real-life self, whose constitutive data traces— those bits and bytes we've left behind—are available for scraping and selling.

We might understand both emergent, empowering forms of digital control—maybe we would like to see more targeted ads for commodities tagged "trans"?—and ongoing histories of analog and digital domination through what Jasbir Puar (2017: 45) calls "trans(homo)nationalism," a capacitating project of recognition by and incorporation into the neoliberal state, in which trans of color bodies form the ground from and against which white normative trans subjects are swept up in the flows of reproduction and wealth accumulation. Puar situates trans(homo)nationalism within a larger weave of debility, capacity, and disability, in which "those 'folded' into life are seen as more capacious or on the side of capacity, while those targeted for premature or slow death are figured as on the side of debility" (13). Thus the promises and perils of identification immanent to trans(homo)nationalism are bound up as well with counterinsurgency, extrajudicial execution, and whatever else might look like an untimely remainder of a long-dead diagram of power. Puar's formulation makes plain that the enabling identifications of trans(homo)nationalism and the debilitating identifications of the Global War on Terror are neither analytically nor practically separable.

Transness conceived as threatening bodily capacity haunts the surveillance and security assemblages making up the biopolitics of identification. I will not dwell on the Department of Homeland Security's (DHS) 2003 warning that "male bombers may dress as females in order to discourage scrutiny," as Toby Beauchamp (2019) has paid it due attention. What I do find remarkable about this announcement, however, is its presumption of passing, the sense it proffers that heightened state scrutiny of gender—through, for example, millimeter-wave scanners that assess bodies against normative schemas of somatic sex at airport security checkpoints—is requisite because potential terrorists might otherwise unproblematically navigate public space as women. Passing's taken-for-grantedness at once disavows the difficulties and the dangers that trans people—and trans women of color in particular, who are foils for the terrorists conjured here—face in public space, and authorizes the surveillance that will only compound those dangers in an attempt to guarantee passing's impossibility. The likelihood of not passing, the reality that trans people often are revealed or must reveal themselves as such at scenes of biometric security, is denied to obscure the ground truth of deviance on which capture systems operate.

As Philip Agre (1994) has suggested, capture requires state change: transition is the condition of possibility of keeping track. Agre's argument is that digital tracking systems do not passively apprehend but, rather, act on their targets, propelling their motion and determining its form, and we might extrapolate this claim from its information studies and business organizational context to say that capture technologies—including data mining algorithms, biometric access control scanners and databases, and the Department of Homeland Security's (2014) as-yet unimplemented Future Attributes Screening Technology, or FAST program, which assembles an array of affective sensors to predict the "mental state" of "malintent"—demand fugitive subjects, or that a degree of deviation is in-built. In other words, capture systems induce the deviant swerves that they discipline: unruly moves do not emerge against a backdrop of normative actions and affective arrangements but produce the very path from which they stray.

Capture systems presume and predict threatening capacities to debilitate trans technicity, or forestall the use of trans to terrorist ends, whether through restricting mobility or exercising lethal violence. And that the same practices of data aggregation and analysis are used by corporate marketing firms to predict likely genders, and by state agencies to predict likely terrorists, to be executed before they can be confirmed as such, suggests that capture aims not for definitive identifications but for actionable predictions, close-enough quantifications of potential that will invite profitable futures and stave off risky ones. If the technical means of capturing the threatening toolness of transness—the biopolitics of identification—were to have a Spinozist slogan, it might go something like "we do not even know what a body is capable of . . . but damned if we won't figure it out."

In a striking confluence of trans(homo)nationalism and the capture of trans technicity, the computer scientist Karl Ricanek (quoted in Vincent 2017) scraped facial image data from transition videos uploaded to YouTube to develop a facial recognition algorithm that could authenticate identities "after" hormone replacement therapy (whenever that is?), motivated by the question: "What kind of harm can a terrorist do if they understand that taking this hormone can increase their chances of crossing over into a border that's protected by facial recognition?" Ricanek extends the presumed pass of the DHS warning cited above, taking trans embodiment while traveling to be a nonissue, and making the problem one of identifying the face of a terrorist, or the likelihood that a given face belongs to a terrorist—the potential for threatening potential.

This attempt to quell the threat of trans technicity through digital capture retools facial recognition's foundational concern with deviance and deviation, with instrumentalizable identities and illicit movements. Physiognomic gender deviance was figured as a sign of criminality in the historical nexus of sexology, criminal anthropology, and eugenics undergirding automated facial recognition: the Italian criminologist Cesare Lombroso, for example, noted the tendency of female criminals to capitalize on their "atavistic diminution of secondary sexual characters" and pass as men to evade law enforcement. Lombroso figured the masculine-faciality-traits-cum-"savage features" of potential or actual female offenders as not only indications of, but also contrivances for, criminality (Lombroso, Ferrero, and Morrison 1895: 112), claims that echo in Ricanek's suspicion that terrorists will transition to evade biometric capture. Indeed, at the origins of facial recognition are the very anxieties that Ricanek expounds: that the toolness of transness will aid and abet criminal action, and that this threat must be captured through facial imaging technology, whether it be the analog practices of criminal physiognomy and composite photography or the digital development of facial image databases and facial recognition algorithms. Normative schemas of gendered faciality emerge out of and against practices of identifying criminal faces, predicting criminal propensities, and preventing criminal activities.

This primacy of deviance-deviation—perhaps of trans technicity as the originary swerve against which the normative is measured—in capture systems recalls Puar's formulation of trans of color bodies as the constitutive biopolitical failures of trans(homo)nationalism, the deviant ground from which some white trans subjects can move on up. The empowering scene of posting a transition video on YouTube, or the potentially capacitating and life-affirming effects of such visibility, are here incorporated into a project of counterterrorism, of the preemption of virtual threats to the nation. Trans(homo)nationalism might therefore name the impossibility of disentangling the "liberal" coupling of control and freedom from illiberal acts of containment and violence.

It is only by attending to how transness cuts across the domains of control and counterinsurgency that we can begin to make sense of identification as both an index of gendered affect and the goal of computational capture. Engaging difficult pop-cultural objects like "I Sexually Identify as an Attack Helicopter,"

I suggest, offers a way through the wider cultural imaginaries (and the attendant material realities) of trans as a tool with which to commit acts of violence against the nation, or crimes against its citizens; of identification as a variably capacitating and debilitating technology, in which the sovereignty of the trans(homo)national subject risks sliding into the aerial sovereignty exercised by the US military. And at a moment when drones have been hailed "genderqueer bodies" (Daggett 2015: 362) in an academic article turned meme itself, it seems imperative that the linkages between control and counterinsurgency, between transgender lives and specters of trans technicity, be further identified.

Harper Shalloe is a PhD student in Modern Culture and Media at Brown University.

Notes

1. "I Sexually Identify as an Attack Helicopter," knowyourmeme.com/memes/i-sexually -identify-as-an-attack-helicopter (accessed June 30, 2019).

2. Trans technicity is a formulation I have picked up from Julian Gill-Peterson, but I run in a different direction with it. For Gill-Peterson (2014: 408), if the body is understood in its originary technicity, "not [as] a passive substrate ruled by a transgendered consciousness but an open technical system with its own implicit forms, its own affects," transgender emerges as both a bodily capacity and a sign of the body's capacity, a way the body differs from itself and an expression of its immanent potential to do so. Following Gill-Peterson, I take trans as something all bodies are capable of, a nonproprietary technical capacity, or a gradation in the capacity of human (and perhaps nonhuman) matter to act, but I focus my analysis on the specter of its direction toward illicit ends. Thus, I use trans technicity to signal the capacity, whether actual or imaginary, of bodies to do things with trans, a capacity at once conjured and disciplined in the discourses and practices of capture under consideration here.

3. For a thorough account of the powers and perils of machine learning's proliferation, see O'Neil 2016.

4. Here I draw on Wendy Chun's (2006) important claim that, in the context of information and communications technologies (though certainly not only in this context), control is dialectically bound to freedom.

References

Agre, Philip. 1994. "Surveillance and Capture: Two Models of Privacy." *Information Society* 10, no. 2: 101–27.

Beauchamp, Toby. 2019. *Going Stealth: Transgender Politics and U.S. Surveillance Practices.* Durham, NC: Duke University Press.

Cheney-Lippold, John. 2017. *We Are Data: Algorithms and the Making of Our Digital Selves.* New York: New York University Press.

Chun, Wendy. 2006. *Control and Freedom: Power and Paranoia in the Age of Fiber Optics.* Cambridge, MA: MIT Press.

Daggett, Cara. 2015. "Drone Disorientations: How 'Unmanned' Weapons Queer the Experience of Killing in War." *International Journal of Feminist Politics* 17, no. 3: 361–79.

Department of Homeland Security. 2014. "Future Attribute Screening Technology." November 18. www.dhs.gov/sites/default/files/publications/Future%20Attribute%20Screening%20Technol ogy-FAST-508_0.pdf.

Gill-Peterson, Julian. 2014. "The Technical Capacities of the Body: Assembling Race, Technology, and Transgender." *TSQ* 1, no. 3: 402–18.

Hu, Tung-Hui. 2016. *A Prehistory of the Cloud*. Cambridge, MA: MIT Press.

Kaplan, Caren. 2006. "Precision Targets: GPS and the Militarization of U.S. Consumer Identity." *American Quarterly* 58, no. 3: 693–713.

Lombroso, Cesare, William Ferrero, and W. Douglass Morrison. 1895. *The Female Offender*. New York: D. Appleton.

Manovich, Lev. 2001. *The Language of New Media*. Cambridge, MA: MIT Press.

O'Neil, Cathy. 2016. *Weapons of Math Destruction: How Big Data Increases Inequality and Threatens Democracy*. New York: Broadway.

Puar, Jasbir. 2017. *The Right to Maim: Debility, Capacity, Disability*. Durham, NC: Duke University Press.

Vincent, James. 2017. "Transgender YouTubers Had Their Videos Grabbed to Train Facial Recognition Software." *Verge*, August 22. www.theverge.com/2017/8/22/16180080/transgender -youtubers-ai-facial-recognition-dataset.

Transgressing the Boundaries of the Borderlands

JACK CARAVES

Post-Borderlandia: Chicana Literature and Gender Variant Critique
T. Jackie Cuevas
New Brunswick, NJ: Rutgers University Press, 2018. 169 pp.

Post-Borderlandia opens up with the case of the "San Antonio Four," which refers to four Latina lesbians—Elizabeth Ramirez, Kristie Mayhugh, Cassandra Rivera, and Anna Vasquez—who were all wrongfully convicted of gang raping Ramirez's two nieces in 1994 and spent almost fifteen years in prison. Cuevas recalls her attendance at Deborah S. Esquenazi's documentary about their struggle, *Southwest of Salem*, where the four were present and openly shared about their ordeal. Ramirez explained to the audience that she had rejected sexual advances from her nieces' father and that he may have manufactured the accusation against Ramirez and her friends. While Ramirez shared this with her attorneys, it was something that was dismissed, along with the fact that some of the jurors were blatantly homophobic and yet allowed to remain on the jury. Cuevas recalls another audience member who asked the four women if they thought they were punished harshly by the criminal justice system because they were lesbians or because they were Latinas, to which Vasquez immediately answered "both" (2). Using a trans analysis, Cuevas reminds the reader that "fear of queer sexuality can bring out the homophobic gender police, but gender nonconformity can disrupt the social order by bringing one's ontological status as a categorizable human being into question and can "render a person illegible" to family and community members (3). It is here that Cuevas begins her broader argument for the book and sets the tone for the extralegal and material consequences of a post-borderlands subjectivity for gender-variant individuals such as the San Antonio Four, whose

TSQ: Transgender Studies Quarterly ∗ Volume 6, Number 4 ∗ November 2019
DOI 10.1215/23289252-7771838   © 2019 Duke University Press

transgression of gendered and racially normative boundaries led to their construction as "dangerously deviant" subjects whose bodies become untrustworthy and thus "disposable" (137).

In juxtaposing the material realities experienced by the San Antonio Four, Cuevas analyzes Chicana literature and cultural production to address how characters are challenging heteropatriarchal norms and standards while also transgressing normative ideals of queer identity and Chicana/o identity. The cultural texts Cuevas analyzes in *Post-Borderlandia* move between fiction, performance art, and film. Cuevas examines plays by Butchlalis de Panochtitlan and Adelina Anthony, as well as Anthony's film *Bruising for Besos* (2016), all which center the urban landscape of East Los Angeles. In addition to these, the fictional narratives capture historical events ranging from US invasion of Mexico in 1846 through the Chicano movement of the 1960s and 1970s and moving through the 1990s punk scene to the September 11, 2001, attacks on the World Trade Center. Ceuvas also examines Jovita Gonzalez's *Caballero* originally written in 1930s but published in 1996, Helena Viramontes's *Their Dogs Came with Them* (2000), and Felicia Luna Lemus's *Like Son* (2007). While these literary productions could be analyzed chronologically, Cuevas employs a queer time line that moves between time and space and layers history, place, and generation, which ultimately complicate generation and lineage of Chicanx subjectivity altogether (22).

Cuevas builds on and moves beyond what she refers to as the limitations that have been placed on Gloria Anzaldúa's borderlands theory[1] and conceptualizes a post-borderlands subjectivity through the use of a "gender variant critique"(4). Anzaldúan borderlands theory—which was developed to understand a mestiza or mixed-race person (i.e., Chicana) on the border —refers to both a physical borderland and a psychic borderland. The physical borderland, Cuevas reminds us, is what Anzaldúa refers to as the harsh conditions that Chicanas experience along the US-Mexico border that create precarity, violence, and extreme marginality. Anzaldúa's conception of a psychic borderland is "where the mestiza and queer must contend with the normalized daily violence and trauma of racism, sexism, and homophobia" (9). Yet in Cuevas's investigation of Chicana literature and cultural production in *Post-Borderlandia*, Cuevas finds that these authors challenge the normative constructions of Chicana/o identity. Furthermore, Cuevas notes that while authors and Chicana feminist scholars like Gloria Anzaldúa and Cherríe Moraga were framing Chicana lesbian subjectivity within the context of pushing back against patriarchal, masculinist Chicano nationalism and white-centered feminism, they did so in a way that relied heavily on a conception of cisgender *mujer*/woman identity that allowed for an analysis only around sexual identity and dismissed possibilities of gender and sexuality outside womanhood. Cuevas argues that authors such as Lemus and others work against these rigid categories of Chicana womanhood and normative gender experiences (10). In doing so, authors like Lemus move beyond the borderlands that have been conceptualized within borderlands theory, and they negotiate a different set of borders beyond the sex/gender binaries constructed for Chicanas and Mexicanas (10).

While Cuevas is speaking to Chicana and Chicano studies and Chicana literature—which, she acknowledges, implicitly make use of the cisgender male/female homosexual/homosexual binary in the field—she draws from queer theory and transgender studies to acknowledge that queer and gender-variant individuals currently exist and have always existed beyond the traditional binary conceptions of queerness (i.e., gay and lesbian) and gender identification (i.e., man/woman) that are rigidly maintained in Chicano studies as well as in Chicana literature and cultural production. In regard to terminology, Cuevas takes up the very debated use of the *x* in *Chicanx* and *Latinx*. Cuevas's use of the *x* in *Chicanx* and *Latinx* is a way to "unsettle the gender binary bound up in terms such as 'Chicano,' 'Chicana' and variations such as 'Chicana/o' and 'Chican@'" (19) and to "move beyond the binary and offer a trans, genderqueer, gender nonconforming, and gender variant intervention that opens up the possibilities of ascribing any gender or none at all" (20). Cuevas contributes to the growing field of critical *jotería* studies that bridges Chicano/Latino studies and queer theory and transgender studies. *Post-Borderlandia* answers to trans Chicano scholar Francisco Galarte's 2014 reflection of jotería studies when he says, "Jotería, listen to what your trans* brothers and sisters are saying, and remember those long forgotten" (229).[2] To do this, Cuevas focuses on texts that are categorized as being Chicana texts and cultural productions that transgress the normative constructions of Chicana womanhood within the cisgender binary to include "suit donning Chicana butch, the ambiguously gendered brown body, the accessibly feminine queer, the transgender Chicanx person" to argue that gender nonconformity has shaped ideas of queerness (5). Moreover, these characters and narratives, Cuevas argues, move us beyond a gender-normative paradigm that has become so entrenched within Chicana/o studies. In doing so Cuevas employs critical jotería studies, which creates a bridge for dialogue between Chicanx cultural studies and queer theory.

In conceptualizing a post-borderlands subjectivity, Cuevas is influenced by Emma Pérez's (1999) idea of the "decolonial imaginary," which extends Anzaldúa's "mestiza consciousness" and Chela Sandoval's (1997) "differential consciousness." Perez's (1999: 15) idea of a decolonial imaginary "helps locate the queer post-borderlands Chicanx subject somewhere between internal colonization and diaspora in a psychosocial place full of potentiality." Cuevas argues that using the post-borderlands lens allows one to read contemporary queer Chicanx texts "beyond the limiting debates of essentialist identity politics" and to further the notion of the borderlands that is always seen as a liberating space. In this way Cuevas argues for a post-borderlands framework that traces and reframes how one looks at Chicana lesbian literature and how that literature actually moves beyond limitations of gender and sexual categories and creates Chicanx community that disrupts binaries (14–15).

Cuevas also builds on José Esteban Muñoz's (1999) notion of "disidentification" to argue that the struggles her characters experience arise from issues surrounding their nonnormative gender expressions or gender identity— and emphasizes that their struggles are not isolated in the identities of either Chicana or queer. Cuevas describes post-borderlandia as expanding "the analytic categories of gender and sexuality to account for the racialized queer genders beyond feminine/masculine and homosexual/heterosexual binaries" (25). The author further argues that post-borderlandia is the site "where gender variance pushes beyond the known frames of meaning and reformulates the potentialities of/for Chicanx. . . . We keep open the radical potentiality of queerness, of gender, of Chicanidades," and, furthermore, gender-variant critique breaks from fixed ideas of ChicanA and ChicanO gender and genders more broadly, that are not yet here (13–14). In so doing, Cuevas' post-borderlands framework moves away from a gender-normative paradigm and toward a more radical notion of gender and gender identity that not only queer sexuality but also gender and through their disidentification with both white lesbianism and heteronormative Chicanidad (10).

Cuevas emphasizes that a gender-variant critique that examines the relationship between gender and sexuality in Chicana cultural productions is significant because within Chicana/o studies scholars have not considered the many genders and ways that gender variance reshapes and makes us rethink notions of Chicano identity (25). In this way, *Post-Borderlandia* becomes a recovery project that allows us to look at Chicana cultural production that one might see as fitting within a Chicana lesbian subjectivity, yet is destabilized by gender variance and moves us toward Chicanx, Latinx, and post-borderlands.

The chapter titled "Chicana Masculinities" juxtaposes a new generation of Chicana writers and performances with the generation of Chicana lesbian writers, who, Cuevas argues, established the butch as a prominent Chicana queer figure as being both sexually and emotional vulnerable. Focusing on contemporary depictions of Chicana butches, Cuevas recounts two plays—Adelina Anthony's *Mastering Sex and Tortillas* and Butchlalis de Panochtitlan's *Barber of East LA*—that show how this newer generation is both building on and critiquing normalized ideas of Chicana butchness.

"Ambiguous Chicanx Bodies" focuses on Viramontes's book *Their Dogs Came with Them*, which examines the queering of racialized gender through the gender ambiguity of the central figure, Turtle, who was raised a girl but presents as a man. Cuevas notes that while Turtle's gender isn't central to their story, what is evident is the inequality in East Los Angeles amidst the Chicano movement in the 1970s. Turtle's character is pushed out from her family because of assumptions of her sexuality and not accepted in her brothers' gang. Cuevas argues that Turtle's body "serves as both a shelter and threat, and her possible queerness hovers as a ghostly possibility that seems inevitably lost" (23). Furthermore, Cuevas highlights Viramontes's use of Turtle's ambiguous racialized queer body to break with traditional conventions of this genre that the book fits into. It does not fit within a queer coming-out story, nor does it fit a Chicanx coming-to-consciousness narrative.

"Transing Chicanidad" looks directly at Chicanx characters who transgress gender boundaries as well as geographic boundaries that are tied to traditional Chicanx characters and narratives centered in the US Southwest. In this chapter Cuevas dives into Lemus's *Like Son*, which centers Frank Cruz, a trans Chicano who moves from Los Angeles to New York as a young adult, but is called to back to his family in Los Angeles to take care of his dying father. Before his untimely death, Frank's father provides him with a clue that Frank traces into his family's queer history. Cuevas asserts that *Like Son* moves away from the borderlands struggle we usually encounter in Chicanx literature, away from the struggle between white feminism and heteronormative Chicanidad to a post-borderlands that centers trans embodiment and gender queerness. Cuevas notes Frank's trans embodiment is not isolated in the struggle of same-sex desire or racism alone, but it is Frank's struggle with gender expression and identity that shifts our understanding of the possibilities of Chicanx identity and what might be possible within this queer time line. Furthermore, not only is his trans body reshaping ideas of gender within Chicanidad, but his family's queer history that Frank uncovers after his father's death also queers and reshapes the traditional heteronormative Chicano family structure that is synonymous and confounded within Chicano identity.

The penultimate chapter, "Brokeback Rancho," centers Gonzalez's historical novel *Caballero*, which was written during the 1930s. Because of its queer content and alternative history, the book remained unpublished until 1996, when it was discovered in Gonzalez's archives by José Limón and Maria Cotera. *Caballero* depicts queer love on the borderlands between Mexican ranchero Luis Gonzaga and the Anglo US military officer Captain Carl Devlin. Cuevas argues that while the novel has been acknowledged as a contribution to the Chicana literary canon, it also serves as part of the queer Chicana literary archive (102) that provides a queer alternative history of the borderlands. The novel resists US hegemonic constructions of history and reshapes our understanding of heteropatriarchical, Chicano masculinity. Cuevas further argues that González's commitment to queerness centers a gender-variant approach that prefigures the Chicana lesbian feminist canon of the twentieth century (117).

In the concluding chapter, Cuevas returns to the work of Gloria Anzaldúa, who is and continues to be a source of inspiration for Cuevas's work. What is most refreshing here is Cuevas's archival finds of Anzaldúa's unpublished writing done prior to and after *Borderlands/La Frontera*. Although her ideas were not fully formed, Anzaldúa too was thinking about gender variance. This finding is grounded in Cuevas's analysis of Anzaldúa's unpublished story "Heche," which stands for "he/she." While "Heche" or "he/she" contains problematic conceptions of intersex and gender-variant identity, Cuevas highlights Anzaldúa's motivations to move beyond a fixed gender binary that disrupts notions of gender, bodies, and literary strategy (125). While Anzaldúa is heavily cited for her borderlands theory and her take on the intersection of race, class, gender, and sexuality, Cuevas notes that her identity is always fixed as a woman, and there is never an interrogation of possibilities of gender queerness or gender variance that she may be referring to. Cuevas highlights that which is often missed in Anzaldúa's work, where she expresses a sense of "dislocation and belonging in relations to normative gender" (126). Cuevas argues that in Anzaldúa's assertion of being "half and half" Anzaldúa is "disidentifying" with the gender binary and is alluding to gender-variant possibilities (126) and creating new possibilities in the post-borderlands.

Cuevas contributes to a growing conversation between Chicana/o studies and queer and trans studies and paves the way for new potentialities of Chicanx identity while recovering histories. The greatest takeaway from this book through the various movements between time, gender identities, and Chicanx embodiments is that gender variance has always been here, but it has been lost in the borders of masculine/feminine and heterosexual/homosexual. Cuevas's gender-variant critique allows us to understand beyond the categories or race, class, gender, sexuality, and nationality and further allows us to understand how gender performance and gender identity become illegible within the normativity of the binary and the material consequences that it has for the characters in the texts she evaluates. Furthermore, Cuevas's use of the San Antonio Four sheds light on the material consequences that exist when we do not interrogate the power embedded in normative gender expectations of racialized beings.

Jack Caraves is an assistant professor of women, gender, and sexuality studies in the Department of Sociology and Interdisciplinary Social Sciences at San José State University. Their research uses community-based mixed-methods approaches to focus on the experiences of trans Latinxs in Southern California and the role of family and spirituality in serving as spaces of empowerment and resistance.

Notes

1.   Described by Cuevas as "both the physical borderlands where Mexico meets the U.S. boundary and the resulting hybrid, dynamic consciousness required of borderlands subjects (i.e. mestiza consciousness)" (9).

2.   In Galarte's (2014) reflection on critical jotería studies in the *Journal of Aztlán*, he draws on Anzaldúa's call in *Borderlands/La Frontera* to Chicano scholars to listen to their *jotería* and include them in their narratives, histories, and cultural production. To this degree, Galarte is asking queer Chicanos to look outside lesbian and gay Chicano identities and open their awareness to the potential of gendered identities, particularly transgender identity that challenges current paradigms grounded in a gendered dichotomy.

References

Galarte, Francisco. 2014. "On Trans* Chican@s: Amor, Justicia, y Dignidad." *Aztlán* 39, no. 1: 229–35.

Muñoz, Jose Esteban. 1999. *Disidentifications: Queers of Color and the Performance of Politics.* Minneapolis: University of Minnesota Press.

Pérez, Emma. 1999. *The Decolonial Imaginary: Writing Chicanas into History.* Bloomington: Indiana University Press.

Sandoval, Chela. 1997. "Mestizaje as Method: Feminists of Color Challenge the Canon." In *Living Chicana Theory*, edited by Carla Trujillo, 353–70. San Francisco: Third Woman.

The Body as Provocation

The Weaponization of Gender in Latisha King's Murder Trial

DIANE DETOURNAY

The Life and Death of Latisha King: A Critical Phenomenology of Transphobia
Gayle Salamon
New York: New York University Press, 2018. 192 pp.

Told in a certain way, the circumstances surrounding the murder of Latisha King and the conflation of gender expression with sexual orientation that took place in the ensuing trial could be a story that trans studies knows all too well—the conclusions familiar, the implications already preset. Latisha, a young, fifteen-year-old black gender-nonconforming teenager, was brutally killed for her defiance of normative sex/gender regimes, only to face further violence in death through the relentless denial and erasure of her gender identity during the murder trial and its subsequent coverage.[1] As Salamon meticulously pulls apart the threads that constitute the tragic unfolding of Latisha's life and murder, however, the frameworks through which we have come to understand violence directed toward trans women, and trans women of color in particular, also begin to unravel. What is it that we think we know about Latisha's death? How do we conceptualize the convergence of racial, gendered, and sexualized power at the site of her body, in all of its materiality? And more precisely, how is it that Latisha's gender, her very movement and presence within the social life of the school, could be constituted as an act of aggression—one that demanded a response, in the form of discipline and lessons about proper ways to take up space by her teachers, bullying and harassment from her classmates, and, ultimately, two shots in the back of the head by a fellow student, Brandon McInerney, twenty minutes into a routine English composition class?

TSQ: Transgender Studies Quarterly ∗ Volume 6, Number 4 ∗ November 2019   **683**
DOI 10.1215/23289252-7771852   © 2019 Duke University Press

Drawing on the conceptual tools offered by phenomenology, Salamon's *Life and Death of Latisha King: A Critical Phenomenology of Transphobia* offers an astoundingly careful analysis of the gestural life of gender, tracing in profoundly beautiful ways how something so minute as the very "click" of high heels could become such a central focus of the hearings and rendered into evidence of an aggression that ultimately positioned Latisha as the author of her own death. In doing such work, Salamon is modeling the provocative account of phenomenology as a method articulated by this book. As Salamon writes, "One of the things that phenomenology teaches us is that observation, that description, is just as likely to get us to a place of unknowing as to a place of knowing . . . to unknow is to revise or undo knowledge that I already have, perhaps to question the epistemological regime that brought that knowing about in the first place" (148). In attending to the register of gestures, sounds, objects, and movement that animated the scene of the trial, Salamon delivers an insight of enormous significance to trans studies: the normative prescriptions of sex/gender, along with its murderous policing, is not only or uniquely consolidated through the invocation of bodily morphology or even anatomy. That a green dress, gifted to Latisha by a classmate, can be revealed in the courtroom to at least one audible gasp, as Salamon shows us, tells us that there is much about what is glossed as transphobia and its violence that we must unknow. Here, "gender is understood as something other than a property of bodies or persons" (14). In short, the tempting conclusion that Latisha was murdered because her gender did not conform to her sex assignment, and hence that the definition of proper embodiment is pregiven, no longer suffices.

The first three chapters of the book compellingly attend to the ways in which bodily modes of expression are central to the construction of Latisha King's gender as an act—and thus a provocation—as well as to the scene of the courtroom itself. Describing this work as a "methodological reversal," Salamon takes the relentless scrutiny, dissection, and parsing of Latisha's body within the trial's unfolding and turns it back onto the witnesses and onlookers. In one particularly memorable moment, Salamon dwells on the condemnation of Latisha's boots by a teacher who symptomatically characterizes the footwear as the case of a "kid" "making themselves a target" (73). Given the sensible shoes worn by this witness, Salamon wagers, her response might betray "a certain measure of gender envy" in relation to Latisha's accomplished femininity (74). Salamon continues, "That the teachers who police Latisha's gender also have a gender is seemingly invisible to them. But when a teacher herself clicks down the hall, or squishes down [it] in practical shoes with crepe soles, she, too, is offering her gender to the world, even if it recedes from her attention in its confirmation with the norms of gender. Even if her shoes—perfectly appropriate, nearly invisible in their dullness—escape attention. Even if they do not make her a target" (87).

In the fourth chapter, the book moves beyond a focus on individual embodiment to the broader social body of the school and the bodies of objects. Through this analysis, Salamon provocatively suggests that the attribution of an excessive presence and attention seeking to Latisha is tied to the understanding of gender as determined by and carried within objects. Here, we return once again to the fixation on a pair of high-heeled shoes, which variously become cast as a safety concern, an intentional auditory distraction, a demand for attention, and the list goes on. Joining together the understanding of gender as an object and gender as a gesture, Salamon writes, "Latisha's gender was not a matter of her sexed body but rather the conjoined effect of her bodily movement and the material signifiers of femininity that were worn on, though not part of, her body" (137). This is where the intervention of phenomenology becomes so critical to conceptualizing the conditions of possibility for Latisha's murder, offering a way to link the scrutiny of the high heels to the final act of violence. As Salamon concludes, "The dress became the gender; the gender became an object; the object became a weapon" (147). In short, the shot fired by Brandon becomes an act of self-defense.

In Salamon's deft hands, Latisha does not emerge from this text as either a model victim or a radically defiant subject. The dangers of making a murdered transfeminine (a term that Latisha did not choose) teenager into the subject of a book project are many. As C. Riley Snorton and Jin Haritaworn (2013) have argued, the lives of trans women of color are all too often granted significance only in death, the consequence of which is to delimit the content of their lives to perpetual victimhood. In its purposeful and deeply caring engagement with the archive of Latisha's life, however, Salamon's book abides by the joining of "life and death" in the title, tirelessly drawing out fragments from the testimonies that provide contours to Latisha's own inhabiting and styling of gender, and her confidence and courage in the face of bullying, harassment, and a perpetual unseeing. Such courage could ultimately only register as a threat, resulting in what emerges as a resolutely collective need to make her figuratively and literally disappear. As such, the book carves out the larger—and devastating—space of violence that shores up Brandon's firing of the shotgun and his articulation in a subsequent statement that "it would make everyone's life at school better" (153).

In harnessing the tools and concepts of phenomenology, Salamon brings forth the embodied logics of gender, race, and sexuality that subtend the violence unleashed onto Latisha. In so doing, the book makes the brave argument that Brandon was not the sole murderer nor fully responsible for the brutal end he brought to Latisha's life. As Salamon writes, "Brandon was following, rather than defying, the desires and expectation of his teachers with their repeated incantation that *Larry had to be stopped*" (156–57). If at one level, following the lead of structural critiques of violence, we know that there is never merely one perpetrator to violence and that the conditions that erupt into any singular event are multiple and complex, Salamon powerfully reveals that how the sound of a shoe registers and a green dress is felt are critical elements to be contended with if we are to fully grapple with the collective imperative to void Latisha's existence.

The Life and Death of Latisha King builds on Salamon's earlier work on the materiality of the body and continues in the same expansive and original way to carve out the thought that emerges at the intersection of phenomenology and trans studies. The earlier *Assuming a Body: Transgender and Rhetorics of Materiality* (2010) offered a critical intervention into the conceptualization of the body as self-evident and immediately accessible, a conceptualization that, at the time, coursed throughout scholarship within trans studies. With the same signature care, Salamon worked to untether "bodily materiality" from "bodily feeling," delivering a profound critique of the ways in which trans studies relied on the collapse of these terms to authorize claims of bodily certainty, while offering the enabling possibilities of posing the body as an object of epistemological uncertainty (9). Reflecting on this impressive corpus of work, I am left wondering about phenomenology's ability and potential to hold race together with sexuality and gender, not only as categories that bear upon one another but that may also radically undo one another.

I have in my mind here the growing body of scholarship that picks up and extends the lineage of Hortense Spillers's (2003) articulation of slavery as an ungendering violence. C. Riley Snorton (2017), Christina Sharpe (2016), and Patrice Douglass (2018), to name a few, all variously conceptualize black gender as "antagonistic" to the paradigm of gender, the nonbeing that makes possible sex/gender coherence as well as its transgressions (Douglass 2018: 114). Douglass, for example, writes: "Gender is a category for Humans. The violence of ungendering is a domain for the captive, those who died in the hold of the ship and continue dying by the wayside of gender" (119). Within the space of phenomenology, by contrast, race appears alongside and adjacent to gender but does not cut across and disrupt the latter. At one point, Salamon makes the brilliant move of connecting the "click" of Latisha's shoes to George Yancy's articulation of the "click" of car doors that follow and echo his movement as a black man through public space (88). In these moments and throughout the text, Salamon relentlessly works to reintroduce the significance of race into the discourse of a trial that has demanded its erasure. Yet, the relationality of race and gender is held apart by what I understand to be the "we"—that is, the definitional contours of the human—that is seemingly required by phenomenology. Salamon reflects in depth on the productivity of this central tension within phenomenology—its impulse toward universality joined to a focus on the "perspectivally specific nature of experience" (105). Following this line of inquiry, I wonder if phenomenology may not also be challenged, perhaps pushed to contend with its own horizons and irresolvable limitations, by the life and death of Latisha King.

Diane Detournay is a lecturer in English and Women's, Gender, and Sexuality Studies at Fordham University and is currently working on a book manuscript titled "Feminism, Race, and the Category of 'Woman': The Civilizational Architecture of Women's Rights."

Note

1. Gayle Salamon offers a thoughtful and lengthy discussion of the book's navigation of the use of names and pronouns when referring to Latisha. In brief, Salamon writes, "I have called her 'Latisha' because that is what she called herself" (24). At the same time, Salamon notes, the book is an effort to contend with the forms of injustices that Latisha faced, including the consistent erasure of her feminine identity by those who surrounded her during her life and in the public coverage of the murder trial after her death: "So in those instances where I do use the male pronoun, I am attempting to describe with most precision exactly how Latisha's gender was read and misread, and I have done my best to do this describing without replicating the violence done to her in the name of gender conformity" (24).

References

Douglass, Patrice. 2018. "Black Feminist Theory for the Dead and Dying." *Theory and Event* 21, no. 1: 106–23.

Salamon, Gayle. 2010. *Assuming a Body: Transgender and Rhetorics of Materiality.* New York: Columbia University Press.

Sharpe, Christina. 2016. *In the Wake: On Blackness and Being.* Durham, NC: Duke University Press.

Snorton, C. Riley. 2017. *Black on Both Sides: A Racial History of Trans Identity.* Minneapolis: University of Minnesota Press.

Snorton, C. Riley, and Jin Haritaworn. 2013. "Trans Necropolitics: A Transnational Reflection on Violence, Death, and the Trans of Color Afterlife." In *The Transgender Studies Reader 2*, edited by Aren Z. Aizura and Susan Stryker, 66–76. New York: Routledge.

Spillers, Hortense. 2003. "Mama's Baby, Papa's Maybe: An American Grammar Book." In *Black, White, and in Color: Essays on American Literature and Culture*, 203–29. Chicago: University of Chicago Press.

The first introductory textbook for transgender/trans studies at the undergraduate level

INTRODUCTION TO TRANSGENDER STUDIES

by Ardel Haefele-Thomas, PhD

with the participation of Thatcher Combs

Foreword by Susan Stryker

This is the first introductory textbook intended for courses in transgender/trans studies at the undergraduate level. It can easily be used in LGBTQ, queer, and gender/feminist studies.

Written by an accomplished teacher with experience in a wide variety of higher learning institutions, it explores not only contemporary transgender issues and experiences but also the history of gender diversity around the world.

It encompasses and connects global contexts, intersecting identities, historic and contemporary issues, literature, politics, art, and culture.

Ardel Haefele-Thomas embraces the richness of intersecting identities—how race, ethnicity, sexual orientation, class, nation, religion, and ability have cross-influenced to shape the transgender experience and trans culture across and beyond the binary.

PRAISED BY LEADERS IN TRANSGENDER STUDIES

"Ardel Haefele-Thomas has given the rising generation a generous gift."
—**Susan Stryker,** coeditor of *Transgender Studies Quarterly,* University of Arizona (from the foreword)

"I can't imagine a better textbook introducing students to transgender studies."
—**Paisley Currah,** coeditor of *Transgender Studies Quarterly,* City University of New York

---

USER-FRIENDLY
- written by a trusted authority
- single-authored
- writings from the community
- inviting, attractive, and reader-friendly design

HARRINGTON PARK PRESS
harringtonparkpress.com   NEW YORK CITY

Distributed Internationally by
COLUMBIA UNIVERSITY PRESS

204

Printed and bound by CPI Group (UK) Ltd, Croydon, CR0 4YY

18/12/2025

14796112-0002